CRISIS AS AN   *Y*

Organizational and Community Responses to Disasters

Edited by

Roni Kaufman
Richard L. Edwards
Julia Mirsky
Amos Avgar

University Press of America,® Inc.
Lanham · Boulder · New York · Toronto · Plymouth, UK

Copyright © 2011 by
University Press of America,® Inc.
4501 Forbes Boulevard
Suite 200
Lanham, Maryland 20706
UPA Acquisitions Department (301) 459-3366

Estover Road
Plymouth PL6 7PY
United Kingdom

Library of Congress Control Number: 2011931484
ISBN: 978-0-7618-5621-4 (paperback : alk. paper)
eISBN: 978-0-7618-5622-1

CONTENTS

iv

PREFACE

This book had its genesis at an international conference with the theme of "Crisis as an Opportunity: Organizational and Professional Responses to Disaster." That conference was held in Jerusalem in January 2009 and was attended by nearly 150 individuals from all parts of the world. The conference was sponsored by the Spitzer Department of Social Work at Ben-Gurion University of the Negev and the School of Social Work at Rutgers, The State University of New Jersey, in collaboration with Magen David Adom International Institute, Israel.

The conference brought together researchers and professionals dealing with post-disaster interventions in various parts of the world. Presenters discussed disaster preparedness, response, and follow-up from a variety of perspectives related to various types of disasters, including wars, earthquakes, hurricanes, terrorist events, and others. A major focus was on how organizations and professionals can most effectively respond to disaster situations. Discussions at the conference led to the conclusion that there was a need for a book that would provide a comprehensive theoretical framework for disaster preparedness and response and which would include various case studies and practice wisdom about post-disaster interventions. This book represents an attempt to meet that need.

ACKNOWLEDGMENTS

This book is the product of the efforts of many people, including those who presented at the conference that spawned this book and all those who attended the conference and contributed to the discussions. We appreciate their willingness to share their knowledge and experiences. We also appreciate all of the many people who have worked in the myriad organizations and communities that have, either directly or indirectly, been affected by disasters, whether natural or human made.

We also want to thank our colleagues who have contributed to our understanding of the long term effects of disasters and the stresses they place on individuals, families, communities, and societies. Our appreciation also extends to the many first responders and caregivers of various sorts who themselves have to deal with the stresses of being victims while at the same time they must play helping roles.

Further, we thank Alexis Biedermann, a graduate student at the Rutgers University School of Social Work, for her assistance with various aspects of the preparation of this book, and Sharon Bear for her excellent assistance with the copyediting and formatting of the materials included in the book.

Roni Kaufman, Richard L. Edwards, Julia Mirsky, and Amos Agvar

INTRODUCTION

Roni Kaufman, Richard L. Edwards, Julia Mirsky, and Amos Avgar

Disasters, both natural and human made, appear to be increasing in frequency and scope. Moreover, whenever a major disaster occurs, it commands media attention, which also has been expanding. Further, there is a growing sensitivity both to issues related to preparedness and to responses on the part of communities and societies confronted with various types of disasters. As a result, interest in disaster preparedness and response is increasing among academics as well as practitioners from various disciplines.

Such major natural disasters as the Asian Tsunami, the devastation wrought on New Orleans and surrounding areas by Hurricane Katrina, the loss of life from mudslides in Brazil, the recent earthquakes in Haiti, Chile, and Japan, as well as earlier earthquakes in places such as Turkey, China, and other countries, have garnered worldwide attention. Likewise, human-made disasters, such as the terrorist attacks on New York's World Trade Center or in Oklahoma City, Spain, England, Sri Lanka, Iraq, Afghanistan, and various other countries around the world, or the attacks on school children in places such as Columbine High School in Colorado and in various communities in China, send shock waves throughout societies.

Whenever a disaster occurs, whether from natural or human causes, there are immediate harmful effects on individuals, families, communities, and societies. However, as Shultz, Espinel, Galea, and Reissman (2006) stated:

> Exposure to disaster impact is only the opening salvo. As the disaster unfolds, and far into the aftermath, the affected populations grapple with loss and change, consequences that persevere long after the risk for physical harm has dissipated. This trilogy of forces—exposure to hazard, massive personal and societal loss, and profound and enduring life change—characterize the nature of disaster. (p. 69)

In terms of responses to disasters, many researchers and commentators have identified three interconnected and overlapping phases (Mileti, Drabek, & Haas, 1975). The most immediate response is what many label *the emergency or rescue phase*, when there is a concentration on saving lives and providing for basic human needs such as food and shelter. This is followed by the *recovery or restoration phase*, often lasting up to a year or more, where there is a focus on resuming normal, basic life activities. Finally, those affected by the disaster may enter what is called the *reconstruction phase*, which can last for years. During this phase, organizations and communities can be reshaped and strengthened, and opportunities for development that may have been presented by the disaster and its more immediate responses may be fully materialized (Coghlan, 1998; Drabek, 1986).

This book addresses various aspects in the development of long-term interventions following natural and human-made disasters, with a particular emphasis on poor or disadvantaged communities (such as villages stricken by the Asian Tsunami and neighborhoods devastated by Hurricane Katrina in New Orleans, among others). Attention is given to the role that change agents, such as local and international non-governmental organizations (NGOs) and psychosocial professionals, can play to ensure that the window of opportunity that is opened following the disaster (i.e., heightened public interest and new resources) is realized and generates not only immediate help but also sustained community development.

Part One of this book includes three articles that address analytic frameworks and perspectives related to disaster interventions.

In Chapter One, *Community and Organizational Responses to Disasters*, Brian W. Flynn reviews the status of the field of disaster preparedness, response, and recovery, considering the significantly increased acknowledgment of the nature and consequences of disasters, the complex challenges that remain, and areas that show especially promising opportunities for collaboration and development.

In Chapter Two, *Intervention in Disasters: An International Perspective*, Joanne Caye discusses current perspectives on interventions after disasters and provides mitigation and prevention examples, suggesting there is an important role for schools of social work in research and the implementation of effective, collaborative disaster response and mitigation efforts.

Part Two of the book includes several chapters that address community development and organizational interventions in disasters.

In Chapter Three, *Challenges for Community Development in Disaster Situations,* Amos Avgar and Roni Kaufman focus on how change agents, such as local and international non-governmental organizations (NGOs) and agencies, can ensure that the window of opportunity which is opened following a disaster is realized and generates future development. This chapter presents a number of physical and socio-political "opportunities" for post-disaster community development, provides an analytical framework for the analysis of post-disaster interventions, with examples from post Asian tsunami and interventions following other natural disasters, and makes recommendations for community practitioners.

In Chapter Four, *Program Logic Modeling as a Tool for Developing a Disaster Response and Mitigation Plan: The Somaliland Experience*, Johny Augustine and Vivek Chemmancheri Kokkammadathil describe an intervention in Somalia whereby a "program logic model" was used to develop strategies for systematic and fair distribution of water through water trucking, construction of more water storage facilities, increased representation of women in the community development committees, and personal and community empowerment.

In Chapter Five, *Planning For The Unimaginable: Having Your Personal, Family, Organizational, and Community Plans*, Howard S. Feinberg discusses issues to consider in disaster preparedness, suggesting that individuals, families, organizations, and communities should use basic planning constructs in developing plans that include consideration of such matters as communications and evacuation protocols. Feinberg also discusses the importance of creating active planning and response networks between similar organizations and various NGOs as well as with first-response organizations (first aid, police, fire, rescue) and local, regional, national, and international authorities.

In Chapter Six, *Taking the Disabled into Account in Preparing for and Responding to Disasters*, Patricia Findley suggests that a framework of principles of community engagement, developed by the U.S. Center for Disease Control, can assist public health professionals and community leaders to engage the community in health decision making and action to serve those with disabilities on a community level in disaster situations.

In Chapter Seven, *Neighbors Helping Neighbors: The Disability Community and Emergency Preparedness*, Jessica Jagger identifies some exemplary projects for and by people with disabilities committed to better emergency preparedness, mitigation, response, and recovery. Jagger suggests that these projects serve as capacity-building approaches, advancing knowledge and bridging the disability and emergency management communities.

Part Three of the book includes four chapters that represent "notes from the field," commentaries from individuals who have been personally involved in disasters as both helpers and victims.

In Chapter Eight, *Mud and Mold: Making Meaning of Adversity in New Orleans,* Ronald E. Marks discusses the impact of Hurricane Katrina on a school of social work located in the affected area from the perspective of an individual who serves as dean of the school, who lived in the affected area, and whose family was affected as well. The author describes efforts to "restart" the school after the hurricane's devastation and the impact of such a disaster on the "helpers," who are themselves also among the victims.

In Chapter Nine, *Words of Wisdom Following the Tsunami: Lessons From Sri Lanka,* Ahangamage T. Ariyaratne discusses, in a personal practical-philosophical account, lessons for practitioners from his perspective five years after the tsunami wreaked so much devastation on so many communities.

In Chapter Ten, *Making the Voices of Victims Heard,* Mihir R. Bhatt suggests that it is important for the voices of victims of disasters to be heard in public and by decision-making bodies so that a crisis may be turned into an opportunity and so that victims can gain greater control of their lives. Bhatt provides examples of how the All Indian Disaster Mitigation Institute has been involved in various disaster situations in and around India, including victims of the Bihar flooding, the Myanmar cyclone, and others.

In Chapter Eleven, *The Human Hand Behind Natural Disasters: The Ugandan Experience,* Benon Musinguzi suggests that most of the recent worldwide disasters that seem to be natural, in fact have a human hand behind them in that those most affected are often the poorest members of their societies, who live in the most vulnerable areas. Using Uganda as an example, Musinguzi contends that it is incumbent upon social and behavioral health professionals to get more involved in prevention activities rather than waiting to manage the post-disaster crises.

Part Four of this book contains four chapters that address psychosocial interventions for post-disaster recovery situations.

In Chapter Twelve, *Cultural Sensitivity in Psychosocial Interventions Following a Disaster: A Tri-national Collaboration in Sri Lanka,* Mooli Lahad, Yehuda Baruch, Yehuda Shacham, Shulamit Niv, Ruvie Rogel, Nitsa Nacasch, Lilach Rachamim, and Dmitry Leykin describe the psychological impact of the Asian tsunami in 2004, emphasizing the importance of mental health system preparedness. Lahad and his colleagues discuss principles of building an intercultural collaboration structure and suggest principles for teaching and training overseas. The authors also explore Sri Lankan cultural competency with regard to the impact of cultural differences and indicate existing sources of coping as well as introduce and interpret adaptations of Western techniques and methods.

In Chapter Thirteen, *Psychological Outcomes of the 2001 World Trade Center Attack,* James Halpern and Mary Tramontin consider the immediate and long-term psychological consequences of the September 11, 2001, attack on the World Trade Center in New York City. The authors offer clinical observations and share research findings and reflections derived from the vantage point of nearly a decade following the disastrous terrorist attack that cost over 3000 lives.

In Chapter Fourteen, *Social Work Students During Wartime: False Effect of Professional Self-efficacy?* Shira Hantman and Miriam Ben Oz explore the experience of social work students from Tel Hai College in Israel who volunteered and provided "pseudo-professional" social work intervention in a "tent city" established for those who had to flee missile attacks in the second Lebanon war. These authors contend that attention must be given to the long-term effects of such extensive experiences on the professional developmental process of students preparing for roles as helping professionals.

In Chapter Fifteen, *Shared Traumatic Reality: Social Work Students and Clients in an Area Under Attack,* Nehami Baum explores the impact of shared traumatic reality on social work students in Israel who studied and worked under terror attacks and who lost someone with whom they were in close "psychological proximity" as well as describes the impact on their professional orientations, identity, and practice.

In Part Five, the concluding section, Chapter Sixteen, *From Helping to Changing,* the editors of this book—Roni Kaufman, Richard L. Edwards, Julia Mirsky, and Amos Avgar—identify two approaches for post-disaster intervention: the "helping and saving" approach and the "changing and developing" approach (Bates & Peacock, 1987; Cuny, 1982). While both approaches have relevance for post-disaster intervention policies and programs, the authors indicate their preference for the "changing and developing" approach, discussing its relevance for each of the three phases of intervention in post-disaster situations.

REFERENCES

Bates, F. L., & Peacock, W. G. (1987). Disaster and social change. In R. D. Russell, B. DeMarchi & C. Pelanda. (Eds.). *Sociology of disasters: Contributions of sociology to disaster research.* (pp. 291-330). Milano, Italy: Franco Angell.

Coghlan, A. (1998). *Post-disaster redevelopment.* Conference Paper, Victoria, Australia: Australian Emergency Management Institute.

Cuny, F. C. (1982). *Disasters and development.* New York: NY: Oxford University Press.

Drabek, T. E. (1986). *Human systems responses to disaster: An inventory of sociological findings.* New York, NY: Spring-Verlag.

Mileti, D., Drabek, T. E., & Haas, E. J. (1975). *Human systems in extreme environment: A sociological perspective* (Monograph No. 021). Boulder, CO: University of Colorado Institute of Behavioral Science.

Shultz, J. M., Espinel, Z., Galea, S., & Reissman, D. B. (2006). Disaster ecology: Implications for disaster psychiatry. In R. J. Ursano, C. S. Fullerton, L. Weisath & B. Raphael (Eds.), *Textbook of disaster psychiatry* (p. 69). New York, NY: Cambridge University Press.

Part One:
Analytic Frameworks and Perspectives

Chapter One
Community and Organizational Responses to Disasters
Brian W. Flynn

The field of disaster behavioral health, in the three decades in which I have been involved, has changed dramatically. While there has been a significant increase in the acknowledgment of the nature, magnitude, and duration of the consequences of disaster, there has not been enough progress in the development of an evidence base and the integration of behavioral health issues into the rapidly expanding fields of disaster preparedness, response, and recovery. As such, serious challenges remain.

In this chapter, I briefly review the status of the field, as seen through my eyes, and provide a perspective on why we have not progressed further or faster. In addition, I will identify emerging challenges for preparedness, response, and recovery that are significantly more complex than those for natural and human-caused disasters. Finally, I will identify ten areas that show especially promising and synergistic opportunities for collaboration and development.

WHERE ARE WE?

Individual and collective trauma have been part of the human story since its beginnings, and humankind has faced emergencies and disasters that threaten our well-being and our very existence since the dawn of time. These struggles are memorialized in art, literature, and especially in archeological remains.

In the approximately 30 years that I have been active in the field of disaster behavioral health, many significant developments have taken place. While much remains to be learned, advancements in the understanding of the nature of, and interaction among, biological, psychological, social, and environmental factors have moved in directions and at a pace largely incomprehensible 30 years ago. In addition, appreciation for the role of psychosocial factors in emergency and disaster situations has increased dramatically. In the United States, that movement has been simultaneously memorialized and led by government law and policy.

In the United States, the following federal initiatives are central:

- The Stafford Act, originally enacted over 30 years ago, provides for federal support of crisis counseling and training efforts in the wake of a disaster significant enough to warrant a disaster declaration by the President (Robert T. Stafford Disaster Relief and Emergency Assistance Act, 2000).
- The Pandemic and All-Hazards Preparedness Act (PAHPA) specifically addresses the emerging threat of a pandemic and integrates behavioral health into its vision and requirements (Pandemic and All-Hazards Preparedness Act, 2006).
- The Homeland Security Presidential Directive-21 (HSPD-21) calls for a comprehensive and integrated federal plan for all disasters and emergencies containing health consequences. Mental health issues are addressed throughout this document as well as in a specific section (Homeland Security Presidential Directive-21, 2007).
- The National Response Plan Framework is the overall template for disaster preparedness and response. Mental health issues and requirements are included in this document (National Response Framework, 2008).

In the context of these initiatives, the following observations can be made:

- There is a dramatically increased understanding of the behavioral health consequences of extreme events
- Behavioral health factors are being increasingly integrated into preparedness and emergency management.
- While the centrality of behavioral health factors to preparedness and response has been increasingly recognized, individual and collective intervention models remain more *practiced* than *researched.*

WHY ARE DEVELOPING AND DELIVERING GOOD PREPAREDNESS, RESPONSE, AND RECOVERY SO DIFFICULT?

Even in light of what most would view as considerable advancement in the field of disaster behavioral health, there are enormous challenges that seem to inhibit the robust development of the field. I propose that these challenges are largely a function of seven factors that can be termed "cracks in the foundation" of the field as well as a function of six areas for which there is a lack of consensus.

Seven Cracks in the Foundation

Crack 1. Lack of Understanding of the Seriousness of Behavioral Health Factors

Even in the face of increasing understanding and repeated experience, for many, there is a lack of understanding that the psychosocial factors are among the most significant in disasters (Norris 2005; Norris et al., 2002). As an example, the behavioral health footprint is consistently larger than is the medical footprint in virtually all disasters in which these issues have been measured. In the case of the Sarin exposure in the Tokyo subway, four times as many people sought medical treatment than had actually been exposed (Kawana, Ishmatsu, & Kanda, 2001). In the SCUD missile attached on Israel, more people died and were injured from stress-related causes than from the physical impact of the missiles (Kron & Mendlovic, 2002).

There is also sometimes a lack of recognition that there is a psychosocial component to virtually every aspect of preparedness, response, and recovery. Efficacious preparedness, response, or recovery cannot occur in the absence of knowledge about how people respond under stress. No response will be optimal unless it reflects knowledge of and the ability to identify stress responses, the ability to promote individual and community resilience, and recognition of the special needs of at-risk populations. Long-term recovery from disasters must incorporate diverse considerations such as individual and collective grief, the psychosocial impact of changed community structure and composition, and changed socioeconomic factors.

While I am unaware of objective data to document this position, it is intuitively clear that, when defined in broad but accurate ways, the economic cost of adverse psychosocial consequences are greater than other types of health costs in a typical disaster. Treatment costs for diagnosed behavioral health disorders are only the tip of the iceberg. If one could accurately capture the costs of absenteeism, decreased job and school performance, domestic and community discord, increased number of accidents due to inattention, to name a few, these costs would be massive.

Finally, there is a tendency to view behavioral health factors as secondary to other "more important" considerations, especially in the early stages of an event. It should be remembered that the behavioral choices that people make, such as decisions to stay in place, evacuate, seek medical care, and search for loved ones, are very real life-and-death decisions.

Crack 2. Lack of Understanding of the Broad Roles that Behavioral Health Experts Can Play

When most people think of the roles that behavioral health experts can play in disasters, they think of direct intervention with victims and survivors. While this role is central and critical, there are other roles that are as critical. In 2001, a group representing a wide range of experts in virtually all aspects of behavioral health reviewed evidence and came to a consensus about early intervention around mass violence (e.g., terrorism). The results of that meeting are captured in *Mental Health and Mass Violence: Evidence-Based Early Psychological Intervention for Victims/Survivors of Mass Violence. A Workshop to Reach Consensus on Best Practices* (National Institute of Mental Health, 2002). One of the most significant contributions of the meeting was to identify, based on evidence and extensive experience, important roles that could be played by behavioral health experts immediately following events. The work of that group identified several roles in addition to the provision of screening, referral, and direct services. These roles include consultation to leadership (e.g., helping leaders become aware of the psychosocial consequences of their decisions, words, and behavior), risk and crisis communication, and program evaluation. My many years of experience led me to the conclusion that there is a potential role for almost everybody in contributing to effective preparedness, response, and recovery but that we are defeating ourselves if we stop at direct service provision. The field needs to promote and educate in regard to the wide range of contributions that can be made.

Crack 3. Leadership Challenges

Effective leadership is critical to disaster preparedness, response, and recovery. This is well documented in the professional literature (Flynn & Lane, 2008; Marcus, Dorn, & Henderson, 2006) as well as in the popular literature (Giuliani, 2002; Ripley, 2008). The same is true regarding leadership for behavioral health efforts. Unfortunately, in far too many cases, leadership has been absent, inconsistent, or lacking the comprehensive vision necessary to lead. In the United States, this has been true in both the executive and legislative branches as well as at federal, state, and local levels of government. The same can be said for academic leadership. It should be noted that effective leadership in disasters is an incredibly complex task, requiring an array of skills demanded by few other roles. An effective leader in this context must be able to integrate, balance, advocate evidence-based approaches (even when the evidence is less than clear), deal with real-world response complexities that are difficult to anticipate, take into account political realities, and have compassion. It is no wonder that quality leadership in preparedness, response, and recovery is so scarce.

Crack 4. Personality Dependent Structures

When progress is made in achieving visibility of, resources for, or expansion of the field of disaster behavioral health, there is typically a strong, passionate, and capable individual behind these achievements. Unfortunately, when that key leader is no longer present (often through assuming a different position or retiring), progress slows, at best, or stops, at worst. It is incumbent on the field to determine ways to institutionalize enhancements and to take successorship issues seriously so that advancement can continue on a more linear path.

Crack 5. Resources

Compared to other worthy stakeholders in disaster health (such as public health and healthcare providers), behavioral health has lacked the resources to reach its fullest potential. Key resources that are lacking include:

Human resources. Few organizations have significantly underutilized general staff or staff with required content expertise to advance the field of behavioral health. Too often, if human resources are assigned, they are assigned to staff with existing pressing responsibilities. There needs to be additional staff with specialized expertise.

Funding. At least in the United States, funding to advance the field and prepare service delivery providers and systems has lagged far behind funding to enhance the capacity of other systems. In many ways, this mirrors the field of mental health in general, which consistently lags behind physical health care in government funding and priority (U.S. Department of Health and Human Services, 1999a). Many causal factors have been proposed, including continued stigma in regard to behavioral health issues as well as an enduring false belief that these issues are not central to efficacious disaster response and recovery.

Time. Even if adequate types and numbers of personnel as well as funds were to be made available, evolving the field takes time. For example, tools to assist in addressing behavioral health factors in hospital triage take time to develop, test, modify, and bring to scale.

Crack 6. Culture

In the United States, our culture of self-sufficiency mitigates against optimal preparedness and response as well as our learning from other cultures. At the risk of oversimplifying, we often tend to seek easy, inexpensive, immediate, one-size-fits-all, doable-by-anyone solutions to complex problems. Unfortunately, the complex issues of human behavior seldom lend themselves to such approaches. Yet, those who play to this cultural bias are often rewarded, and precious time and funding are lost.

Crack 7. Failure to Meaningfully Engage the Public

The New York Academy of Medicine (Lasker, 2004) published a landmark study in which they determined the extent to which citizens would comply with instructions to "shelter in place," finding that few would. Among the reasons for this finding was a lack of trust and confidence in the planning of government authorities. It was further determined that this lack of trust was, in large part, a result of government planning *for* people rather than *with* people. People feel more confident in plans and instructions if they have been part of the development process. Overall, the study demonstrated that failure to meaningfully engage the public results in inaccurate assumptions about human behavior; reduced compliance, trust, and confidence; and a lack of understanding of the factors influencing comfort with and confidence in planning.

Six Areas Lacking Consensus

The field of disaster behavioral health is hampered by a lack of consensus in many areas, of which appear primary.

Area 1. Preparing for What?

While the all-hazards approach has been nearly universally and appropriately adopted, it is impossible to prepare for all disastrous eventualities; there would never be enough people, time, or money to truly prepare for everything, even if we could somehow create a comprehensive list. Because, in some ways, planners are always playing the odds, hazard risk analysis is a key component of preparedness. It is also important to recognize that, while many preparedness and response factors are similar for a variety of events, the same models of response and recovery may not apply in different situations. For example, models for preparing and responding to a tornado may be quite different than for a pandemic.

Area 2. Planning to Do What?

There is little agreement regarding what behavioral health interventions are, or should be, intended to accomplish. Are we attempting to treat a disorder, prevent a disorder, provide comfort and support, accelerate recovery, change the trajectory of psychosocial response, or promote mental health/resilience? All of these are noble goals, but each may call for a different intervention methodology. Without clarity of purpose, the field will never be able to develop evidenced based interventions tailored to the intervention's purpose. Progress is being made, however. The seminal work of Hobfoll et al. (2007) represents the type of considered analysis of early intervention methodologies that should lead to a model of how to guide interventions.

Area 3. Planning within What Context?

Where should the locus of responsibility for preparedness reside? Should it be with hospital personnel and other health care providers, or with public health officials, school personnel, emergency management personnel, natural support systems (e.g., faith community), or other key groups or individuals? Each has a role, but preparedness must also be horizontally integrated. This horizontal integration is where many, if not most, complex systems need the greatest improvement.

Area 4. Services Provided by Whom?

There is a lack of consensus about who is best qualified, or even minimally qualified, to do what to whom when it comes to service provision. Should it be mental health professionals, trained paraprofessionals, healthcare professionals, clergy/chaplains, teachers, peers, or others? Part of the difficulty in making this determination is based in long-standing professional rivalries as well as in the relative absence of evidence to support differential impact as a function of profession or training.

Area 5. Preparing and Responding Using What Strategies?

There are many perspectives within the disaster behavioral health field, and among nations, regarding what strategies should be used and/or have priority. What interventions (e.g., crisis counseling, psychological first aid, cognitive behavioral therapy) work best for whom, when, and under what circumstances? Should our approaches be population based or risk based? What about primary prevention efforts? What about other less commonly thought about strategies such as fostering and training leadership, consultation to leadership, and risk and crisis communications? All have their role; it is a matter of matching based on a commitment to comprehensive approaches and a sound evidence base.

Area 6. Strategies Based upon What?

Upon what should our strategies be based? Ideally, all strategies should be based upon sound evidence. However, we are not yet at that point. Where an evidence base exists, it should be put into practice and brought to scale. Where it does not exist, there is a dilemma. Do we do nothing until the evidence is available? Few, although some, would advocate this position. What, then, should be the criteria? Most would agree that evidence-informed interventions are acceptable. There is less consensus, however, on the appropriateness of basing strategies on expert consensus, experience, and belief. Unfortunately, some interventions appear to be based on effective marketing more than other factors. While most would agree that marketing-based approaches are inappropriate, there is debate about the legitimacy of other criteria.

I would now like to turn my attention to ten areas of priority in disaster preparedness, response, and recovery.

Ten Priority Areas for Productive and Synergistic Development

Priority Area 1. Preparedness and Planning

While progress is being made, it is frustrating to see the relatively low priority placed on behavioral health, generally, and mental health, specifically. This frustration is aggravated by, or perhaps reflected in, a pervasive lack of human resources and funding. The result is a lack of consistency and coordination at all levels of government. With assertive leadership in the field of disaster behavioral health and collaboration with colleagues in other related efforts, this situation can change.

Priority Area 2. System Integration

This is a good news/bad news area. The good news is that everybody is planning and that planning is becoming more sophisticated. The bad news is that there is far too little horizontal integration (stove piping) and that key sectors, such as small businesses and many special needs populations, are not adequately included.

Priority Area 3. Expand and Apply the Evidence Base

While growing, the evidence base (Norris et al., 2002; U.S. Department of Health and Human Services, 2008) has a long way to go. There must be expanded research in areas such as medical, public health, and behavioral health interaction, risk, and protective factors, interventions (individual and collective), short- and long-term consequences, and understanding and serving special populations. In addition, every effort must be made to bring science to practice in more timely and effective ways.

Priority Area 4. Leadership

Leadership matters. I have found this to be a consistent observation. As noted earlier, the importance of leadership in a crisis is also widely reported in the professional and popular literature. Preparation, response, and recovery can succeed or fail as a function of leadership. This perspective is seen in Amanda Ripley's widely acclaimed book on who survives disasters and why (Ripley, 2008). She states, "After preparation, the next best hope is leadership" (p. 177). Leadership can be studied (Marcus et al., 2006) and developed. Different leadership characteristics can be utilized for different tasks in different phases. Leadership warrants increased attention, study, and application in disaster behavioral health.

Priority Area 5. Communication

The importance of effective communications before, during, and following crisis situations is well documented (Covello, 2003; Meredith et al., 2008; Vineburgh, Ursano, Hamaoka, & Fullerton, 2008). Nevertheless, few fully appreciate that communication is a behavioral health intervention. Communications inform people in ways that influence life-changing behavioral choices. Effective communication can promote self-efficacy and provide anticipatory guidance, leading to positive outcomes. Effective communication can manage hyper-arousal so that stress-related cognitive decline is minimized. In this regard, behavioral health providers can gain much from collaboration with communications experts.

If I have one criticism of current risk and communications practice, it is over-reliance on the written and spoken word. Much is communicated (often more powerfully) through behavior that is witnessed, symbols and rituals, and images. Communication can be enhanced by understanding the power of these other ways of communication and linking them appropriately and creatively with the more traditional written and spoken word. One also should not forget the impact of the new and continuously emerging social media as an important communications factor with behavioral health implications.

Priority Area 6. Engaging Consumers/Community Involvement

The *Redefining Readiness* study (Lasker, 2004), as presented earlier, explains the situation well: "The American public has had little or no role in helping government and private organizations develop terrorism plans" (p. 59). As will be discussed at the conclusion of this chapter, the field of social work, due to its long-standing involvement with communities, may have a special contribution to make in this area.

Priority Area 7. Public/Academic Linkage

If individuals and systems value sharing expertise between public sectors and academic settings, tremendous cross-fertilization can occur. Opportunities include shared complementary expertise, integrated and complementary curricula, fellowships in various settings, and joint planning and training as well as collaborative and applied research. In the behavioral sciences, we seldom tend to think beyond collaborations with traditional fields such as social work, psychology, and psychiatry. While important, these are only the beginning. Invaluable collaboration can take place by linking behavioral health interests with the resources of law, economics, theology, sociology, anthropology, education, risk and crisis communication, political science, business, journalism, and public health, to name just a few.

Priority Area 8. Public/Private Linkages

On September 11, 2001, the world witnessed the walls between the public and private sectors literally come down. When the World Trade Center Towers fell, most of the occupants were private sector organizations; the building, however, was managed by a public entity. The response and recovery required the resources, commitment, and collaboration of both public and private entities. While the need to link these two sectors seems obvious, and some have addressed this need (Center for the Study of Traumatic Stress, 2006; Flynn, Flanigan, & Everly, 2005; Vineburgh et al., 2008), there is unfortunately little linkage and collaboration between them. The potential reasons for this are many, including biases, negative stereotyping, and historical precedents that must be maintained. Public and private sectors are dependent on each other, however, for survival. Organizational isolation in any sector works against an integrated response.

Priority Area 9. Redefining Special Populations

I see two problems in the way that we have traditionally viewed special populations. First, we have used special population and high-risk population as synonyms. Where there is overlap, there is also an important distinction. Being in a special population does not necessarily mean that one is at higher risk. It means that one may be part of a group of people whose needs may require additional, customized, or specialized approaches in preparedness for, response to, and recovery from extreme events (Flynn, 2007; Shultz, Espinel, Flynn, Hoffman, & Cohen, 2007). For example, members of a minority ethnic or cultural group may very likely need specialized or tailored approaches. They are not, solely by virtue of their ethnic identity, more at risk.

Second, traditional notions of special populations have been almost exclusively determined by pre-event demographics. These demographics include race and ethnicity (U.S. Department of Health and Human Services, 2001, 2003, 2009), age (Brown, Cohen, & Kohlmaier, 2007; Pynoos et al., 200; U.S. Department of Health and Human Services, 1999b), and various types of disabilities (American Red Cross, 2004; U.S. Department of Health and Human Services, 1996). During many years of disaster behavioral health work, I have found this demographically based view to be too limiting. People who may never have been considered as having special needs before a disaster could find themselves categorized as part of a special population based on what they experience during a disaster. Examples of events that would result in such categorization include injury, loss of home, displacement, and bereavement. In addition, people who would not be considered as having special needs, either before or during a disaster, could find themselves with special needs during the longer-term recovery period. Examples of special needs include permanent relocation, job loss, degradation of support network, and long-term economic decline.

Priority Area 10. Prevention

The best disaster behavioral health interventions are those that never have to be delivered. While natural disasters will always happen, there are efforts that can be made to minimize, or even prevent, large-scale adverse psychosocial consequences. This can be accomplished, however, only if the social sciences begin to foster collaborations and become involved with issues not typically in their domain, such as levee design, architectural standards, licensing and placement of energy-related facilities, and city/community planning. Social scientists need not become experts in these often very specialized and technical areas but should become involved in the service of reminding others of human consequences and the value of reducing physical as well as psychological trauma.

What is needed overall is a fundamental change of model as well as an expansion of the nature of the roles played by behavioral health professionals and those in the social sciences, more generally.

To effect such change, we must first rediscover community mental health and commit to a public health model of preparedness and response. A reminder of the value of a public health model for mental health services is included in *Mental Health: A Report of the Surgeon General* (U.S. Department of Health and Human Services, 1999a). In addition, Ursano, Fullerton, Weisaeth, and Raphael (2007) and the Institute of Medicine (2003) discuss the public health model as it relates specifically to disaster behavioral health. The community mental health model as envisioned and implemented decades ago was based on a public health model. That model incorporates many elements no longer embraced by many training programs or service delivery systems. These elements, however, as listed below, need to be embraced:

- Use of population-based approaches
- Inclusion of individual and collective interventions
- Focus on interactions between individuals and their surroundings
- Recognition and inclusion of a large numbers of stakeholders
- Recognition of a wide range of service providers
- Promotion of the value of prevention
- Promotion of the broad roles for the social and behavioral sciences

Second, we must expand the roles that we play. Most commonly, when one thinks of the roles that behavioral health professionals can play, individual psychotherapeutic or psychosocial interventions come to mind. If we become trapped by the vision that these are our only, or even most important, roles, we will be missing significant opportunities to make a difference in the lives of individuals, communities, and organizations.

In a widely referenced and respected publication, Mental Health and Mass Violence: Evidence-Based Early Psychological Intervention for Victims/Survivors of Mass Violence. A Workshop to Reach Consensus on Best

Practices (National Institute of Mental Health, 2002), the various roles that be-havioral health professional might play are presented as follows:

- Needs assessment
- Monitoring the recovery environment
- Outreach and information dissemination
- Technical assistance, consultation, training
- Fostering resilience, coping, and recovery (facilitating natural support networks)
- Triage
- Treatment
- Psychological first aid

Social Work Is Uniquely Situated

While every professional discipline has a unique role to play in disaster prepar-edness, response, and recovery, social work as a profession is uniquely suited to meet the field's complex challenges. Social work has, arguably, the greatest number of specialties within the profession (e.g., clinical, research, community organization, policy). Social work enjoys a long and distinguished professional culture of working across professional, organizational, and international bounda-ries. A review of degree programs, as well as continuing education offerings, reveals a rich, diverse, and comprehensive training curriculum. Social work also enjoys a high diverse work force.

Ironically, in the view of many, social work as a field has been late in com-ing to the table in the field of disaster preparedness. It is time for that to change.

WHAT IS AT STAKE?

The stakes involved in optimizing the potential of behavioral health in disasters are huge. If we fail, we can anticipate increased fear, pain, suffering, and loss, potentially severe social and economic decline or collapse, and continued or accelerated loss of confidence in community and government systems. Perhaps most disturbing, the potential exists for fear-based behaviors and choices that could kill more people and do more socioeconomic damage than the events themselves.

The potential consequences of our success, however, are even more pro-found. We have the opportunity to reduce death, loss, and suffering, to reduce adverse socioeconomic adverse impacts, to promote economic growth, and to facilitate the development of stronger and more resilient individuals and com-munities. We can restore confidence in leadership by promoting pro-social and adaptive behavioral choices leading to the enhancement of the public's health.

REFERENCES

American Red Cross. (2004). *Preparing for disaster for people with disabilities and other special needs* (Pub. No. A4497). Retrieved from http://www.redcross.org/www-files/Documents /Preparing/A4497.pdf

Brown, L. M., Cohen, D., & Kohlmaier, J. (2007). Older adults and terrorism. In B. Bongar, L. M. Brown., L. Beutler, P. Zimbardo & J. Breckenridge (Eds.), *Psychology of terrorism* (pp. 288-310). New York, NY: Oxford University Press.

Center for the Study of Traumatic Stress. (2006). *Workplace preparedness and response for disaster and terrorism: Creating a community of safety, health and security through integration, knowledge and evidence-based intervention.* Uniformed Services University of the Health Sciences, Bethesda, MD. Retrieved from http://www.centerforthestudyoftraumaticstress.org/downloads/CSTS%20Leadership %20Planning%20for%20Workplace%20Preparedness.pdf

Covello, V. T. (2003). Best practices in public health risk and crisis communication. *Journal of Health Communication, 8*(Suppl. 1), 5-8, 148-151.

Flynn B. W. (2007). Meeting the needs of special populations in disasters and emergencies: Making it work in rural areas, *Journal of Rural Mental Health, 31*(1), 12-20.

Flynn B. W., Flanigan S., & Everly, G. S. (2005). Fostering human continuity: An essential element in workplace crisis intervention. *International Journal of Emergency Mental Health, 7*(3), 187-194.

Flynn B. W., & Lane, C. F. (2008). Integrating organizational and behavioral health principles to promote resilience in extreme events. In C. Cooper & R. Burke (Eds.), *International terrorism and threats to security: managerial and organizational challenges.* Cheltenham, UK: Edward Elgar.

Giuliani, R.W. (2002). *Leadership.* New York, NY: Hyperion.

Hobfoll, S. E., Watson, P., Bell, C. C., Bryant, R. A., Brymer, M. J., Friedman, M. J., et al. (2007). Five essential elements of immediate and mid-term mass trauma intervention: Empirical evidence. *Psychiatry, 70*(4), 283-315, 316-369.

Homeland Security Presidential Directive-21. (2007). *Public health and medical preparedness.* Retrieved from http://www.dhs.gov/xabout/laws/gc_1219263961449.shtm

Institute of Medicine. (2003). *Preparing for the psychological consequences of terrorism: A public health strategy.* Washington, DC: National Academies Press.

Kawana, N., Ishmatsu, S., & Kanda, K. (2001). Psychophysiological effect of the Sarin attack on the Tokyo subway system. *Military Medicine, 166,* 23-26.

Kron, S., & Mendlovic, S. (2002). Mental health consequences of bioterrorism. *The Israeli Medical Association Journal, 4,* 524-527.

Lasker, R. D. (2004). *Redefining readiness: Terrorism planning through the eyes of the public.* New York, NY: New York Academy of Medicine.

Marcus L. J., Dorn, B. C., & Henderson J. M. (2006). Meta-leadership and national emergency preparedness: A model to build government connectivity. *Biosecurity and Bioterrorism: Biodefense Strategy, Practice, and Science, 4*(2), 128-134.

Meredith, L. S., Shugarman, L. R., Chandra, A., Taylor, S. L., Stern, S., Burke E. B., Parker, A.M., & Tanielian, T. (2008). *An analysis of risk communication strategies and approaches with at-risk populations to enhance emergency preparedness, response, and recovery-final report* (RAND Working Paper). Santa Monica, CA: RAND Corporation.

National Institute of Mental Health. (2002). *Mental health and mass violence: Evidence-based early psychological intervention for victims/survivors of mass violence. A workshop to reach consensus on best practices* (NIH Pub. No. 02-5138). Retrieved from http://www.nimh.nih.gov/health/publications/massviolence.pdf

National Response Framework. (2008). *Public affairs support annex.* Retrieved from http://www.fema.gov/emergency/nrf

Norris, F. H. (2005). Range, magnitude, and duration of the effects of disasters on mental health: Review update 2005. *RED: Research, Education, Disaster Mental Health.* Retrieved from http://www.redmh.org/research/general/effects.html

Norris, F. H., Friedman, M. J., Watson, P. J., Byrne, C. M., Diaz, E., & Kanzysztof, K. (2002). 60,000 disaster victims speak: Part I & Part II. An empirical review of the empirical literature, 1981-2001. *Psychiatry, 65*(3), 207-239.

Pandemic and All-Hazards Preparedness Act of 2006, Pub. L. No. 109-417, 109th Cong., 2nd Sess. S 11220-11237. (2006).

Pynoos, R., Schreiber, M., Steinberg, A., Pfefferbaum, B., Saddock, B., & Saddock, V. (Eds.). (2005). *Children and terrorism. Comprehensive textbook of psychiatry* (8th ed.). New York, NY: Lippincott, Williams and Wilkins.

Ripley, A. (2008). *The unthinkable: Who survives when disaster strikes and why.* New York, NY: Crown.

Robert T. Stafford Disaster Relief and Emergency Assistance Act, 42 U.S.C. 51221, et seq., as amended by the Disaster Mitigation Act of 2000, Pub L. No. 106-390, 114 Stat. 1552 (2000) (the Stafford Act).

Shultz, J. M., Espinel, Z., Flynn, B. W., Hoffman, Y., & Cohen, R. E. (2007). *DEEP PREP: Disaster behavioral health all hazards training.* Miami, FL: Center for Disaster and Extreme Events Preparedness (DEEP Center), University of Miami, Miller School of Medicine.

U.S. Department of Health and Human Services. (1996). *Responding to the needs of people with serious and persistent mental illness in times of major disaster.* Rockville, MD: U.S. Department of Health and Human Services, Substance Abuse and Mental Health Services Administration, Center for Mental Health Services. (DHHS Pub. No. SMA 96-3077)

U.S. Department of Health and Human Services. (1999a). *Mental health: A report of the surgeon general.* Rockville, MD: U.S. Department of Health and Human Services, Substance Abuse and Mental Health Services Administration, Center for Mental Health Services, National Institutes of Health, National Institute of Mental Health.

U.S. Department of Health and Human Services. (1999b). *Psychosocial issues for older adults in disasters.* Rockville, MD: U.S. Department of Health and Human Services, Substance Abuse and Mental Health Services Administration, Center for Mental Health Services. (DHHS Pub. No. SMA 99-3323)

U.S. Department of Health and Human Services. (2001) *Mental health: Culture, race, and ethnicity—A supplement to mental health: A report of the surgeon general.* Rockville, MD: U.S. Department of Health and Human Services, Substance Abuse and Mental Health Services Administration, Center for Mental Health Services.

U.S. Department of Health and Human Services. (2003). *Designing culturally competent disaster mental health programs.* Rockville, MD: Center of Mental Health Services, Substance Abuse and Mental Health Services Administration. (DHHS Pub. No. SMA 3828)

U.S. Department of Health and Human Services. (2008). *Disaster mental health recommendations* (Report of the Disaster Mental Health Subcommittee of the National Biodefense Science Board). Retrieved from
http://www.hhs.gov/aspr/conferences/nbsb/dmhreport-final.pdf

U.S. Department of Health and Human Services. (2009). *Cultural competency curriculum for disaster preparedness and crisis.* Retrieved from
https://www.thinkculturalhealth.org/ccdpcr/

Ursano, R. J., Fullerton, C. S., Weisaeth, L., & Raphael, B. (2007). Public health and disaster mental health: Preparing, responding and recovering. In R. J. Ursano, C. S. Fullerton, L. Weisaeth & B. Raphael (Eds.), *Textbook of disaster psychiatry.* London, UK: Cambridge University Press.

Vineburgh, N., Benedek, D., Fullerton, C., Gifford, R., & Ursano, R. (2008). Workplace resources for crisis management: Implications for public-private sector planning, policy and response to disasters. *International Journal of Public Policy, 3*(5/6), 378-388.

Vineburgh, N., Ursano, R., Hamaoka, D., & Fullerton, C. (2008). Public health communication for disaster planning and response. *International Journal of Public Policy, 3*(5/6), 292-301.

Chapter Two
Interventions in Disasters:
An International Perspective
Joanne S. Caye

Many scientists and disaster responders think that the number of natural disasters is increasing worldwide. Disaster briefs produced by Oxfam (Goneshan & Diamond, 2009; Magrath, Bray, & Scriven, 2007) state that the number of natural disasters has quadrupled in the last two decades. The group reports that the costs associated with disasters also have gone up, largely due to the frequency of events. When writing about disaster risk management in Southeast Asia, Loh (2005) noted that the number of reported natural disasters "significantly increased to 383 in the last decade (1995-2005), from 270 disasters between 1985 and 1994 and 107 disasters between 1975 and 1984" (p. 230). Although Loh's statistics refer specifically to Southeast Asia, Oxfam, as noted above, reported that the increase is worldwide.

In an editorial for the *Journal of Disaster Management and Response*, McMahon (2007) cited several factors that influence the development and consequences of disasters, including "geography, climate change, personal resources, infrastructure, and political instability" (p. 95). The rise in casualties and costs also can be attributed to the increasing development of high-risk locations (Kahn, 2005; Spence, 2004). Such growth is supported by both the very wealthy, who have the resources and interest in building on relatively inaccessible sites, and the very poor, who often are pushed out of their neighborhoods and forced to find new housing in places that are prone to natural hazards. "The increasing proclivity of Americans to build and dwell along hurricane-ravaged coasts, in fire-prone semi-deserts, and bestride earthquake faults ensures that catastrophes of a similar magnitude are likely to occur in the not-too-distant future" (Landy, 2008, p. S187). In keeping with this, McMahon stated:

> Lacking resources, the poor often live where the work is, such as fishermen living on the beach, predisposing them to tidal waves, tsunamis, and flooding, or where the land is more affordable because it is less desirable, such as at the base of volcanoes, in flood plains, or in seismically active areas. Out of neces-

sity for economic survival, the environment also may be exploited, predisposing areas to disaster, such as landslides and flooding. (p. 95)

The argument that natural disasters are occurring more frequently is challenged by scientists such as David Morrison, senior scientist with the National Aeronautics and Space Administration (NASA), who stated that costs are increasing because reconstruction is more expensive and because rare, severe events, such as Hurricane Katrina and the 2004 Indian Ocean Tsunami, are skewing the numbers of those affected (Morrison, 2009). Others argue that the appearance of more disasters can be attributed to the availability of continuous, global news coverage as well as to an expanding population along the nation's coastlines and in other higher risk areas (Kirschenbaum, 2004).

Moving away from the natural disaster discussion, experts argue that human-caused disasters are both decreasing and increasing, depending on the context. Specifically, interstate conflicts are decreasing while regional conflicts and within-country displacements to avoid conflict are increasing (Human Security Brief Project [HSBP], 2008). For example, in May 2009, hundreds of thousands of individuals in Sri Lanka abandoned their homes to avoid the escalating violence in that country (Nelson, 2009).

Despite differences of opinion surrounding the number of natural or human-caused disasters worldwide, there is agreement regarding the enormous increases in the number of people affected and the financial costs of recovery and reconstruction (Haddow, 2008; Spence, 2004; van der Vink et al., 1998). Earthquake losses in the United States between 1987 and 1997 increased from about $4 billion per year to $13 to $20 billion, depending on the figures used to determine costs (Department for International Development, 2006). In a 2007 report, Oxfam (as cited in "Climate Feedback," 2009) estimated that the number of people affected by climate-related disasters will increase 54% in the next six years. Munich Re, one of the world's largest reinsurance companies, saw economic losses from disasters worldwide total more than $608 billion (U.S. dollars) during the 1990s (White et al., 2004). From 1990 to 1999, the Federal Emergency Management Agency spent more than $25.4 billion to provide disaster assistance in the United States (White et al., 2004).

Researchers also generally agree about the uneven costs paid by the rich and poor after disasters. Risk factors for adverse outcomes, including loss of life, livelihood, and property in both natural and human caused disasters, are consistently greater for those with (a) lower socioeconomic status, (b) lower education, and (c) high levels of pre-disaster stress as well as among (d) ethnic minorities, all of which are risk factors generally found in developing countries and among poorer populations (Norris, Stevens, Pfefferbaum, Wyche, & Pfefferbaum, 2008). According to Schilderman (2004), "Natural disasters are on the increase, not so much because natural hazards are growing in number, but because poor people are becoming more vulnerable" (p. 414). Of the approximately 128,000 disaster-related deaths that occurred annually from 1971 to 1985, 97% involved the Third World and were mostly due to poverty (Schilderman, 2004). The Center for Research on the Epidemiology of Disasters (CRED, as cited in White et al., 2004) provides a stark example of the ways that disasters hurt poor people the most. They noted that two high-density population centers had earthquakes four days apart in 2003. The first, a 6.5 quake, struck Southern California, killing two people and injuring 40. Four days later, a 6.6 earthquake occurred in a poor area of Iran, killing at least 40,000 individuals. There are many opinions about why Southern California fared well as compared to Iran, including (a) quality of building materials and infrastructure, (b) quick access to tools and technology that assist in finding survivors, (c) communication access and good roads, (d) mitigation efforts in the area prior to the event, and (e) the predisaster health and status of the population.

What is the appropriate response from the rest of the world after a disaster? The expectations regarding the speed and intensity of disaster response has changed considerably over the past quarter-century (Kirschenbaum, 2004). Prior to the 1960s, disaster events, even the most severe, were local events; local governments, communities, and individuals primarily handled the recovery and cleanup efforts (Kinnevy, 2009; Kirschenbaum, 2004; Platt, 1999).

The federal government resisted becoming involved in disaster response for one or more potential reasons: (a) the government did not see it as their responsibility, (b) officials expressed concern about the financial drain of disaster response, or (c) there simply were not enough resources to react without undermining other pressing needs. A 1934 U.S. law authorized the Bureau of Public Roads to use federal funding to repair highways and bridges damaged by natural disasters ("History of Federal Disaster Mitigation," 2005), but overall response remained fragmented and piecemeal. In the U.S., it took four major hurricanes and two earthquakes in 10 years for federal response to become the norm, including presidential disaster declarations that activated national response and financial support.

Prior to the 1960s, the lack of advanced communication technology meant that information spread slowly, also preventing a more widespread disaster response. "A hundred years ago, the terrible earthquake in Pakistan might not have been reported until weeks after the fact. By then, it would simply be a couple of paragraphs in the major newspapers. Most would never note the event" ("EPIC Disasters: The World's Worst Disasters"). Telephones and telegraphs were landlines, dismantled by high winds, floods, and earthquakes. Newspapers depended on these same sources for their information. Television was in its early days and did not have the resources or capacity to deliver news from around the world quickly.

Years later, with the advent of a 24/7 news capacity, saturation of access to cell and satellite phones with cameras, and computer access across the world, information is available almost instantaneously. Even victims have access to the media in unprecedented ways, although such access has repercussions. Media reports repeatedly broadcasting or publishing scenes of death and tragedy can raise emotions, resulting in traumatized victims and observers who demand a response (Straussner, 2009). Some experts say that the result of the increase of response from governments and nongovernment organizations (NGOs) is increased costs over time (Kirschenbaum, 2004). Hurricane Katrina is an example of an increased response, combined with tremendous cost. "Measured in dollar terms, Katrina was the worst natural disaster in American history; its $96 billion price tag is more than three times greater than the second most expensive disaster, Hurricane Andrew" (Landy, 2008, p. S187).

Governmental response to disasters of human intention worldwide continues to be controversial. Current activities, including international involvement in Iraq and Afghanistan, clashes between Israeli settlement inhabitants and Palestinians, Sudan's position regarding Darfur, and Sri Lankan government activity with Tamil Tigers, underscore the precarious political balance between straightforward humanitarian assistance for those who are victims in these situations and respect for national sovereignty and self-rule.

Despite the general public's expectation that federal governments will respond comprehensively post-disaster, there is considerable ambivalence regarding the perspective that widespread national response is always the most favorable course to take. Concerns fall into specific categories, which are described below.

FEDERAL INVOLVEMENT

One concern involves the perspective that the federal government, in its wish to alleviate suffering and respond to public demand, intrudes on activities better handled by local residents. According to Kelly (2008), post-disaster damage assessments must operate on two levels: clarifying the magnitude of the damage attributed to the disaster event and identifying what resources are needed that the community does not already possess. To accomplish these tasks well, local agencies and residents must be a necessary part of the process. As the response to disasters moved from a largely local situation to a national, federal activity, planning became incredibly difficult. CRED (as cited in White et al., 2004), one agency that maintains emergency events data, stated, "Planning became so complicated that planners forgot the individuals who would carry out the plan, as if they would have no part in their own survival or safety during and after a disaster" (p. 12).

Less Flexible Response

Large agencies and governments often use a top-down approach (Loh, 2005), with the result that they are less able to change protocol quickly to meet the specific needs of diverse local communities. Smaller organizations may be more nimble, culturally sensitive, and flexible to the needs of more remote, specialized communities and situations (Oprisan, 2009). Knowing the informal structures of a community and the community leaders is vital when the army of volunteers arrives after a disaster. For external responders, a lack of flexibility and local knowledge may be especially critical in times of complex disaster and civil unrest as well as when the factions and tensions involved in the development of the current situation are not obvious or clearly understood.

Nevertheless, governments and large agencies can gather huge banks of data, which can be used to understand and ultimately predict hazardous zones, thus focusing preparation efforts. At first, this ability seems to be very beneficial, and many times it is. Data can be extremely helpful when planning response efforts. Loh (2005), however, suggests that the emphasis on definitions of hazard zones, rather than on mitigation, maintains the status quo for the population. Over time, scientifically based data collection about disasters and disaster response replace generic, more user-friendly community sources of information (Kelly, 2008). However, these data, which may be very useful when studied, can also be ignored when politicians have other agendas. Further, when large bureaucratic organizations are responsible for disaster response, interagency conflicts and organizational problems develop (Spence, 2004). In some cases, sporadic funding of pet projects occurs due to political expediency rather than proven effectiveness and efficiency (Haddow, 2008). One example is Project Impact, which was developed in the 1990s to partner with local businesses and community organizations to reduce the effects of future disasters across the country. Using seed money sent directly from Washington, DC, communities designed projects that promoted resilience to the types of disasters that most often affected local residents (Haddow, 2008). Seattle, Washington, utilized the funding to develop a series of warning systems that proved extremely effective. The program was considered a model, but when federal administrations changed, so did the political emphasis of the new administration. As a result, much of the mitigation funding was cut, what was left over was directed to the state, and virtually all resources to Project Impact community partners were cut, despite evidence that the program worked beyond expectations.

Finally, there has been significant concern about shrinking private insurance coverage following disasters. In years past, many survivors had access to private insurance to recover losses after a disaster event. Others received some government support or made their way without assistance. However, insurance companies are increasingly withdrawing from high-risk areas due to the losses that they have experienced, and there is some interest in having governments assume most of the risk involved (Kirschenbaum, 2004). As governments provide more grants or low-cost loans to disaster victims to cover gaps created by the lack of private insurance, the programs have become quite costly. "In both Florida and California, insurer unwillingness to renew policies was exacerbated by premium rate caps imposed by state insurance regulators. Both states responded to insurer flight by establishing state-level natural disaster reinsurance pools" (Barnett, 1999, p. 149). According to Barnett, "disaster relief sends distorted signals. The availability of grants and low-interest loans allows individuals to pay less than the total cost associated with their risky activities. The remainder of the cost is borne by taxpayers" (p. 145). Barnett suggested that "the financial performance of government natural disaster insurance programmes, both in the US and around the world, has been less than impressive" (p. 153) and that other plans are necessary. It is unclear, however, whether private insurance companies are willing or able to provide comprehensive coverage at reachable premium prices.

As the evidence shows, costs in lives affected and property damage as a result of disasters are undeniable. Poor people suffer more, and developing countries are more affected. It is also unlikely that disasters, natural or human caused, will decrease markedly in the future. The population of the world is increasing, and an increasing number of people are living along coastlines, in other risk heavy areas, and along fault lines. The facts support a change from a culture of reaction to a culture of prevention. Cited in the *UN Report on Armed Conflict*, the 1997 Carnegie Commission stated that prevention is not just a good idea; it is cheaper than reaction after a disaster. For example, the economy of Lebanon was so damaged by the warfare that occurred there for 15 years that, by 1990, the GDP was 50% lower than it was before fighting started in 1974 (HSBP, 2008). To move toward a culture of prevention requires individuals, agencies, and governments to take the notion of disaster mitigation more seriously.

Disaster mitigation is an absolute necessity for developing countries, donor governments and agencies, and inhabitants worldwide. Mitigation, however, requires a paradigm shift that comprises a particular set of skills, including (a) the ability to engage the general population when there is no disaster looming (Stehr, 2006); (b) the willingness to take the time to create relationships with local communities (U.S. Agency for International Development, 1998); (c) the ability to garner funding that supports necessary changes to the topography, housing stock, and cultural habits of communities; and (d) the ability to build the political will to make the legal and policy changes necessary to carry the process forward for the long term. Each of these skills has both a rationale and potential pitfalls.

PLAN WHEN THERE IS NO DISASTER

Regardless of the inherent logic of beginning when there is no disaster, completing such peacetime planning has been extremely elusive. According to Stehr (2006), "The history of disaster relief . . . can be characterized as having brief periods of intense political activity typically following a major disaster . . . followed by longer periods where interest in the subject wanes" (pp. 493-494). Lindell and Prater (as cited in Stehr, 2006) highlight important linkages between hazard mitigation and preparedness practices as well as between community recovery and reconstruction outcomes. If mitigation is so useful and there is evidence to support its effectiveness, including the ability to save lives and reduce property destruction, why don't governments and individuals support it more actively? The reason is that effective mitigation takes time, staff, financial resources, and development and purchase of technologies to assist in timely warning and dissemination of information. Cash-strapped governments and municipalities have little money to spare and are more likely to focus on immediate, more pressing public needs. Local residents are much more likely to complain about access to water, utilities, and education than about disaster planning, except when there has been a major event.

Build Relationships

Regardless of the urgent calls for help after a significant disaster, survivors may still see the involvement of outsiders as an intrusion. After both the Indian Ocean Tsunami and Cyclone Nargis, the government of Burma refused entry to aid agencies or seized food sent to victims (Seekins, 2009). According to the U.S. Agency for International Development (1998), "Effective planning recognizes that the impact of external aid is rarely neutral" (p. 6). There is abundant evidence that aid can increase tensions between countries, regions, clans, and tribes, change power relationships, and involve activities that prolong conflict. Kemmelmeier, Broadus, and Padilla (2008) described the conflict that immediately developed in New Orleans between Katrina survivors and rescuers when gun-toting rescuers, who were focused on protecting property and preventing looting, presented themselves in a position of power. Tensions escalated until Lieutenant General Russel Honoré (U.S. Army) "arrived in the city. . . and ordered all military, indeed any armed rescuer on whom he laid eyes, to put their weapons down, reminding them that they were on a rescue mission and not at war" (Kemmelmeier et al., 2008, p. 240).

Lee (2008) noted similar issues during rescue efforts after the 2004 tsunami. "Aid aggravated social tensions and the lack of community engagement led to grievances. There was a perceived lack of transparency, beneficiary expectations were not always met, and it was difficult to match aid to needs" (p. 1410).

However, such problems can be avoided. Avgar (2009) encourages responders to take time to get what he calls "buy in" from the local community. In this regard, humanitarian aid agencies need to better understand the context and culture in which aid is delivered (Lee, 2008). In all disaster response situations, but especially in those involving conflict, "aid workers should attempt to understand the local culture, the strategies of competing forces in areas of conflict and coping strategies of vulnerable groups . . . Aid may exacerbate rather than ameliorate conditions for vulnerable populations" (U.S. Agency for International Development, 1998, p. 6). Following through with these recommendations takes time, resources, and cultural sensitivity on the part of donor nations and agencies.

Ultimately, international partners in disaster response and mitigation are responsible for effectively reaching out to local communities and strategically coordinating with governments and NGOs around the world and for ensuring that their programs have a positive impact. The focus must be on assistance to communities to strengthen their abilities to prevent and mitigate emergencies. Following a fact-finding mission to Indonesia after the tsunami, Tyler (2009) described what can result when things go well. Tyler noted that the national redevelopment authority of Sri Lanka recruited local residents in each community to guide and perform rebuilding efforts. Planners were flexible and community-driven, and local liaisons using resident labor supervised village rebuilding. At the time of Tyler's visit, over 90,000 homes had been rebuilt, and several villages in western and central Sumatra had been relocated. Tyler stated, "I was impressed by the ingenuity and sophistication of the planning approaches used in the most challenging situations and the tangible, positive impacts our international colleagues are making in people's lives" (p. 56).

Garner Funding

Funding is necessary to mitigation efforts to build appropriate housing, encourage development in less-risky neighborhoods, and enhance collaboration and understanding among diverse groups that frequently face conflicts. Applying for and receiving adequate funding for mitigation projects has been an ongoing concern.

Providing adequate shelter for survivors after a disaster and constructing disaster-resistant housing to minimize future loss remain prominent issues. Schilderman (2004) laments that, too often, emphasis is placed on establishing adequate building codes, without giving equal attention to the socioeconomic realities and challenges of such policies. In developed countries, rules and regulations that support the construction of disaster-resistant buildings within hazardous zones are fairly universal. According to Spence (2004), "In Japan's Kobe earthquake of 1995, building damage was concentrated among the older buildings built before the new quake-resistant building regulations in 1981. In spite of the substantial ground accelerations experienced, buildings built according to those regulations performed well" (p. 393). The same was true for buildings struck by a category-5 cyclone that hit Australia in 1998. However, when building code regulations are applied to countries with fewer resources, such as materials and highly skilled labor, the results are quite different. A 7.4 earthquake in Gölcük, Turkey, cost 17,000 lives and destroyed over 66,000 buildings. Many of those killed were living in new apartment blocks that were supposedly earthquake resistant, but the housing was built without the needed technical expertise or required building materials to actually render the buildings quake resistant. The results of India's 2001 Bhuj Bujarat earthquake were similar; modern structures built of reinforced concrete crumbled in the major quake. Until that year, compliance with an existing building code regarding quake resistance was voluntary and left to the discretion of the owner. After 2001, the building codes became mandatory (Spence, 2004).

Like building changes taken to reduce damage from natural disasters, initial building or retrofit building to increase resistance to bombing and other terror attacks demonstrates the same affordability gap between rich nations and poor localities. Based on experiences with bombings in London, Oklahoma City, and, most recently, New York, construction officials have developed codes and protocols that render structures less accessible and less vulnerable to internal and external attacks. Buildings constructed with rebar, heavily protected elevators, shatterproof glass, computerized entrance screens, and a location away from streets have all proven effective (McManamy, Post, Ichniowski, & Reins, 1995). However, such complicated security systems and tools require expensive materials and extensive expertise to install.

As noted above, most money is spent in response to a major event. The Bipartisan Task Force on Funding Disaster Relief (as cited in Stehr, 2006) reported that, between 1977 and 1994, three-quarters of all U.S. federal spending on disasters paid for post-disaster recovery. The task force report also noted that such a massive outpouring of financial support from "the federal government discourages state, local, and individual self-reliance by offering federal disaster assistance too readily" (p. 494). Researchers call this the *Samaritan's dilemma,* an issue debated nationally and internationally. As a result of relying on other national governments and organizations, most localities, and especially poorer countries, under-invest in risk reduction, thus perpetuating existing risks. The Office of U.S. Foreign Disaster Assistance (OFDA) encourages responders to "recognize the challenges of providing assistance that helps without doing harm" (U.S. Agency for International Development, 1998, p. 2). OFDA works to provide resources for whatever disaster situation is the focus but simultaneously emphasizes taking steps to meet future needs.

There also has been a shift in disaster recovery funding. Until recently, OFDA spent most of its resources responding to natural disasters that occurred around the world. That changed in the 1990s, when requests for assistance increasingly came from people involved in war, armed conflicts, and other complex situations. According to the U.S. Agency for International Development (1998), "In 1997, 78 percent of OFDA's emergency response resources were dedicated to complex emergencies" (p. 3). Mitigation focused on peacemaking and peacekeeping is even more fraught with difficulties than is prevention focused on climate, weather, or geographic risk. Building relationships in a culture of distrust, civil unrest, and assumption of malicious intent can be frustratingly slow, with little apparent sign of success, and disasters of human intention often incite blaming behaviors and a wish for retaliation (Rosenfeld, Caye, Ayalon, & Lahad, 2005). Moreover, mitigation does not always stand firm against the wrath of righteous indignation.

The United Nations named the decade 1990-2000 the *International Decade for Natural Disaster Reduction* and focused on the chronic escalation of vulnerability to loss in the economically less developed countries (ELDCs; Degg & Chester, 2005). It has been estimated that "86% of the most populous cities in ELDCs are exposed to natural hazards of significant loss-inflicting potential compared with 65% of the largest cities of the North" (Degg & Chester, 2005, p. 125). Degg and Chester described a significant change in the mitigation thinking that has occurred over the last 10 to 15 years in Peru. Like so many countries, the most hazardous parts of Peru are also the most densely populated. For over 20 years, the emphasis in regard to disasters was the development of hazard zones and "a top down hazard planning and regulation approach" (p. 133), neither of which has been effective. Andrew Maskrey, a former director of Intermediate Technology in Peru, suggested using a community-based approach to disaster mitigation. Maskrey strongly believes that people most frequently live in risky areas, unsafe buildings, and disaster-prone conditions because they perceive that they have no other choice. Maskrey would agree with the view of Avgar (2009) that "government-backed mitigations are often ineffective . . . because of their failure to engage with ordinary people" (p. 140).

As a result of Maskrey's influence, Peru's National Program for Disaster Mitigation has started to "place more emphasis on the value of a 'bottom-up' incultured approach to mitigation" (Degg & Chester, 2005, p. 141). Education initiatives were started in early elementary school grades, as poor children do not frequently progress beyond elementary school. "The overall aim has been to shift the local civil defense system away from defending people from external factors towards defending people against their own vulnerability" (p. 141). Local groups highlight the local social, economic, political, and cultural conditions of an area and determine which options are viable for assisting people to live in locations of lower risk.

Mitigation or reduction of risk, where inter-group conflict is the basis for war, civil strife, or the development of large refugee camps, has proven elusive and extremely difficult. When one considers the protracted conflicts between the Israelis and Palestinians as well as other Arab states; the conflicts between the Northern Irish Catholics and Protestants; and the struggles in Darfur, Sudan, among others, the complexity involved in breaking through the long-term entrenched positions of these groups cannot be overemphasized. The U.S. Agency for International Development (1998) supports Maskrey's perspective on topographical mitigation in Peru. Attention to basic needs of shelter, security, and safety produce situations in which people are less vulnerable to regional violence. According to the agency, "Populations in disaster-prone areas are most vulnerable when they are weakened by hunger and disease, incapable of generating the means to solve problems, and prevented from producing sufficient food by a degraded resource base" (p. 59). Thus, in Niger, "the intervention chosen was a combination of food delivery, productivity-enhancing interventions, increased civil participation and self-determination" (p. 59).

POLITICAL WILL

Stehr (2006) stated that there are "strong political and economical forces at work that will make widespread urban hazard mitigation difficult to achieve" (p. 497). He could easily have left out the words *urban hazard*. All mitigation efforts are subject to the ebb and flow of attention and resources, as discussed below.

Changes in administrations within a government can disrupt projects or funding already in place. If political perspectives have changed, a new government may not be willing to continue what the previous administration was doing. An example is Project Impact, mentioned earlier, a hazard mitigation program started during the Clinton administration to provide grants to communities to reduce future disaster effects. Project Impact was eliminated in 2001, even though it was costing only $20 million per year and was highly evaluated for its effectiveness. The elimination occurred because the Bush administration put forth a new urban policy that expected cities to take on added responsibility for protecting their own citizens (Stehr, 2006).

There are ongoing efforts to increase collaborative responses to disasters and areas of armed conflict around the globe. Martti Ahtisaari, former President of Finland and 2008 Nobel Peace Prize Laureate, oversaw an initiative by the Finnish government to begin discussions on what has been termed the Comprehensive Approach. The purpose of this project is to urge governments and NGOs to begin developing agreed-upon methods for responding to the complex conflicts and crises ongoing in the world, a pursuit "aimed at integrating the political, security, development, rule of law, human rights and humanitarian dimensions of international missions" (Rintakoski & Autti, 2008, p. 9).

The underlying idea of the Comprehensive Approach is to operationalize effective coordinated disaster response as well as enhance the chances for effective disaster mitigation efforts. As such, the program seeks ways to utilize a consensus-based response to natural and complex disasters within the "three dimensions of security: the politico-military, the economic-environmental, and the human dimension" (Rintakoski & Autti, 2008, p. 15). The project is "beneficial on all levels of crisis management: strategic, operational and tactical . . . linking security and development together in fragile states and taking the local population and authorities increasingly into consideration in the field" (p. 23).

The Organization for Security and Cooperation in Europe (OSCE) and the North Atlantic Treaty Organization (NATO), along with the United Nations (UN) and the European Union (EU), are taking steps to use the Comprehensive Approach as an operational concept. The process, however, has not been without its difficulties. According to Rintakoski and Autti (2008), "The strength and weakness [of the Comprehensive Approach] is for some observers the same issue, that of inclusiveness" (p. 15). Building and maintaining momentum for cooperation and collaboration across international borders and finding the political will to persevere in the face of other pressing time and manpower needs have been difficult for all the organizations involved. "The UN, EU, and OSCE suffer from internal, institutional and interagency rivalry and all suffer from disagreement and fragmentation between member states . . . there is still an ideological gap between political/military actors on the one side and humanitarian actors on the other" (p. 17). The Comprehensive Approach often has been constructed somewhat differently with each organization because each member country develops the concept so as to be compatible with its national interests. In times of crisis management, for example, "[t]he donor's unity of effort is especially at risk when there are tensions between the donors' national political and/or security and development interests, or when there are tensions between short- and long-term needs" (p. 18). Despite these very real obstacles, those who support the Comprehensive Approach hope to achieve better outcomes and resolve crises in sustainable ways. In particular, they hope to develop a culture of cooperation, moving from a need-to-know to a need-to share approach. "Effective multilateralism is the way forward . . . A Comprehensive Approach cannot be based on command and control. It requires facilitative leadership that balances the need to respect the independence of the participating agencies while at the same time manages their interdependencies" (p. 31).

For the Comprehensive Approach to be successful, the governments, NGOs, and academic institutions involved must collaboratively develop, teach, and evaluate mitigation interventions to learn what actually works. As was stated earlier, all disasters are ultimately local, and part of the planning involves training all responders in culturally sensitive ways (Rintakoski & Autti, 2008). Mitigation is only as strong as the willingness of local residents in an area to change their living patterns. Both local and international leaders are required to explain and engage others in sustainable development, mitigation, and disaster response. Academia is a necessary partner in the process—as a teacher, planner, and evaluator. Thus, for all parties, the ability to speak and work respectfully across disciplines and cultures is critical to any success. Social work, planning, community organization, anthropology, medicine, and psychology each have a place. Participatory change provides an excellent model to approach mitigation from a bottom-up perspective. Social work has the capacity to provide holistic thinkers who can advocate for fragile families and communities as well as to empower those same individuals and communities to utilize the skills and assets that they already possess. Planners and geographers identify and clarify risk. Anthropologists highlight ethnic patterns and honor local traditions and beliefs, while medicine and psychology focus on the physical and mental health of survivors and responders. The cooperation of many professions is needed to move forward to prevent and to respond effectively to disaster events locally and around the world.

REFERENCES

Avgar, A. (2009). *A model for community intervention in disaster situations.* Presentation at the Rutgers School of Social Work and the Ben-Gurion University International Conference on Crisis as an Opportunity: Organizational and Professional Responses to Disaster, Beer-Sheva, Israel.

Barnett, B. J. (1999). U.S. government natural disaster assistance: Historical analysis and a proposal for the future. *Disasters, 23,* 139-155.

Climate feedback: The climate change blog. (2009, May 22). Retrieved from http://blogs.nature.com/climatefeedback/2009/04/climate_disasters_increasing_w.html

Degg, M. R., & Chester, D. K. (2005). Seismic and volcanic hazards in Peru: Changing attitudes to disaster mitigation. *The Geographical Journal, 171*(2), 125-145.

Department for International Development. (March 2006) *Reducing the risk of disasters—helping to achieve sustainable poverty reduction in a vulnerable world: A policy paper.* London, UK: Author.

EPIC disasters: The world's worst disasters. (n.d.). Retrieved from http://www.epicdisasters.com/

Goneshan, S., & Diamond, W. (2009) *Forecasting the numbers of people affected annually by natural disasters up to 2015.* London, UK: Oxfam International. Retrieved from http://preventionweb.net/go/9064

Haddow, G. A., Bullock, J. A., & Coppola, D. P. (2008). *Introduction to emergency management* (3rd ed.). Boston, MA: Butterworth-Heinemann.

History of federal disaster mitigation: Evolution of the Federal Emergency Management Agency. (2005, November). Washington, DC: Congressional Digest.

Human Security Brief Project. (2008). *Human security brief 2007.* Retrieved from http://www.humansecuritybrief.info/HSRP_Brief_2007.pdf

Kahn, M. E. (2005). The death toll from natural disasters: The role of income, geography, and institutions. *Review of Economics and Statistics, 87*(2), 271-284.

Kelly, C. (2008). *Damage, needs or rights? Defining what is required after disaster* (Working Paper 17). Benefield UCL Hazard Research Center, Disaster Studies and Management, University College, London, UK. Retrieved from http://www.reliefweb.int/rw/lib.nsf/db900sid/FBUO-7HWHG9/$file/Benfield-Jul 2008.pdf?openelement

Kemmelmeier, M., Broadus, A. D., & Padilla, J. B. (2008). Inter-group aggression in New Orleans in the immediate aftermath of Hurricane Katrina. *Analysis of Social Issues and Public Policy, 8,* 211-245.

Kinnevy, S. C. (2009). *The Feldman Initiative: Helping Katrina survivors in Mississippi.* Presentation at the Rutgers School of Social Work and the Ben-Gurion University International Conference on Crisis as an Opportunity: Organizational and Professional Responses to Disaster, Beer-Sheva, Israel.

Kirschenbaum, A. (2004). *Chaos organization and disaster management.* New York, NY: Marcel Dekker.

Landy, M. (2008, December). Mega-disasters and federalism. *Public Administration Review* (Suppl.), S186-S198.

Lee, A. C. K. (2008). Local perspectives on humanitarian aid in Sri Lanka after the tsunami. *Public Health, 122,* 1410-1417.

Loh, B. (2005). Disaster risk management in Southeast Asia: A developmental approach. *ASEAN Economic Bulletin, 22*(2), 220-239.

Magrath, J., Bray, I., & Scriven, K. (2007) *From weather alert to climate alarm* (Oxfam Briefing Paper). London, UK: Oxfam International. Retrieved from http://www.oxfam.org.uk/resources/policy/climate_change/downloads/bp108_weather_alert.pdf

McMahon, M. M. (2007). Disasters and poverty. *Disaster Management & Response, 4,* 95-97.

McManamy, R., Post, N. M., Ichniowski, T., & Reins, P. (1995). Weighing future safety of federal buildings. *Engineering News-Record, 234*(18), 8-12.

Morrison, D. (2009). *Is the rate for natural disasters increasing?* National Aeronautics and Space Administration, Astrobiology. Retrieved from http://astrobiology.nasa.gov/ask-an-astrobiologist/question/?id=5452

Norris, F. H., Stevens, S. P., Pfefferbaum, B., Wyche, K. F., & Pfefferbaum, R. L. (2008). Community resilience as a metaphor, theory, set of capacities, and strategy for disaster readiness. *American Journal of Community Psychology, 41*(1/2), 127-150. doi:10.1007/s10464-007-9156-6

Nelson, D. (2009, May 27). More than 280,000 Sri Lankan refugees could be held in camps for up to two years. *The Telegraph.* Retrieved from http://www.telegraph.co.uk/news/worldnews/asia/srilanka/5357104/More-than-280000-Sri-Lankan-refugees-could-be-held-in-camps-for-up-to-two-years.html

Oprisan, A. (2009). *Reporting IBC-A Turkish NGO's response to the 2005 Pakistan earthquake.* Presentation at the Rutgers School of Social Work and the Ben-Gurion University International Conference on Crisis as an Opportunity: Organizational and Professional Responses to Disaster, Beer-Sheva, Israel.

Platt, R. H. (1999). *Disasters and democracy: The politics of extreme natural events.* Washington, DC: Island Press.

Rintakoski, K., & Autti, M. (Eds.). (2008). *Comprehensive approach: Trends, challenges and possibilities for cooperation in crisis prevention and management.* Comprehensive Approach Seminar, Helsinki, Sweden. Retrieved from http://www.reliefweb.int/rw/lib.nsf/db900sid/YSAR-7LPT6W/$file/comprehensive-approach.pdf?openelement

Rosenfeld, L. B., Caye, J. S., Ayalon, O., & Lahad, M. (2005). *When their world falls apart: Helping families and children manage the effects of disasters.* Washington, DC: NASW Press.

Schilderman, T. (2004). Adapting traditional shelter for disaster mitigation and reconstruction: Experiences with community-based approaches. *Building Research & Information, 32*(5), 414-426.

Seekins, D. M. (2009). State, society and natural disaster: Cyclone Nargis in Myanmar (Burma). *Asian Journal of Social Science, 37*(5), 717-737.

Spence, R. (2004). Risk and regulation: Can improved government action reduce the impacts of natural disasters? *Building Research & Information, 32*(5), 391-402.

Stehr, S. D. (2006). The political economy of urban disaster assistance. *Urban Affairs Review, 41,* 492-500.

Straussner, L. A. (2009). *Preparing social work students to work with clients traumatized by disaster.* Presentation at the International Conference on Crisis as an Opportunity: Organizational and Professional Responses to Disaster. Ben-Gurion University of the Negev, Beer-Sheva, Israel.

Tyler, E. (August, 2009). What I did on my summer vacation. *Planning,* 56-57.

U.S. Agency for International Development. (1998). *Mitigation practitioner's handbook.* Retrieved from http://www.usaid.gov/policy/ads/200/hbkoct18.pdf

van der Vink, G., Allen, R. M., Chapin, J., Crooks, M., Fraley, W., Krantz, J., Lavigne, A. M., LeCuyer, A., MacColl, E. K., Morgan, W. J., Ries, B., Robinson, E., Rodriquez, K., Smith, M., & Sponberg, K. (1998). *Why the United States is becoming more vulnerable to natural disasters.* Princeton, NJ: Department of Geosciences, Princeton University. Retrieved from http://www.agu.org/sci_soc/ articles/eisvink.html

White, P., Pelling, M., Sen, K., Seddon, D., Russell, S., & Few, R. (2004). *Disaster risk reduction: A development concern.* United Kingdom Department for International Development (DFID Policy Paper). Retrieved from http://www.dfid.gov.uk/ Documents/publications/drr-scoping-study.pdf

Part Two:
Community Development and Organizational Interventions

Chapter Three
Challenges for Community Development in Disaster Situations
Amos Avgar and Roni Kaufman

INTRODUCTION

The information in this chapter is intended to assist disaster intervention agents, including local and international non-governmental organizations (NGOs), policymakers, managers, and community leaders, to better understand the processes and dynamics that are at play after a disaster. We believe that such understanding can lead to better decision making, leading to the achievement not only of post-disaster recovery but also of long-term development and renewal. Thus, this chapter focuses on a critical question in post-disaster interventions: How can local and international change agents ensure that the opportunities that present themselves following disasters are realized as well as facilitate the generation of future community development?

Pursuing opportunities for local community development following disasters presents a major challenge to communities, as they need to resist outside forces that are pursuing their own interests, trying to take advantage of the disaster in ways that are detrimental to local development (Anderson, 2008; Bolin, 2006; Klein, 2007). The examples and many of the insights presented below are based on the involvement of the American Jewish Joint Distribution Committee (JDC)[1] and TAG International Development[2] in post-disaster intervention programs worldwide. Most of the examples are from recent post-disaster assistance programs following the 2004 tsunami in India, Thailand, Sri Lanka, and Indonesia (for a comprehensive review, see Telford & Cosgrave, 2007; Telford, Cosgrave, & Houghton, 2006), the 2005 earthquake in Pakistan, the 2008 cyclone in Myanmar, the 2008 floods in Bangladesh, the 2010 eruption of Mt. Merapi in Java, Indonesia, and the resettlement of internally displaced persons in Sri Lanka following decades of civil war. In addition to our immediate personal involvement in these programs, we interviewed over 40 informants from local and international NGOs and reviewed relevant reports from NGOs.

In this chapter, we will present a number of physical and sociopolitical opportunities for post-disaster community development and suggest an analytical framework for a post-disaster intervention analysis. We will conclude with recommendations for community practitioners and policymakers.

DEVELOPMENT CHALLENGES FOLLOWING DISASTER

Following are examples of how the potential for development is missed when post-disaster opportunities are not identified. It should be emphasized that many such opportunities are time limited and are often irreversible.

Physical Development

Land Use Planning

The tsunami in South Asia washed away virtually all villages and structures situated on the shorelines. It presented an opportunity for local communities along the beautiful shores of Thailand, Sri Lanka, and Indonesia to redesign them and to build safer houses on higher ground to mitigate the impact of future disasters. This also presented an opportunity to take advantage of the economic potential of these shores for the development of tourism.

These communities needed to resist local and national pressure to provide immediate permanent shelter to the displaced persons, which would involve the building of unsafe structures and the endangering of the population in the event of futures disasters. They also needed to resist outside capitalist forces that tried to take advantage of the disaster and to "rob" the indigenous population of the one resource that they had, namely, the shores, which became temporarily unpopulated. Some communities had the vision to enact and enforce new zoning regulations, allowing for development, and to resist the natural tendency and pressure to rebuild quickly. Other communities, due to lack of vision or power to redirect the recovery, simply built in an unplanned fashion, exposing the residents to future hazards and foregoing economic opportunities.

In Sri Lanka, immediately following the disaster, an ordinance prohibiting the rebuilding of houses 100 meters from the shoreline was enacted. It served two functions—to protect against future flooding and, for the most part, inhibit hostile takeover of the shores by major tourist businesses. Similarly, in Jannu-Kasmir in Pakistan, safe housing codes were enforced, preventing the building of homes on the steep slopes and requiring earthquake-resistant materials and building techniques. The social and human cost of seizing these opportunities was to prolong the discomfort of the victims who were forced to stay in temporary shelters.

Infrastructure Development

Disasters can cause a serious destruction of physical infrastructure and communications systems. At the same time, however, they present an opportunity for technological innovations and development. In Kashmir, Pakistan, for example, following the devastating earthquake of 2005, roads were destroyed, and communication and electrical lines were cut. One of the results was the quick introduction of technological innovations such as cellular phones.

In Indonesia, following the eruption of Mt. Merapi in 2010, and in Sri Lanka, following the tsunami, it became apparent that the existing physical infrastructure could not accommodate the urgent need to alert the population and to guide it before, during, and after disasters. This situation provided a unique opportunity to use digital smart phones for social networking and disaster warning. Similarly, in Thailand, following the tsunami, the entire fresh water systems in the Krabi region were destroyed. Rather than rebuilding the existing systems, new pipelines and reservoirs were constructed, with the participation of the community. Thus, the disaster not only enabled the upgrading of the water system and the improvement of health conditions but also strengthened the community organizational structure.

Sociopolitical Development Challenges

Social Change and Community Integration

Following the floods in Bangladesh and the tsunami in Sri Lanka, local women whose families were affected assumed leading roles and became the driving force in the recovery efforts of their communities. This opened up a unique opportunity for social change, strengthening the status of women and fostering the development of women's movements. In Sri Lanka, the centrality of a local women's movement increased dramatically as a social force in the rural society and continued well into the reconstruction phase. Subsequently, community leaders realized the critical role of women in the recovery processes and legitimized the more open, visible, and active involvement of women in their respective communities.

The process of rebuilding the embankments in Bihar, India, following the floods of 2008 was, in itself, an exercise in community development. The community was mobilized through a series of meetings, and both men and women volunteered to participate. The stressful situation and, subsequently, the leading roles that the women assumed overcame the traditional norms that prevented women from taking an active role outside their homes. The result was a significantly reduced level of marginalization of women in those communities.

These examples demonstrate how a community's response to disaster may lead to significant social change and open the way to new patterns of social interaction. In the cases presented above, community leaders realized the critical role of women and the need for change as well as seized the opportunity to develop mechanisms for their social mobility. Communities are often comprised of distinct social and religious groups, with clear boundaries between them. During the period following a disaster, when people of all social classes and faiths face a common threat, the divisiveness becomes less obvious, and collaboration bears fruits for all groups concerned. Because the floods in Bihar, India, affected all social classes and castes, and the recovery necessitated the joint efforts of all those affected, community meetings, for the first time, included people of all castes. The inclusive participation in planning the recovery process demonstrated the advantages of local cooperation across social divisions and resulted in greater social cohesion and a relaxing of class barriers.

In Bangladesh, following the floods of 2008, the whole community was mobilized in an integrated fashion, bringing together Muslim, Christian, and Hindu religious leaders as well as "secular" leaders such as teachers and village heads. An unprecedented all-inclusive community forum for planning and follow-up was formed. It increased the level of community integration, allowed for a smooth recovery process, and, by virtue of its continued existence, had a long-term impact on the community.

Political Change

On the political level, disasters that affect diverse populations in a given region may cause a process of rapprochement between rival groups, enhance reconciliation, and help facilitate a peace process. In Banda Aceh, Indonesia, the tsunami resulted in a significant and long-term change in the hostile relationship between the Free Aceh Movement, a Muslim movement, and the central government. Muslim militants who suffered from the disaster quickly congregated throughout the devastated Aceh province. During the emergency and the recovery phases, they were provided with immediate relief and temporary housing from the Indonesian government and the military. Similarly, they took an active role in the emergency efforts, working side by side with the rest of the emergency forces. The surge in the spirit of cooperation was capitalized on by the government and brought about a dramatic attitude change among the rebels, resulting in long-term cooperation. The former rebels gained political power in a democratic way and continue to collaborate with the national government. In contrast, in Sri Lanka, a country that has suffered from decades of civil war, the opportunity for long-term cooperation was not seized, and the reduced tension between the Tamil Tigers (LTTE) and the government following the tsunami was short-lived, and the hostilities were resumed at an even higher level.

Community Sustainability

Sustainable development meets the needs of the present without compromising the ability to meet future needs. In the developing world, disasters can present opportunities for overcoming the poverty that characterized a region prior to the disaster and that deepened immediately afterwards.

In southern Thailand, following the tsunami, the recovery-renewal measures included the teaching of new fishing techniques, the introduction of microfinance programs, and the construction of new fresh water systems. These measures improved the livelihood of the population, reduced poverty, and ensured sustainability and long-term development. Similarly, in Bangladesh, following the recent floods, fishing cooperatives were established, and the villagers were taught the skills of building and mending their boats as well as improved fishing techniques.

In contrast, in Banda Aceh, Indonesia, following the tsunami and the destruction of the local fleets of boats, foreign aid agencies purchased and imported boats from abroad. The boats however, did not comply with local fishing practices, and training courses were not offered to introduce the new technology. This represented a lost opportunity for local development and dozens of broken boats in the river leading to the sea, preventing safe passage.

In Sri Lanka, following the tsunami, to get the villagers back on their feet, the farmers were taught new baking techniques using the abundance of rice rather than the imported expensive wheat, thus changing consumption patterns and increasing local income. In India, following the floods, a women's large cooperative was developed. The cooperative, which included thousands of women, used its power and the post-disaster solidarity to negotiate successfully with a large insurance agency to insure the women who were previously considered uninsurable because of their lower status and dependence on men. These examples demonstrate how disasters present opportunities for leveraging and mobilizing local assets for community development.

Disaster Mitigation and Preparedness

A disaster, with its devastating effects, also provides opportunities for developing better preparedness and mitigating mechanisms for protecting against future disasters. Recognizing and seizing these opportunities takes an articulated vision from leaders as well as political will. In Sri Lanka, the tsunami resulted in a greatly enhanced awareness of the effects of natural disasters and significantly increased the introduction of new disaster-mitigation and management practices.

For example, Sarvodaya, a leading community-based NGO (Sarvodaya, 2010), developed, as part of its core structure, a new community disaster management center. The center became engaged in both preparedness and mitigation activities and significantly improved the response to subsequent disasters. In India, the All India Disaster Mitigation Institute (AIDMI, 2010) significantly increased its professional level and geographic involvement following the tsunami, including their school safety programs and their work on an international level. AIDMI also became a source of knowledge to disaster-stricken countries in the region, including the Maldives, Myanmar, and Bangladesh.

The degree to which challenges and opportunities materialize is influenced by the ability of leaders, organizations, and communities to understand the significance and interrelationships between a number of key factors that are at play following a disaster and how to manipulate them. These factors are presented and discussed in the next section.

KEY FACTORS AFFECTING POST-DISASTER DEVELOPMENT

Avgar, Kaufman, Iecovich, and Mirsky (2004) present a conceptual model for community development in the aftermath of a disaster. The model seeks to answer the questions: How do communities utilize critical factors that are at play in a post-disaster situation to achieve community growth, development, and transformation? The factors discussed in that conceptual model include solidarity, integration, linkages, social entrepreneurship, leadership, and outside intervention. As our experience expanded, we identified developmental community vision as an additional critical factor that influences the response to and the redevelopment of communities following disasters.

In the following section, we demonstrate how these factors and their interrelationships during the three phases of post-disaster response, namely, emergency, recovery, and renewal, play key roles in long-range community development. We suggest how these factors can be manipulated so as to become an integral part of the intervention strategies. In light of our "opportunity orientation" approach, we also emphasize the importance of the continuity of responses in the intervention process, from the emergency and recovery to the renewal phases.

Community Development Vision

The development vision of a community can be defined as the desired long-term future state of the community. It reflects the orientation and aspiration for a better future, as perceived by the community, suggests directions as to how to achieve the desired future state of affairs, and articulates the underlying values of the community. A common vision serves as a beacon for decision makers throughout the community. The vision is often the prism that serves to identify opportunities and challenges. The community vision, at its best, is holistic and encompasses all aspects of human life, including interrelationships between social, economic, and spiritual spheres as well as the relationship to the environment.

Having a clear vision of "the community at its best" can guide intervention activities during the emergency and recovery phases and set the stage for the third phase of reconstruction and renewal. In the final analysis, it is what happens during the renewal phase that makes the difference between development and stagnation.

A common community developmental vision can be developed before a disaster or can emerge following the disaster. A clear vision prior to the disaster is often difficult to achieve due to existing constraints such as intra-community tensions, political rivalries, and physical constraints such as proximity of residential areas to the shorelines. A disaster may shatter the prevalent worldview, free post-disaster efforts from some of the constraints, and enable the community to perceive the future differently, specifically, to identify and mobilize local assets that were previously unrecognized or ignored, thus facilitating growth.

Often the major community development agents that are active in the post-disaster development process are the local NGOs. Their activities during disaster situations are influenced by their former vision of community development. For example, the activities of Sarvodaya in Sri Lanka and Population Development Association (PDA, 2010) in Thailand, both leading NGOs that were intensively involved in the post-tsunami response, are indicative of a pre-disaster community development vision. Sarvodaya, as a grassroots organization, was always committed to local capacity building and building strong, cohesive, and independent as well as integrated local communities. The organization had a clear community vision and access to the corresponding institutions and programs that were needed to achieve it. In its activity following the tsunami, Sarvodaya was able to direct the international resources that it raised for rural growth and development, thus moving toward realizing their vision.

New social structures, such as multi-purpose community centers and an institute for higher learning, were established to increase social integration, professionalization, and community building. Sarvodaya also established a community disaster management center that helps local communities to prepare for future disasters and enlightens community leaders as to how to quickly respond to future disasters and utilize opportunities for local development.

PDA, like Sarvodaya, had a development vision and has aspired to work throughout Thailand to disseminate its programs and message. The tsunami and the resources that they were able to mobilize were used to expand its operation into new geographical areas and to build new sustainable programs, such as pure water systems and income-generating ventures in schools and communities situated in disaster-stricken areas.

Following a disaster, the vision of a community organization can change dramatically. For example in the Maldives, Care Society (Care, 2010), a local NGO, added disaster preparedness and response to its major social mission and vision, which is to promote the conditions needed to support the disabled. The expansion brought about a significant change in the structure and functioning of the organization, which now functions as a multi-issue organization.

The direct operational intervention of outside agencies, and the degree to which they try to impose their vision or formulate it in a dialogue with the community, is a critical factor in post-disaster recovery. Some agencies arrive with their own sociopolitical agenda and vision of the future. They try to impose the vision on the affected community and its social structure and design relief-recovery efforts based on their vision. To be effective and to have a long-term impact, however, "buy in" by local organizations or communities is needed. An example is the development of the Hesed community centers network in the former Soviet Union (FSU; Mirsky, Kaufman, & Avgar, 2006). In the 1990s, following Perestroika and the breakdown of the Soviet Union, Jewish communities faced a disastrous situation due to the collapse of social services, the breakdown of ideology, and lack of support systems. American Jewish Distribution Fund (AJDC) operated in the Former Soviet Union as an International NGO and, in partnership with the local population, became involved with community development. Together with local leadership, a vision of the desired character of this Jewish community welfare institution was crystallized, and the appropriate response and reorganization needed to achieve the vision were developed. The response took the form of the Hesed model, a welfare service based on Jewish values, voluntarism, and community orientation. It was implemented successfully and took root in hundreds of communities because the vision on which it was based was shared and further developed by local communities.

Lappin (1985) recommended that disaster intervention agents adopt the role of enabler, undertaking a proactive institution-building approach, with constant dialogue with community-wide leadership, who should make the final decisions. Outside agencies should be attuned to the local community's vision and assist in further crystallizing that vision.

External and internal agencies involved with disaster must not be fixated at the recovery phase and need to consider the impact of short-term policies on long-term development. An example of such fixation on recovery that hampered long-term development was seen in Banda Aceh, where first-rate temporary barracks were built for internally displaced people. These barracks were equipped with running water, good lighting, and overall adequate services. The good conditions of the temporary housing prevented people from leaving them and rebuilding their homes. In contrast, those who were housed in less-desirable temporary housing conditions resettled and rebuilt. The first-rate barracks remained heavily populated, slowly turning into a slum.

Solidarity

Solidarity, on both the local and national level, is of critical importance to a community's development subsequent to disasters. At the community level, solidarity can be defined as the degree to which members of the community are unified in pursuit of common interests and goals (Avgar et al., 2004). It reflects feelings of identification with a meaningful reference group. Solidarity can be seen as the energy that enables people and communities to thrive. As a form of spontaneous energy, solidarity enables people to put aside self-interests and to come together in a common effort. It is a force that enables communities and organizations to confront both physical repercussions and the social-psychological traumas.

The resilience of people struck by disaster is a powerful force for the rehabilitation and reconstruction of their societies. The higher the level of solidarity that is exhibited after a disaster and mobilized for relief and reconstruction, the greater the resilience of the community. Solidarity as a spontaneous, unstructured form of energy is, in and of itself, an opportunity with tremendous potential for change, growth, and development. To sustain solidarity and ensure that it has a long-term impact, it needs to be structured and institutionalized. If organized structures and mechanisms are not developed as vehicles for channeling this energy, it will fade out relatively quickly, without leaving a lasting impact. This energy can and often is directed toward the establishment of new structures (e.g., committees, standing task forces, new organizations) or is absorbed and integrated into existing organizations, particularly local NGOs. Institutionalizing solidarity also increases the potential for the rise of a new energized cadre of leadership. The channeling and structuring of solidarity provides a framework for increased grassroots participation and involvement in the recovery. Similarly, greater local participation often leads to increased economic activities and to more constructive and sustainable development. A clear, crystallized community vision can serve as an effective platform to harness, structure, and mobilize solidarity as additional resource to further development and growth.

One of the most obvious manifestations of solidarity is the phenomenon of volunteers and volunteerism (Mirsky et al., 2006). For example, in the implementation of recovery programs, we have witnessed, in Sri Lanka, Bangladesh, and Thailand, the establishment of new committees and task forces on the basis of the increased number of volunteers. When these new organizational forms were structured and institutionalized, they facilitated renewal in four significant ways:

1. They provided a desirable arena for local participation in the planning and decision-making process. They placed the beneficiaries in the role of resource and agents of change, a level of involvement and participation that contributes to recovery by restoring people's sense of meaning and value, which the disaster had damaged.
2. They provided a more structured, institutional channel for the rising scope of citizen participation and a sense of solidarity that needed a framework. These committees continued to function in the renewal phase and served as a catalyst for the establishment of new services and activities.
3. They presented additional frameworks for the emergence of new local leadership.
4. They served as self-help groups or acted as a safety net for their members and their families as well as others who were in need of assistance.

At the national level, solidarity is defined as the degree to which different governments and local organizations, often with diverse goals and interests, are unified in pursuit of a common goal (Avgar et al., 2004). A disaster can bring about a significant increase in the cooperation between the government and NGOs. It can also, however, increase the hostility and rivalry between the sectors due to competition over the influx of new resources. For example, in Sri Lanka, the entire NGO sector came under heavy criticism because, for the first time, the government felt that the NGO sector received more resources than did the government.

At the national level, the sudden rise in solidarity after a disaster can also bring significant structural changes and new policy guidelines in the service sector, particularly in the services related to the disaster. In Chile, for example, the rise in solidarity that occurred following the mining crisis in 2010 resulted in structural and policy chances with regard to mining practices at the national level.

Integration

Integration is defined as the degree to which organizational divisions, subgroups, and institutions within the community are connected to each other (Avgar et al., 2004). Organizations, communities, and societies differ with respect to the degree of their internal animosity and fragmentation as well as their inter-organizational linkage and cohesiveness. A high degree of integration, inter- and intra-community, and organizational cooperation allows for the high degree of resource mobilization needed to meet common goals and confront potential threats. A disaster often shatters existing coalitions and the social equilibrium and disrupts familiar modes of operation. New patterns of inter- and intra-community and organizational interaction may be revealed, while old ones may be either strengthened or abandoned.

For example, following the tsunami, we witnessed the rise of coordinating structures in an attempt to bring together the host of organizations operating in response to the disaster. These structures were organized by local or outside bodies such as the UN. In Kashmir, it was the UN that assumed the role of coordination, and in Sri-Lanka, it was Consortium of Humanitarian Agencies (CHA). We believe that, when such roles are performed by local agencies, which are an integral part of the community, the long-term changes are greater.

Linkages

Communities and organizations should be viewed within a larger social context, and linkages are the relationships or communication channels between communities and organizations in a regional, national, or international context (Avgar et al., 2004). Globalization is the ultimate manifestation of linkages between societies, communities, and organizations. Linkages are potential or actual resources for development, growth, and response to threats and disasters. Following a disaster, both dormant and active linkages may be used to mobilize outside support. The effect of linkages is cyclical. The disaster, as noted earlier, is followed by an influx of outside agencies, many of which have not had any linkages to organizations in the affected areas. The newly established contacts, however, often result in long-term relationships, allowing for continued support for long-term development. Clearly, the more linkages that the community had before the disaster, the greater the potential for recruiting help. However, it is not just the number of linkages that is important. Prior intensive contacts and collaboration with outside organizations increase the propensity for the interaction between the recipients and the outside organization to be harmonious. Additionally, those outsiders may have greater appreciation for local conditions.

The impact of linkages on development is closely related to vision. A clear, unifying vision of the community is often accompanied by forceful enthusiasm that, in turn, serves as a magnet in attracting outside organizations and resources. A clear vision can strengthen the impact of linkages in two ways. First, having a vision highlights the kind of resources required to bring development to its materialization and thus acts as a directive force in identifying and mobilizing the needed resources. Second, the force of this enthusiasm is contagious, thus facilitating the mobilization of outside resources needed for achieving its goals.

In an interview, Dr. Ahangamage Tudor Ariyaratna, the chair of Sarvodaya, emphasized that, following the tsunami, as usually happens following disaster situations, the number of partners of the organization tripled. Their vision allowed for mobilizing existing as well as new partners and the use of outside expertise toward their development goals.

Social Entrepreneurship

Social entrepreneurship leads to the establishment of new social organizations, programs, and services as well as to continued innovation and restructuring of existing ones. As part of shaking the existing social structure, a disaster presents opportunities for entrepreneurs. Social entrepreneurship, like linkages, is also highly related to developmental vision (Kaufman, Mirsky, &Avgar, 2007). Entrepreneurs, by virtue of being innovators, are motivated and oriented by a clear vision of the future. Following a disaster, when old ways of operation are often inadequate, the new situation of uncertainly provides fertile ground for both socially and economically oriented entrepreneurs who are sensitive to new opportunities.

Following the tsunami in Krabi, Thailand, the vocational training frameworks were drastically changed with the introduction of information technology and computers by external entrepreneurs. In Sri Lanka, community tourism rose as a new venture led by local entrepreneurs. In Indonesia, a local entrepreneur was one of the driving forces in the recovery and development efforts in Banda Aceh, introducing new methods to the fishing industry in the region.

In summary, the interrelationships between these factors are critical and have significant influence on response and long-term development. Some of the factors, such as integration and linkages, which influence organizational response and development, are related to conditions that prevailed before the disaster. Others, such as solidarity and outside intervention, are consequences of the disaster.

CONCLUSION

Post-disaster situations create tremendous devastation and chaos, with the result that individuals, organizations, and communities are thrown into a state of shock. At the same time, a flood of outside agencies and organizations sweep the region (often referred to as the secondary disaster). It is at this point that visionary leadership is critical for recovery, renewal, and long-term development. From a religious-historical perspective, viewing disaster as an opportunity is as old as the world itself. Out of chaos, God created the world. Similarly, the devastation following the Biblical flood served as an opportunity for establishing a new covenant between God and man. The challenge is, of course, to create a visionary response out of disaster.

REFERENCES

All India Disaster Mitigation Institute. (2010). Retrieved from www.southasiadisasters.net

American Jewish Joint Distribution Committee. (2010). Retrieved from www.jdc.org

Anderson, W. A. (2008). Mobilization of the black community following Hurricane Katrina: From disaster assistance to advocacy of social change and equity. *International Journal of Mass Emergencies and Disasters*, 26(3), 198-218

Avgar, A., Kaufman, R., Iecovich, E., & Mirsky, J. (2004). Social disaster as an opportunity. *Social Development Issues*, 26(1), 1-13.

Bolin, R. (2006). Race, class, ethnicity, and disaster vulnerability. In H. Rodríguez, E. L. Quarantelli & R. R. Dynes (Eds.), *Handbook of disaster research* (pp. 113-129). New York, NY: Springer.

Care Society. (2010). Retrieved from www.caresociety.org.mv

Kaufman, R, Avgar, A. & Mirsky, J. (2004). A brigade model for the management of service volunteers: Lessons from the former Soviet Union. *International Journal of Nonprofit and Voluntary Sector Marketing*, 9(1), 57-68.

Kaufman, R., Mirsky, J., & Avgar, A. (2007). Social entrepreneurship in crisis situations. *International Journal of Diversity in Organisations, Communities and Nations*, 7(3), 227-232.

Klein, N. (2007). *The shock doctrine: The rise of disaster capitalism*. New York, NY: Knopf.

Lappin, B. (1985). Community development beginning in social work enabling. In R. W. Roberts & S. H. Taylor (Eds.), *Theory and practice of community social work* (pp. 59-94). New York, NY: Columbia University Press,.

Mirsky, J., Kaufman, R., & Avgar, A. (Eds.), (2006). *Social disaster as an opportunity*. Langham, MD: University Press of America.

Population Development Association. (2010). Retrieved from www.pda.org.th

Sarvodaya. (2010). Retrieved from www.sarvodaya.org

Telford, J., & Cosgrave, J. (2007). The international humanitarian system and the 2004 Indian Ocean earthquake and tsunamis. *Disasters, 31*(1), 1-28.

Telford, J., Cosgrave, J., & Houghton, R. (2006). *Joint evaluation of the international response to the Indian Ocean tsunami: Synthesis report*. London, UK: Tsunami Evaluation Coalition.

NOTES

1. The American Jewish Joint Distribution Committee is the overseas arm of the American Jewish community. Its core mission is to assist Jewish communities in distress. As part of its core mission, AJJDC has provided humanitarian aid on a non-sectarian basis throughout the world.

2. TAG International Development is an English/Jewish NGO. Its core mission is to export Israeli expertise and best practices to Third World Countries. It aims to promote peace and reconciliation as well as community development and to build professional regional networks and cooperation in the area of disaster response.

Chapter Four
Program Logic Modeling as a Tool for Developing a Disaster Response and Mitigation Plan: The Somaliland Experience

Johny Augustine and Vivek Chemmancheri Kokkammadathil

Lack of or limited capacity to curb the impact of hazards remains a major hurdle for the Horn of Africa, especially Somaliland, which attained sovereign state status by separating itself from war-torn Somalia in 1991. Despite being a relatively peaceful nation and having over 35 international and 90 national non-governmental organizations (NGOs) engaged in humanitarian relief work (United Nations Office for the Coordination of Humanitarian Affairs [UNOCHA], 2005), the country has been struggling to deal with the perilous impact of the repeated droughts and flash floods hitting the country for decades. Institutional deficiencies and financial constraints remain the major factors that severely limit the extent of governmental involvement and institutional responses to cataclysmic events such as these.

   The purpose of this chapter is to illustrate the development of a drought response and mitigation plan for Somaliland using logic modeling (Kellogg Foundation, 2004) as one of the key methodologies. We argue that a well-developed emergency response and mitigation plan, utilizing the principles of logic modeling, could be a starting point to address some of the most pressing needs of the vulnerable communities of this region.

   This chapter is organized into an introduction and major five sections. The introduction presents the setting in which we did our study and the major purpose of the chapter. Because we were unable to locate much scholarly literature specific to Somaliland, section one attempts to provide a general overview of the disaster trend in the Horn of Africa. Key social, economic, and political issues that necessitate the need for a comprehensive drought response and mitigation plan for the region are also explored, including the impact of these disasters on the lives of the vulnerable communities in the region. Section two concerns the institutional response to drought and flood in the Horn of Africa. Particular attention is given to the focus of ActionAid International Somaliland (AAIS) in

Somaliland, including a discussion of challenges and the need for best practices. Section three presents the method used to obtain the background and contextual information for development of the Drought Response and Mitigation Plan for Somaliland, utilizing the principles of logic modeling and based on the results of rapid vulnerability assessments (RVAs) of five drought-stricken villages in the region. Section four is centered more specifically on logic model development. Section five, the final section, provides the major implications of our work, specifically for social workers, NGO personnel, and others who are engaged in disaster response services.

BACKGROUND AND OVERVIEW

Natural disasters such as droughts and flash floods have been on the increase in the Horn of Africa—the region containing the countries of Eritrea, Djibouti, Ethiopia, Somalia, and Somaliland—and continue to affect the vulnerable communities in the region. Drought disasters are the most common, with debilitating social and economic impacts on the lives of the rural communities. Somaliland, a break-away region from Somalia and a self-declared republic, has witnessed three harsh droughts since 2000 that have resulted in massive asset loss, increased livestock mortality, and, in severe situations, human death. In 2008, this semi-arid region received very little rainfall during the two major seasons locally known as *Gu'* (April-June) and *Dyer* (September-November) (AAIS, 2008), portending a precarious year ahead for Somaliites. In the ensuing sections, we attempt to portray the key social, economic, and environmental impacts of these extreme climatic changes on the people in the region.

ECONOMIC, SOCIAL, AND POLITICAL IMPACTS
OF DISASTERS

The effects of prolonged drought and erratic rainfalls on the rural communities in the Horn of Africa are multifarious: devastation of pastoral land and crops, emaciation of livestock, famine and hunger, and, in severe cases, livestock and human death (Speranza, Kiteme, & Weismann, 2008; Wakabi, 2006). In addition, cyclical droughts result in a loss of biodiversity, deforestation, temporary-distress migration, poor productivity of land (Balleh, 2008; Morrissey, 2008), and increased conflict, particularly over pastoral land access and rights (AAIS, 2007, 2008). Further, the UN's World Food Program (WFP) is claiming that, in Ethiopia, approximately 17.5 million people will be affected by the severe and extended drought of 2008. The present drought is the worst since 1984, during which approximately 1 million people starved to death due to famine and hunger ("The tragedy of the decade," 2008; Zarocostas, 2008).

In addition to the cyclical droughts, the flash floods induced by torrential rains are a source of major concern for the people living in this region. In 2009, flashfloods resulted in the displacement of several hundred families and deaths of a minimum 5,700 livestock ("BBC monitoring Africa," 2009) in Somaliland. The livestock, weakened by the prolonged drought, were unable to survive the 72 hours of torrential rain. In many parts of the world, including the Horn of Africa, flash floods are followed by numerous public health issues, such as compromised personal hygiene, poor sanitary conditions, contaminated water sources, inaccessibility to health care services, and the spread of disease (Keim, 2008). Responses to such crisis situations are severely limited, particularly in the Horn of Africa, due to inadequate surveillance measures implemented by the government and the lack of awareness and preparedness plans of the communities.

THE IMPACT OF DROUGHTS AND FLASH FLOODS ON SOMALILAND

Somaliland people's ability to make a living is severely challenged by periodic droughts and flash floods. Kabubo-Mariara and Karanja (2007) reported that flash floods and droughts are the two major disasters that adversely affect the agricultural sector and livestock production of the African region. This holds true for Somaliland, whose economy relies almost entirely on livestock production, agriculture, and remittance from abroad. For instance, the majority (60-65%) of the people of Somaliland rely on livestock for their livelihood (UNOCHA, 2005). The continuing droughts have caused a huge depletion in the livestock (60-80% of herds) due to a lack of quality feedstuffs and an increase in the severity and spread of disease and parasites in the drought-affected regions. Even though the poor wanted to hold on to their livestock assets until the drought was over, the cost of fodder and food for survival forced them to sell their livestock for cheap prices, usually less than 30% of the normal rates (Little, Stone, Mogues, Castro, & Negatu, 2008). Further, the severe crop loss, combined with soaring food prices, has resulted in an acute food and livelihood crisis throughout northern Somalia. For the first time, as a recent Food Security Assessment Unit (FSAU) rapid assessment (AAIS, 2008) estimates, 20% of the total urban population living in the urban areas are facing humanitarian emergency conditions.

The depletion of ground water level is another major source of concern for the people of Somaliland. The drought assessment conducted by ActionAid in the three regions of Sanag, Togdheer, and Hargeisa reveals that the depletion of the water level can have both direct and indirect effects on the lives of Somaliland people. Direct effects are an acute shortage of water for drinking and irrigation. Indirect effects include poverty; increased conflict over pastoral land; declined productivity of land; depleted assets; crop loss; food crisis; malnourished children; increased school dropouts, especially during drought periods; spread of water-borne diseases and other ailments; and weakened condition and production of livestock (AAIS, 2008). Unlike in the past, even the coastal and mountain regions are affected by the current crisis.

Getting potable water has always been difficult in the eastern regions of Somaliland. Families depend on rainwater for drinking, and very few communities have boreholes. Water from shallow wells is normally used for watering livestock and not for drinking purposes due to its high calcium and magnesium content. Shallow wells and barkades (water catchment areas) have dried up. When we did our study, a barrel of potable water cost about 80,000 to 160,000 Somali shillings (1 US dollar = 28,000 Somali shillings) compared with 20,000 to 35,000 shillings during the normal season. Water trucking from water-rich villages to dried-up villages has always been impeded by an insufficient infrastructure and poor coordination of service delivery. In addition, financial constraints and local community involvement still remain the two main stumbling blocks to attaining hydrological security in the region. For example, the construction of barkades, shallow wells, and earth-dams to improve availability and accessibility to water sources has always been hindered by lack of investment from the government and national and international NGOs.

Women and children of Somaliland are disproportionately affected by the drought and flash flood disasters. Weak political representation, inaccessibility to education and training, and ineffective land reforms that would have enabled women's access to farm lands are cited as some of the reasons for women's disadvantaged position in the region (AAIS, 2007, 2008; Mensah, 2008). In addition, a lack of milk and nutritious food, a reduced number of and low-calorie meals per day, and hardships associated with fetching potable water have resulted in serious malnutrition among pregnant and lactating women, complicated pregnancy, increased maternal mortality, low birth weight, and undernourished children under 5 years of age. Women's employment, education, and training needs have never been the focus of the emergency preparedness plans of any governmental or non-governmental agencies and hence remain a concern.

THE INSTITUTIONAL RESPONSE TO DROUGHT AND FLOOD IN THE HORN OF AFRICA

Even though almost all of the southern African countries have some sort of formal drought response and mitigation plan (Wilhite, 2002), the countries in the Horn of Africa, particularly Somaliland, do not have an institutionalized disaster response system. As Wilhite further indicates and as shown in the literature, the impact of droughts is seriously felt by countries that lack institutional capacities or human and monetary resources to mitigate the impacts of such events. Although advanced methods and technologies are available to combat such extreme events, the implementation of those methods has been either slow or extremely difficult in the Horn of Africa. For instance, in 2003, the government of Somaliland created the National Environment Research and Disaster Preparedness Authority (NERAD) to coordinate the disaster management efforts of Somaliland government and over 90 national and international NGOs working in the region. However, due to insufficient financial support from the government and lack of technical know-how, NERAD has been struggling to develop a comprehensive disaster response and mitigation plan for the country. In addition, the efforts of national and international organizations to fight extended droughts have been seriously challenged by lack of community involvement, insufficient monetary resources, and lack of skilled manpower (AAIS, 2007, 2008).

THE FOCUS OF AAIS IN SOMALILAND: CHALLENGES

AAIS operates in the four regions of Somaliland: Sool, Sanaag, Togdheer, and Hargeisa. Currently, the activities of AAIS are focused on the following issues: (a) emergency relief services, (b) women's rights, (c) food rights, (d) governance, (e) education, (f) HIV/AIDS, and (g) human security in emergencies. Out of 13 local partners, two long-term partners—the community-based organizations at Sanaag and Togdheer, and one national NGO (HAVOYOCO)—have implemented emergency drought relief operations with the support of AAIS.

Even though the interventions carried out by AAIS and partner organizations have been effective in addressing the emergency needs of the three regions mentioned above, our critical review of the interventions revealed several challenges and the need for best practices. First, as revealed by our review, the highly sensitive and volatile security condition prevailing in the country represents one of the major challenges for implementing the rights-based program in the region, the key elements of which are community participation, accountability, involvement of vulnerable groups, and personal and community empowerment. Second, the partner agencies would certainly benefit from advanced methodological input, including development of sustainable programs, creation of a carefully crafted monitoring and evaluation plan, and capacity building. Further, we realize that capacity building should be scientifically based and should aim at building skills that enhance the integration of scientific knowledge with indigenous knowledge to provide a more effective and efficient response to crisis events. To that end, we have attempted to incorporate an evaluation tool, frequently used in program evaluation, the *program logic model*, in the development of a drought response and mitigation plan for the region. Third, and most importantly, there is the need for increased community involvement in the design, implementation, and evaluation of rights-based emergency response programs to make this a sustainable endeavor. We recognize that crafting a new approach to find solutions to the above problems would require deliberate and concerted efforts among AAIS, its partner organizations, government agencies, and, above all, the people of Somaliland to make those solutions sustainable, locally relevant, and acceptable.

USE OF THE PROGRAM LOGIC MODEL

The program logic model is a schematic representation of how an organization achieves its mission and objectives. The logic model illustrates how program outcomes are linked with its activities/resources, problem statement, and philosophical assumptions (Kellogg Foundation, 2004; Royse, Thyer, Padget, & Logan, 2006). The program logic model is a handy tool for any researcher/practitioner interested in program development and appraisal for several reasons (Kellogg Foundation, 2004). First, it helps in charting the course of the project, anticipating the challenges ahead and resources available, and in staying focused on program goals and activities. Second, it is an important tool in empowering the community because, with the use of this model, the participants are more aware of their role in the program and, hence, are more likely to be actively involved in the program development process. Third, this model provides a timeline to accomplish the goals and to let the participants know when they have accomplished the goals. Fourth and finally, it can strengthen program planners' as well as the participants' voice in the different phases of program development.

Even though the program logic model has been used in numerous program evaluation efforts (e.g., see Kellogg Foundation, 2004; Mulroy & Lauber, 2004) and is regarded as an effective evaluation tool, it has never been used, as revealed by our review, in the development of a disaster response and mitigation plan. Utilizing an evaluation tool such as this could increase community involvement, strengthen participants' voice, and utilize resources optimally in developing and implementing the program, especially in countries such as Somaliland, where resources are scarce and agencies lack appropriate tools for demonstrating their program effectiveness.

METHOD

Background and contextual information required for this chapter were collected primarily through RVAs of five drought-stricken villages in the regions of Sanag, Togdheer, and Hargeisa of Somaliland; participant observation; and in-depth interviews with the people of and staff at the partner organizations in Somaliland by the disaster preparedness fellow (one of the authors) during his period of assignment from June 6, 2008, to July 17, 2008, at AAIS. The primary criteria for selecting these regions included (a) the gravity of the crisis, (b) the extent of AAIS involvement in the region, (c) community accessibility, and (d) recommendations by partner organizations. Additional materials were garnered through a diligent review of AAIS project activities and program documents since the year 1992.

Over the past few years, participatory RVAs have become a major tool for researchers in the development arena to collect and analyze information at the community level. Focus group discussions (FGDs) represent one of the major techniques used by the researchers in conducting the RVA. In the present study, we organized five FGDs in the five villages of Togdheer, Hargeisa, and Sanag. While selecting the focus group members, efforts were made to include women, elderly, community leaders, and youth to bring in diverse perspectives. The FGDs lasted for 1-1/2 to 2 hours. Mapping of hazards, vulnerabilities, and resources in the communities, exploring existing preparedness and coping practices, and identifying key solutions to combat the impacts of drought and flash floods were the key foci in each FGD. In addition to the five focus groups held, the fellow visited each village to do a critical appraisal of the major drought mitigation measures employed by the villages. Participant observation and in-depth interviews with beneficiaries helped to accomplish this objective. Further, discussions with local partners, AAIS team members, civil society representatives, and government officials assisted in exploring the current level of preparedness and local capacities as well as potential limitations and challenges to the development and implementation of a disaster mitigation plan.

LOGIC MODEL DEVELOPMENT AND DISCUSSION

Seven major themes emerged from the analyses of the qualitative data obtained through interviews, focus groups, and participant observation: (a) create more and repair available water sources, (b) address the basic needs of women and children during and after extreme events, (c) explore alternative livelihood strategies, (d) preserve rangelands to prevent out-migration and conflict, (e) increase women's participation in the CDCs, (f) build up capacity among the local partners and community, and (g) establish monitoring and evaluation of partner organization activities and programs.

The Emergency Response and Mitigation Program Logic Model (Figure 8.1) thus developed establishes strategies for systematic and fair distribution of water through water-trucking; construction of more barkades, shallow wells, and earth-dams for water storage; a pilot demonstration of "farming-based livelihoods" in addition to "livestock-based livelihoods" in one of the villages; development of rangelands in one of the villages to prevent out-migration; the conducting of periodic social audits; and empowerment of the community through engaging people, especially women, in the decision-making and implementation processes, forming community development committees (CDCs), increasing women's representation in the CDCs, and capacity building among partner organizations through intensive education and training.

Problem Statement: Culturally appropriate, locally developed, and scientifically based disaster response and mitigation plans are needed to prevent the social, economic, and political impacts of cyclical droughts and flash floods in Somaliland.	Underlying Assumption: Implementing a disaster response plan will improve accessibility to water sources, reduce malnutrition among women and children, enhance community involvement, and increase political participation of minority groups.

Resources	Activities	Outputs	Short- and Long- Term Outcomes
Contingency funds from AAIS and Strategic Crisis Program fund of IECT (up to 40,000 pounds) and from sources such as EC, DFID, SIDA, and ECHO Technical and logical support from AAIS, IECT, and local partners and government Service of the community development committees (CDCs)	Provide potable water through water trucking Construct more barkades, shallow wells, and earth-dams Provide food relief and nutritional and medicinal supplies to the most vulnerable families Design and implement capacity building and training among local partners and volunteers	No. of families/ village supported by water supply No. of water sources repaired and created/village No. of women and children supported by emergency relief supplies/year No. of trainings imparted to local partners/volunteers No. of partners trained in fund raising and writing research proposals Pilot demonstration of a livelihood program in one village	Increase in the number of days families supported through water trucking Increased number of water storages Increase in the number of families, especially women and children, supported by relief supplies Increase in the number of local partners trained in emergency response

Resources	Activities	Outputs	Short- and Long-Term Outcomes
Active involvement of local partners with experience in relief services Trained community health and capacity-building staff, and RVA facilitators from AAIS	Design and implement a pilot livelihood training and rangeland development program Form/reorganize community development committees (CDCs) to increase women's participation Design and implement capacity building among CDCs Design and implement an evaluation plan	Pilot demonstration of rangeland development in one village No. of CDCs formed/village No. of women membership/CDC No. of social audits performed	Increase in the number of CDCs Increase in the number of social audits performed by CDCs Maintenance of a distribution register Expansion of livelihood programs Creation of a disaster response and mitigation plan in place for one village Increased representation of women and elderly in the CDCs

Impact: Improved individual and family well-being; personal and community empowerment; improved livelihood and poverty reduction; decreased vulnerability to disasters.

Figure 4.1 Disaster Response and Mitigation Plan Program Logic Model

AAIS and partner organizations put particular emphasis on strengthening community involvement in all the phases of the emergency response and mitigation plan logic model development. While ensuring local involvement in the process, efforts were made to build up the capacity for community members through education, training, and skill-building activities. In July 2008, AAIS conducted a major training program specifically aimed at capacity building among the partner organizations in emergency response. Use of English as a medium of communication in training and workshops poses a serious challenge for most of the partner members (AAIS, 2007). Therefore, developing program manuals and brochures in the local language and building capacity among local volunteers conversant in both English and their native language are priorities in the action plan that we have developed. In addition, efforts were made to engage minority groups, such as women and the elderly, in the program development efforts of AAIS, particularly in regard to increasing women's membership in the CDCs. For instance, women's membership in CDCs increased from literally 0% in the 1990s to 30-40% in 2008. One goal is to increase their membership to 50% by the end of 2009.

In accordance with the goal of empowering the community, AAIS and partner organizations encourage the establishment of CDCs to build up the capacity for community members to assess, prioritize, plan, develop, implement, monitor, and evaluate development programs. Representations among these CDCs vary from women and the elderly to "opinion" leaders in the community. CDCs also undertake project activities aimed at resolving community issues. For instance, the CDC in the district of Koryale in Togdheer, after conducting an RVA with support from partner organizations, submitted a proposal to AAIS for the construction and maintenance of a water source—an earth-dam—to improve accessibility to water. AAIS approved the project, and the CDC monitored the progress of the construction effectively and efficiently. After completion of the project, the CDC assigned a community member to monitor and maintain the dam. The local community contributed to the entire process through labor in addition to their involvement in project planning, implementing, and monitoring.

The livelihood strategies envisioned by the local community, with input from AAIS and partner organizations, vary from building water storages for drinking and irrigation purposes to strengthening social networks (e.g., formation of CDCs and local disaster preparedness committees) and livelihood diversification (e.g., forming cereal banks and exploring alternative livelihood options, such as farming-based livelihood in addition to livestock-based livelihood). The immediate goal is to demonstrate a pilot crop-diversification program in one of the villages, namely Shaahid, in the Togdheer region of Somaliland, with the active involvement of the CDCs.

IMPLICATIONS

The ever-increasing frequency of disasters, the ongoing struggle to deal with the adverse impacts, and the inability of relief organizations to develop and implement sustainable programs to combat poverty and social injustice raise many challenges and opportunities for social workers and other professionals engaged in disaster service and social development, particularly in the poor countries around the globe where resources are scarce, and power and opportunities are concentrated in the hands of just a few. The struggle to mobilize monetary and other resources, secure support from local and national governments, and build capacity in the community to attain these goals will require the integration of scientific knowledge with traditional knowledge, development of new skills, and committed and coordinated efforts of various stakeholders in the field. In this context, the significance of social work is paramount; social workers have the potential to assume leadership, and in turn, design policies and interventions in order to address the issues more holistically. Although numerous practice and policy issues that require attention have been identified, only a few critical implications pertaining to disaster service effectiveness are discussed here.

Although NGOs are not mandated to coordinate with other organizations— local, national, or international—many recognize that each organization can benefit significantly from others' expertise, information, knowledge, skills, and technological equipment (Coppola, 2007). Sharing of resources is important to cutting costs without compromising service efficiency. This cooperation and sharing of resources will become ever more important in precarious economic situations, such as the current global financial crisis, wherein the social welfare and developmental sectors in every nation, rich or poor, will have to struggle and rigorously compete for the ever-diminishing economic resources. Moreover, cooperation among organizations at the local, national, and international levels would help to identify innovative disaster response service models, as various organizations have their own ways of dealing with a crisis. Social workers in the field should promote policy changes at the national and international levels, aimed at mandating coordination and cooperation among humanitarian agencies, and will need ever-increasing knowledge and skills in organizing, relationship-building, advocating, and communicating to be effective in such endeavors.

Effective program development requires effective evaluation of the program outcomes. This is possible only if the program goals and objectives are clearly stated, the activities to accomplish the goals are outlined, the timelines to attain program goals are specified, the indicators to evaluate the program are identified, and the results are promptly documented and reported. Although various humanitarian and development organizations are involved in emergency relief and response services in the Horn of Africa, the effectiveness of such interventions has not been evaluated or documented appropriately. Only when evidence of program or practice effectiveness is shown can social workers know whether the goals that they stated have been accomplished or the services that they provided have been helpful to their clients. In addition, continued funding is always contingent on demonstrated program effectiveness and is crucial for sustaining any program. Therefore, social work practitioners working in the social developmental sector should be open to integrating research with their practice and be aware of advanced research tools and technologies as well as be effective program appraisers. Finally, disasters are one of the major causes and results of poverty.

Whereas the emphasis of most of the disaster management work is on addressing the immediate humanitarian needs of the people, such as basic needs (food, clothing, and shelter), health, and mental health issues, holistic programs aimed at a sustainable solution to the problem are still missing in the disaster management arena. Recent efforts sponsored by United Nations International Strategy for Disaster Reduction (UNISDR) have resulted in increased attention to disaster risk-reduction initiatives in poor countries. The challenges experienced by such initiatives include involving the local community throughout the program development, implementation, and evaluation process; integrating indigenous knowledge with scientific knowledge; and building capacity at the local level. By improving knowledge about organizing the community; building skills to create culturally acceptable assessment tools, programs, and solutions; and developing a strong role in developing community networks and structures to respond to crisis events, social work practitioners can become an effective contributor to risk reduction and social development.

Using tools, such as logic models, in disaster response and mitigation program development is an important and innovative beginning in addressing the diverse needs of the disaster-afflicted community in the Horn of Africa. Such a well-developed model provides a concise, yet precise, description of the program objectives, resources available, challenges ahead, and process and outcome indicators to be tracked and evaluated. The logic model is also a strong tool for social work professionals in communicating with diverse audiences in the area of program development and appraisal. Further, as the *W. K. Kellogg Foundation Logic Model Development Guide* (2004) indicates, the logic model is an important tool in empowering the local community because it builds community capacity, strengthens community voice, and enhances community participation in the program development process.

Note: The views and opinions expressed in this paper are purely those of the authors and do not necessarily state or reflect those of ActionAid International.

REFERENCES

ActionAid International Somaliland (AAIS). (2007). *Annual report.* Hargeisa, Somaliland: Author.

ActionAid International Somaliland (AAIS). (2008, March). *Drought assessment report.* Sanag, Somaliland: Author.

Balleh, A. (2008). From cattle to crops in Ethiopia. *Contemporary Review, 290*(1688), 68-70.

BBC monitoring Africa: Floods cause havoc in western Somaliland. (2009, April 3). Retrieved from ProQuest Central database. (Document ID: 1672404991): http://0-search.ebscohost.com.bianca/penlib.du.edu/login.
aspx?direct=true&db=a9h&AN=35039609&site=ehost-live

Coppola, D. P. (2007). *Introduction to international disaster management.* Amsterdam, Netherlands: Elsevier

Kabubo-Mariara, J., & Karanja, F. (2007). The economic impact of climate change on Kenyan crop agriculture: A Ricardian approach. *Global and Planetary Change, 57,* 319-330.

Keim, M. E. (2008). Building human resilience: The role of public health preparedness and response as an adaptation to climate change. *American Journal of Preventive Medicine, 35*(5), 508-516.

Kellogg Foundation. (2004). *W. K. Kellogg Foundation logic model development guide.* Retrieved from http://www.wkkf.org/Pubs/Tools/ Evaluation/Pub3669.pdf

Little P. D., Stone, M. P., Mogues, T., Castro, A. P., & Negatu, W. (2006). "Moving in place": Drought and poverty dynamics in South Wollo, Ethiopia. *Journal of Development Studies, 42*(2), 200-225.

Mensah, S. A. (2008). Experts address the question: "What are the most important constraints to achieving food security in various parts of Africa?" *Natural Resources Forum 32,* 163-166.

Morrissey, J. (2008). Rural-urban migration in Ethiopia. *Forced Migration Review, 31,* 28-29. Retrieved from http://0-web.ebscohost.com.bianca.penlib.du.edu
/ehost/pdf?vid=2&hid=113&sid=4e04abf4-2bfl-4b52-951a-a-
=0346e07f762%40sessionmgr103

Mulroy, E. A., & Lauber, H. (2004). A user-friendly approach to program evaluation and effective community interventions for families at risk of homelessness. *Social Work, 49*(4), 573-586.

Royse, D., Thyer, B. A., Padget, D. K., & Logan, T. K. (2006). *Program evaluation: An introduction.* Belmont, CA: Thomson Brooks/Cole.

Speranza, C. I., Kiteme, B., Wiesmann, U. (2008). Droughts and famines: The underlying factors and the causal links among agro-pastoral households in semi-arid Makueni district, Kenya. *Global Environmental Change, 18,* 220-233.

The tragedy of the decade? (2008). *Economist, 389*(8604), 58. Retrieved from http://0-search.ebscohost.com.bianca.penlib.du.edu/login.aspx?direct=
true&db=a9h&AN=35039609&site=ehost-live

United Nations Office for the Coordination of Humanitarian Affairs (UNOCHA). (2005). Overview of humanitarian environment in Somaliland. Retrieved from http://ochaonline.un.org/OchaLinkClick.aspx?link= ocha&docid=15117

Wakabi, W. (2006). "Worst drought in a decade" leaves Kenya crippled [World report]. *Lancet, 367,* 891-892.

Wilhite, D. A. (2002). Combating drought through preparedness. *Natural Resources Forum, 26,* 275-285.

Zarocostas, J. (2008). UN warns of millions at risk of starvation in Ethiopia and Somaliland. *BMJ: British Medical Journal, 337*(7661), 73-73. Retrieved from EBSCO*host.*

Chapter Five
Planning for the Unimaginable:
Having Your Personal, Family, Organizational, and Community Plan
Howard S. Feinberg

> You're sleeping soundly in your fourth-floor flat when suddenly you're dreaming that your bed is shaking on a roller coaster ride and you're floating on air—only to wake up and realize it's not a dream. An earthquake has leveled your building and many others in your city. You miraculously survived the collapse with minor injuries.

> While sitting in a café in Haifa, Paris, Sau Paulo, or New York, the building across the way suddenly explodes in front of your eyes, throwing debris all over you and killing or wounding hundreds sitting within a block of the explosion. A gas leak? A bomb?

> There's a spontaneous fire erupting from the trash bins in the basement of your school or 30-story office building. Fire and heavy smoke quickly spread up trash chutes, stairwells, and elevator shafts, permeating the entire building. All exits are cut off!

The time for deciding what to do, who to call, where to get assistance, and how to react is not in the minutes before, during, or after a natural or man-made disaster. Plans and strategies should be well established, documented, and practiced on all levels—personal, family, organizational, and communal—well in advance.

To achieve this state of readiness, thoughtful consideration must be given to several questions:

1. What are the likely and unlikely circumstances that I/we might face (e.g., storms, earthquakes, fires, bombings, war, epidemics)?

2.   What are the potential needs related to various scenarios (e.g., personal, family, organizational, communal, societal, governmental)?
3.   What relationships, protocols, and resources currently exist to help me/us react preparedly and effectively?
4.   What must I/we do today and in the future to move from the current state of readiness to a more sophisticated position that will increase my/our likelihood of surviving and therefore being able to effectively contribute to the larger responses in emergency response, recovery, and rebuilding?

The remainder of this chapter will present basic planning constructs and areas to consider, including communications, evacuation protocols, mission-critical functional redundancy and continuity, relationships with first-response and municipal authorities, and equipment and supplies. The goal of this chapter is to provide information that will help community organizations plan for and implement a disaster preparedness and response plan that focuses on the organization's role as a community coordinating and facilitating entity.

The objectives of this chapter are, first, to provide a blueprint for discussion and action by key staff and leadership in assessing an organization's state of preparedness in the event of an emergency. The second is to identify what the organization must do to ensure that it is prepared to seamlessly maintain its operational integrity so that it can react to and lead the community in times of natural and man-made disasters.

The focus of this chapter is less on security and more on business continuity. As such, the sections below, on operational readiness and recovery, are structured to reflect infrastructure, systems, and training/practice issues. This list should be considered a working draft, and it is not, nor can it be, all-inclusive. However, certain emergency-preparedness issues listed below will have an impact on any organization's ability to respond to all emergencies, including those involving security situations.

Finally, as we consider the following issues, please bear in mind that these are not prescriptions. Rather, they are suggestions on how the community organization might immediately address issues in its control while creating relationships and systems that can react and function in situations not of the organization's making and likely out of its ultimate control. By preparing now and sequentially building in additional layers of preparedness and training, an organization should be better prepared to maintain seamless operations, even if all its physical locations become unusable.

My experience in this area came from early training as a first responder in the 1970s and then as lead staff of the Emergency Preparedness and Disaster Response portfolio for United Jewish Communities (now Jewish Federations of North America) from August 2005 through June 2008. The Jewish Federations of North America represents 157 Jewish Federations and 400 independent Jewish communities. The Federation Movement, collectively among the top 10 charities on the continent, protects and enhances the well-being of Jews and others worldwide through the values of *tikkun olam* (repairing the world), *tzedakah* (charity and social justice), and *Torah* (Jewish learning). This role required that I coordinate the strategic and operational responses of the Jewish Federation system and its partner agencies in response to Hurricanes Katrina, Rita, and Wilma; the Virginia Tech massacre; and several other natural and man-made disasters. This included emergency response, fundraising, fund distribution, and establishing immediate and long-term service priorities for victims and first providers who themselves became secondary victims through PTSD and other conditions.

SUGGESTED ACTION STEPS FOR ALL ORGANIZATIONS

In responding to a disaster, there are five critical functions: Emergency Protocols, Communications, Information Technology, Physical Plant Core Functions and Equipment, and Staff Training, the steps of which are presented below.

Emergency Protocols

1. Create a simplified operations protocol that identifies how to react in an unfolding crisis, if staff and clients are on site, and if and where staff is to report in times of crisis, if off-site.
   a. Using pre-established communications modalities (e.g., website and email announcements, 800-number messaging service, PDA PIN messages), inform staff of unfolding emergencies and any immediate instructions.
   b. Make certain every staff person is aware of building evacuation procedures and meeting locations. In the event of an evacuation, the meeting location should be a safe distance from the affected building.
   c. If locking down or sheltering in place, make sure all in the facility are safe and accounted for.
   d. If there is an incident within any building, staff that can evacuate safely should do so, and anyone able to contact outside authorities should also do so. Be certain to identify yourself and explain the exact nature of the incident and location.
   e. A leadership team should be designated for each geographic facility that is within reasonable commute (by foot, bike, or whatever is available).
   f. Consider winterizing remote camp locations as an alternative operations center should the greater metropolitan area be unusable for a time.
   g. Team leaders for each site (and other mission-critical staff) should have at least two modes of reliable communications, e.g., PDA and satellite phone. An alternative to satellite phones is high-powered

walkie-talkies with a 100-mile (160 kilometer) or more range, without need for radio repeaters.

h. Team leaders also should have access to a stockpile of supplies, as noted in emergency preparedness manuals on the U.S. Homeland Security and FEMA websites (www.DHS.gov / www.FEMA.gov), Canadian government website (http://www.safecanada.ca/menu_ e.asp), American Red Cross (http://www.redcross.org), and other preparedness websites.

i. Cash reserves need to be available for team leaders in the event that they need to operate a facility or remote location for an extended period of time.

2. Train and cross-train all senior management staff and others so that any one of the senior management team can function as team leader of the entire organization's operation and/or a satellite operation at remote location.

3. Review and revise, if necessary, existing chains of command so that staff realize who might be in charge in a crisis and that management decisions might well be made and passed through managers other than those in charge of the usual operations.

4. Over the next six months, establish or enhance working relationships with local law enforcement, federal police, emergency response organizations, local military bases, universities, and other non-profit organizations so that they understand your role in the community and how, in times of need, your organization can help them and they can help you. Key staff should have a list of contacts at other institutions that can be contacted.

5. If not already doing so, consider access protocols to all institutions. Limiting access to campuses and buildings and showing a visible presence of a guard has been a proven deterrent to domestic terror attacks in Los Angeles and Chicago over the past few years.

Communications

1. Train key senior managers in the methodology of sending a mass message and devise a chain of command for times of emergencies.

2. Make sure all staff are in possession of a staff contact list that has at least four modes of contacting individuals (phones: cell and home; email: work and home; instant message contact; other) as well as an emergency contact outside of the community who will be a person whom staff member will contact to leave word if communications are down in your area.

a. Create blast email lists for email and PDA PIN users that can be accessed and used by all staff.

3. Make sure that each staff person has a designated staff team contact tree and leader to contact in times of crisis.
4. Investigate and purchase satellite phones and/or high-powered walkie-talkies for key staff. Train all recipients in their use. Provide extended batteries and consider low-cost generators for key staff.
5. Investigate and purchase an 800 (toll free) number to be used to communicate information should normal modes of communication fail.
6. Investigate and purchase a rapid-message system that can instantly send quick notifications to hundreds of people via phone, instant message, PDA PIN messages, or email.

Information Technology

1. Immediately cross-train several people from the organization to make certain that IT integrity is maintained should the IT director and staff be out of commission.
2. Investigate whether a human interface is necessary to point URLs to back-up servers in times of a power failure. The back-up system should ideally be triggered by remote sensors immediately upon main servers either crashing or going off-line. Perhaps a 5- to 10-minute delay or even up to one hour is prudent, but if a major power outage occurs, back-up servers should be triggered immediately and without human interface.
3. In addition to existing back-up sites, consider establishing another site outside of your metropolitan area that can replicate your servers for instant access from remote locations.
4. Make back-up tapes/disks/jump drives as well. Consider on-line automated back-up systems.
5. If not yet capable, your existing web capacity should be upgraded to include a two-way communications portal for users so that message posting can be utilized as means to track community members' whereabouts as well as to post important messages.

Physical Plant Core Functions and Equipment

1. Identify the physical space in each facility to be developed into the mission critical command center. These spaces need independently functioning power and HVAC in the event of a major campus or grid power failure.
2. Provide back-up generators for each command center with ample fuel supplies and access to outside sources for additional fuel when supplies dwindle.

3. Make certain that IT interfaces in the command centers can be switched to primary command status in event of emergency. Ensure that core servers in all locations have adequate air conditioning.

4. Make certain there is at least one phone line "hard-wired" into the local phone company, with a direct line, and not through a switchboard or other electric-powered device. Check with your phone carrier to make sure that this arrangement will allow the line to be self-powered.

5. Additional hard-wired phones should be in several identifiable locations in each facility.

6. Have at least one additional communications tool available at each command center (high powered walkie-talkie and/or satellite phone).

7. Have water and food stockpiled to allow mission critical staff to occupy the command centers for at least 7-10 days without replenishment. In addition, have more than 10 days' worth of non-perishable food items available.

8. Have a full first-aid kit, with the latest equipment, available. As new emergency response protocols are available from the Red Cross, consider updating supplies and training regularly.

9. Have approved masks available for staff that must be in command center in times of epidemic or chemical/biological emergency. Follow all public health recommendations on staff deployment in times of epidemic or chemical/biological emergency.

10. Have cots and blankets for staff available at each site should sheltering in place become necessary.

11. Consider winterizing any remote camp locations and establishing a potential command location should evacuation of your metropolitan area be necessary.

12. If not already doing so, reconsider access protocols to all institutions. Limiting open access to campuses and buildings and showing a visible presence of a guard has been a proven deterrent to domestic terror attacks in Los Angeles and Chicago over the past few years.

Staff Training

1. As protocols are updated, arrange periodic staff training and drills in all key areas (evacuation, building access procedures, communications with outside agencies and communications "within the family").

2. Cross-train top staff in mission critical functions, especially IT.

3. Consider training entire staff (voluntary) in CPR and basic first aid.

4. Consider inviting the FBI, Department of Homeland Security, Royal Canadian Mounties, and/or local domestic terror experts to do an in-depth security installation and procedures evaluation and then training for staff on responding to an incident in process.

Additional Resource for Community Organizations:

United Jewish Communities Emergency Preparedness Manual http://www.ujc
interofficorg/local_includes/downloads/5819.pdf

CONCLUSION

Emergency preparedness must be a high priority for community organizations of
all types. The ability to function internally and to effectively respond to crises
depends on the organization's staff being trained and ready to respond and lead.
Hopefully, the items discussed in this chapter will help those in organizational
leadership determine which areas they need to address and update in their institution's emergency preparedness playbook.

Chapter Six
Taking the Disabled into Account in Preparing for and Responding to Disasters
Patricia A. Findley

Currently, in the United States, 54 million individuals with disabilities, or about one in five, live with a variety of impairments that have an impact not only on their daily lives but also may require special consideration in times of emergency (U.S. Census Bureau, 2008). In the United States, disaster preparedness and response for those with disabilities has historically been relegated to those with disabilities themselves as well as to their family members and trusted friends, with very little responsibility being taken on the federal level (Waterstone & Stein, 2006). In July 2004, President Bush issued an executive order titled *Individuals with Disabilities in Emergency Preparedness* (U.S. Department of Homeland Security, 2005a), which requires administrative agencies to address the safety and security issues of those with disabilities in case of disaster. Nevertheless, the National Response Plan from the U.S. Department of Homeland Security issued in December of that same year did *not* mention individuals with disabilities (U.S. Department of Homeland Security, 2005b). Finally, in July 2005, the Interagency Coordinating Council (ICC), comprised of senior leadership and nearly two dozen federal departments and agencies, put forth a document on emergency preparedness that included those with a disability (Interagency Coordinating Council on Emergency Preparedness and Individuals with Disabilities, 2005-2006). It took nearly a year after the first executive order for recognition that individuals with disabilities require special attention during times of disaster.

To date, very little has been done on a community level to support this vulnerable and growing population in times of disaster or emergency. The Federal Emergency Management Agency (FEMA) has made few materials available to assist individuals with disabilities (Federal Emergency Management Agency, 2006), and there has been little focus on working with the community to prepare for groups of individuals with disabilities. Therefore, the purpose of this chapter is to provide an application, on a community level, of the Centers for Disease Control's (CDC, 1997) *Principles of Community Engagement*, a framework developed to assist public health professionals and community leaders engage the community in health decision making and action for individuals with disabilities.

DEFINITION OF DISABILITY

Each disability requires its own emergency preparations, and managing in times of disaster can be quite challenging. To help communities plan for disaster, it may be useful to define disability in such a way as to facilitate planning. In the literature, definitions of disability range from references to individuals who are unable to work (Findley & Sambamoorthi, 2004) to those with minor impairments that allow them to still function fairly easily with some simple accommodations (Dell Orto & Power, 2007). Disability, for our purposes, is defined broadly to include individuals with impairments from chronic illnesses and conditions that affect the individual's level of participation in his or her environment, according to the guidelines of the International Classification of Functioning, Disability and Health (World Health Organization, 2001). This definition includes physical, mental, sensory, or cognitive limitations as well as psychiatric and emotional disabilities. Additionally, because older individuals may also have these same conditions, the elderly also will be considered within this discussion but not directly; consideration for the care of the elderly requires some of the same preparations and implementation as would a younger population with disabilities, but this does not negate that fact that differences do exist between these populations and that separate and directed planning should occur for the elderly.

DISASTER PREPAREDNESS AND DISABILITY

As noted earlier, FEMA does provide some educational materials to assist those with disabilities to prepare for disasters (Federal Emergency Management Agency, 2006). Additionally, the U.S. Department of Homeland Security's website (www.ready.gov) provides some tips for preparedness and response for individuals with disabilities. Fifty years ago, in a now-classic article, Friedsam (1961) stated that the elderly with chronic conditions that affect physical mobility are more vulnerable in case of disaster. This observation was made at a time in which it was becoming clear that individuals were living longer with chronic illness. More recently, however, it has been noted that there has been limited research in the area of disaster preparedness and safe evacuation of those with disabilities who also have conditions that affect their mobility (Fox, White, Rooney, & Rowland, 2007; Spence, Lachlan, Burke, & Seeger, 2007). Further, it has been noted that a large portion of emergency managers do not have the specific training to work with those with mobility impairments in the face of response, recovery, and mitigation situations (Rooney & White, 2007).

Individual Preparedness

Planning for an individual with a disability does take special measures. The U.S. Department of Homeland Security's website (www.ready.gov) suggests that individuals with disabilities create an emergency kit and develop a plan of what to do in case of emergency, including developing a social network and a family communication strategy. This emergency kit needs to be adapted for the individual's needs, based on his or her condition. It is important that the kit includes at least a week's supply of medications as well as instructions on how to use adaptive devices and to attend to any other special-care needs. It is also essential to develop a plan that includes ways to effectively connect with others in case of disaster when usual systems do not work. This is particularly important for individuals with disabilities, who are nearly twice as likely to live alone as compared to their non-disabled counterparts (Kaye, 1997). Further, their living alone may add to their need for assistance in emergencies. Importantly, social networks, from which younger individuals can receive support, are less likely to be utilized by the elderly, causing them additional stress in emergency situations (Gignac, Cott, & Badley, 2003). Additionally, it is important to be aware that individuals with disabilities may be more concerned about their own condition than events around them as much of the rehabilitation process following catastrophic injury is focused on helping individuals learn to care for themselves and their impairments (Lin, 2003; Rosenthal, 1999).

It is also important to note that a disaster can affect an individual for a number of years, which has implications for the community. For example, Phifer and Norris (1989) reported that older individuals with chronic illnesses who were victims of a flood had worse physical functioning post-disaster (post-flood), with a peak in that worsening occurring in the year post-flood, then diminishing, with greater disaster experiences being related to greater health effects. Notably, the presence of a vulnerable population can affect the overall community, and, as a result, managing emergency situations requires not only an understanding of the vulnerable individual but also a coordinated effort by the community.

Working with the Community on Preparedness

Although it is not realistic to plan for each individual, it is possible to plan for subgroups, such as those with disabilities, in the overall community plan. As noted earlier, the CDC (1997) has developed *Principles of Community Engagement* based on insights drawn from the literature on the critical facilitators of community engagement. These principles, as presented below, were developed to facilitate community collaboration in pursuit of health initiatives but can be easily applied to disaster preparedness for those with disabilities.

Occur Prior to the Engagement Process
1. Be clear about the goals and the communities to be engaged
2. Become knowledgeable about your community

Necessary for the Engagement to Occur
3. Work with your community to build a relationship with formal and informal leaders
4. Respect the right for self-determination within the community
5. Establish partnerships to create change and to promote health

Necessary for the Engagement to Succeed
6. Recognize community diversity
7. Sustain community engagement through resource and capacity development
8. Allow the community the locus of control as needs change
9. Maintain a goal of long-term commitment and sustainability

As seen above, steps 1 and 2 need to be considered prior to the engagement effort, steps 3 through 5 are necessary for the engagement to occur, and steps 6 through 9 are needed for the engagement to succeed. The inherent message of this process is that it can enhance communication, support a common under-standing, and create and fortify community partnerships in the name of shared planning efforts. Below, each of the steps is presented and discussed in terms of how they would need to be modified to address those with disabilities.

1. Be clear about the goals and the communities to be engaged

The disaster preparedness process begins with the community. First, the com-munity needs to be defined, with a focus on which specific segment(s) of the population that the community agrees with whom to work (e.g., is the focus on those who have difficulty with walking or on those with cognitive impair-ments?). Frequently this decision is made based on local needs and budget-related issues. This focusing and refining process usually means learning more about the members of the community (the domain of step 2). But in step 1, the community (or the communities) needs to be clear about the scope of their in-tended involvement so as to not go beyond their resources and abilities. Meet-ings of officials with decision-making power help to facilitate step 1, although the original impetus for the action may come from any level within the commu-nity, including those with the disabilities, advocates, or even family members.

Another component of this step is the inclusion of a formal or an informal evaluation of the organization(s) wishing to engage the community. This re-quires examining the *values* of the organization to understand how it views the issue of disaster preparedness and response as well as how it views partnering. This step also involves an examination of the *intent, operations, resources, and expertise* of the organization. In other words, how does the organization strate-gize, and what resources does it have? This includes having an understanding of the types and the reliability and validity of data that have been collected about the community as well as about the financial resources available for the efforts.

2. Become knowledgeable about your community

One method by which to become more knowledgeable about a community is to conduct a needs assessment or, more specifically, a community vulnerability inventory (Morrow, 1999). Many communities may already have lists of individuals with disabilities who may need additional assistance in times of emergency. These types of activities help the community to understand the needs of individuals with disabilities as well as how well equipped the community is to respond to disasters. Assessing needs facilitates the development of targeted goals for the community.

Moreover, a vulnerability inventory that collects information on a neighborhood level, rather than on an individual level, may be more feasible (Morrow, 1999). A crucial aspect of this process is to collect information from individuals with disabilities as well as from community leaders. Not only will this allow greater understanding of needs and available resources, but it may also allow planning to include those individuals who may be empowered to create or recommend action steps. This speaks to the feeling of "nothing about us without us" that is central to the disability empowerment movement (Charlton, 2000). Further, planners who fully engage citizens will achieve greater outcomes in the safety and survival of their communities (Morrow, 1999).

The data collection for the inventory needs to be sensitive to the various forms of communication techniques needed for those with disabilities. A variety of survey methods, including mail, online, or telephone, is needed to reach the greatest number of individuals. Additionally, the use of a secondary contact may be necessary. Advertisement of the survey is also important to reach as many individuals as possible. Notices should be placed at local hospitals, schools, churches/religious communities, grocery stores, and other places of known community gathering. Additionally, this is a good opportunity to engage with other community agencies who are a part of the larger community infrastructure in planning and preparedness.

A database of names can be created for easy access to information in case of emergency. The website (www.ready.gov), sponsored by U.S. Department of Homeland Security, provides links to databases in most states where individuals can register their emergency contact information. Locally, a database can be maintained on a secure computer, but a backup generator needs to be available or an alternative system of accessing the saved information needs to be developed (e.g., printing a hard copy on a quarterly basis). The database contains contact information and some general demographic information such as age, the individual(s) with whom a person lives, secondary contact information, the individual's impairment, the type of assistance needed, and key contact information on the agencies that serve such individuals. It is understood that agencies may not be available in times of disaster, but such information does provide emergency responders with an idea of the type of agencies on which the individual relies.

This step also includes becoming knowledgeable about the community with respect to economic conditions, norms and values, changes in demography, history, and any past experience with this type of community engagement over disaster preparedness and planning. However, this is not as straightforward as one might expect. Those within the disability community may not wish to see themselves as "disabled" or to avail themselves to additional services. For example, those with a hearing impairment may have assimilated into the "hearing society" and do not perceive themselves as members of a separate culture (Tucker, 1998). Similarly, the experience of having a disability may vary by the ethnic background of the individual, suggesting that a stance of cultural competence, which considers the disability within the context of the ethnic background, be taken when working with individuals with disabilities. This also extends to language and family structure (Stone, 2005). We need to be respectful of how an individual perceives his or her culture for us to interact with the person. This is why it is important to truly understand the community when you begin to plan and to be careful to do *with* the individuals and not *for* the individuals. This may include activities to develop courses and/or overviews of cultural, language, and disability/limitation competencies that can be shared with the professional teams.

3. Work with your community to build a relationship with formal and informal leaders

This step involves a proactive stance, using meetings to engage the community and to help to create a milieu that supports the group process, leading toward planning and preparedness. Meetings need to occur with some regularity to make the process effective. The meetings should involve health care professionals, police, mental health professionals, schools and teachers, spiritual/religious groups, governmental agencies, non-governmental agencies, social service organizations, state representatives, and individuals with disabilities and their family members. It is important to include decision makers within the community to ensure necessary action following recommendations. It is essential to become knowledgeable about lifestyle and healthcare needs by inviting to these meetings individuals who have impairments or disabilities (e.g., those with visual impairments, those who use wheelchairs, those who have psychiatric disabilities). It is worth noting that some individuals with psychiatric disabilities may be the most challenging because they may not understand and/or follow directions, which may put them and others in jeopardy.

4. Respect the right for self-determination within the community

Respect for the community and its right to self-determination is crucial, and it is important to build a relationship with formal and informal community leaders. It may be helpful to identify key community members to act as "ambassadors" to help facilitate a sense of community on the neighborhood level. Community here refers both to the agency and to the business partners within the communities who might collaborate as well as to the sub-community of those with disabilities and the smaller communities within those with disabilities. Those with disabilities are not a homogenous group, so it is important to include good representation of a variety of disabilities when in the process of planning. Partnering with formal and informal leaders and involving local advocacy groups (e.g., National Spinal Cord Injury Association, Brain Injury Association, Multiple Sclerosis Society) helps community members become knowledgeable about specific disabilities.

5. Establish partnerships to create change and to promote health

Partnering should occur on both the community level through organizations that are part of the plan or who will be decisions makers and/or funders of the plan. Community engagement through the participation of individuals, community-based organizations, and institutions is more likely to produce successful mobilization of the community for the planning efforts. Most important to the success of planning and programs are relationships of mutual cooperation and responsibility.

For individuals with disabilities, partners include agencies and programs that understand the needs of those with disabilities. Such partnering will allow for the recognition of special needs and how they affect communication. For example, individuals who are blind can be reached through radio and television announcements, and individuals with hearing impairments can be reached through closed captioning, the use of sign language on television, or text or e-mail messages. Individuals with mobility impairments will require special attention in terms of transportation or evacuation, and individuals with cognitive impairments (both young and old) need an identified contact/family member and repeated communication provided in simple ways. Most important, as discovered in other emergencies, individuals with disabilities may not be able to use the usual resources available to them so alternatives need to be taken into consideration before a disaster.

6. Recognizing community diversity

Along with recognizing self-determination within a community, it is also important to understand diversity particularly in terms of the facilitators of and barriers to reaching people with disabilities. The Americans with Disabilities Act of 1990 prohibits discrimination against individuals with disabilities in the areas of return to work, access to public buildings, and educational opportunities as well as in emergency programming. Further, Section 504 of the Rehabilitation Act of 1973 protects individuals with disabilities from discrimination in all programs receiving funds from the federal government or operated by the federal government. Section 508 of that law prohibits discrimination against persons with disabilities in regard to federally operated technology systems (Federal Emergency Management Agency, 2006). Therefore, it is not just a consideration to include those with disabilities; many emergency programming efforts receive funding through FEMA, and the inclusion of those with disabilities is a requirement.

There are several sources of information about activities to support community emergency preparedness and response programs for those with disabilities. For example, the U.S. Department of Justice offers *An ADA Guide for Local Government* (U.S. Department of Justice, Civil Rights Division, Disability Rights Section, 2008). This guide encourages communities to evaluate their shelters and other locations of evacuation to ensure that they are accessible as well as suggests training for first responders on the needs of those with disabilities. The guide states that planning needs to incorporate accessible communication techniques (e.g., note writing when speech is impaired, the reading of printed material to those with visual impairments) as well as backup generators for refrigerators for medicine or durable medical equipment that requires electricity. Additionally, measures to assist those with mobility impairments need to be readily available (e.g., availability of ramps, wheelchair lifts on vehicles). Similarly, FEMA and the U.S. Department of Homeland Security's Office for Civil Rights and Civil Liberties (CRCL) are developing the Comprehensive Preparedness Guide (CPG) 301 for state, territorial, tribal, and local emergency managers to use in the development of emergency operations plans that include the entire population, with specific recommendations for planning for special-needs populations (Federal Emergency Management Agency and DHS Office for Civil Rights and Civil Liberties, 2008). This interim guide is currently under public review.

7. Sustain community engagement through resource and capacity development

This step involves encouraging the development of and engagement with multiple networks for resource and capacity development. Spence et al. (2007) noted that interpersonal networks, especially those networks that exist beyond the immediate family (e.g., informal caregivers, personal assistants) are critical for individuals with disabilities. The mass media has played a role in how those networks are connected (Spence et al., 2007); however, currently, most connections to family and friends are made via cell phones (Bracken, Jeffres, Neuendorf, Kopfman, & Moulla, 2005). As with other aspects of disaster preparedness and planning for those with disabilities, information-seeking and network-using behaviors have not been reported in the literature; however, it has been noted that those with disabilities may have different informational needs than those without disabilities and that those needs have not been fully addressed (Spence et al., 2007). Targeting these specialized needs is vital for those with disabilities (Lachlan & Spence, 2007). This also means that it is crucial to identify key collaborators to ensure effective information sharing.

8. Allow the community the locus of control as needs change

This step fits with the empowerment movement of those with disabilities, which encourages them to take charge of their own lives, rather than being passive participants. Having those with disabilities helping to craft the direction of the needs and goals of the community encourages empowerment and mitigates marginalization in times of crisis. A lack of inclusion in planning was seen during Katrina, when the vulnerable poor population was unable to evacuate due to a lack of transportation, and 29 lives were lost (Phillips, Morrow, & Fear, 2007). Further, the inclusion of individuals with impairments who have survived a disaster allows them to contribute their insight to planning efforts for future catastrophic events (Rooney & White, 2007).

9. Maintain a goal of long-term commitment and sustainability

Effective emergency preparedness and response begins with directed planning and involves an awareness and understanding of the interrelation of social, economic, and political structures within a community that can create the differences in the vulnerabilities of those with disabilities (Morrow, 1999). Accounting for these differences and working with the community on an ongoing basis will add to the sustainability of the disaster preparedness programming, particularly by taking into consideration that the work occurs on multiple levels or in communities within communities. Sustaining ongoing communication with community organizations, government agencies, first responders, and other service providers also contributes to a longer-term commitment.

Utilizing the above steps may provide a more effective path toward disaster preparedness. To sustain planning and preparedness efforts, involvement and leadership at the local level (Morrow, 1999) as well as the higher levels are required. Further, vulnerable populations need to become part of the planning process (Geis, 1997). Morrow (1999) asserts that, when planners or leaders utilize the strength and expertise of the community, it increases the likelihood that the community will survive a disaster.

CONCLUSION

Although the focus of this chapter has been on those with disabilities, the overall theme in disaster planning and preparedness is the same regardless of the population. Utilizing the *Principles of Community Engagement Process* (CDC, 1997) may assist with the planning, organization, and implementation of disaster preparedness and response, especially when individuals with disabilities, their families, and the organizations that serve them are part of those activities. Planning and preparedness require continual review and revisions to update components of the plan. For example, once an initial database is developed, it should be reviewed on a regular basis to keep it current. Staying current also means staying in touch with communities to keep up to date on their activities and changes. Additionally, medical technology and assistive devices, as well as communication systems, need to be continually upgraded. Moreover, making the entire process part of a regular routine keeps disaster preparedness and planning part of ongoing communication that may facilitate a higher level of awareness and proactive involvement that may reduce stress at the time of disaster.

REFERENCES

Bracken, C. C., Jeffres, L., Neuendorf, K. A., Kopfman, J., & Moulla, F. (2005). How cosmopolites react to messages: American under attack. *Communication Research Reports, 22*(1), 47-58.

Centers for Disease Control. (1997). *Principles of community engagement.* Retrieved from http://www.cdc.gov/phppo/pce/

Charlton, J. I. (2000). *Nothing about us without us: Disability oppression and empowerment.* London, UK: University of California Press.

Dell Orto, A. E., & Power, P. W. (Eds.). (2007). *The psychological and social impact of illness and disability.* New York, NY: Springer.

Federal Emergency Management Agency. (2006). *Your civil rights and disaster assistance.* Retrieved from
http://www.fema.gov/assistance/process/assistancerights.shtm

Federal Emergency Management Agency and DHS Office for Civil Rights and Civil Liberties. (2008). *Interim emergency management planning guide for special needs populations, version 1.0.* Retrieved from
http://www.fema.gov/pdf/media/2008/301.pdf

Findley, P. A., & Sambamoorthi, U. (2004). Employment and disability: Evidence from the 1996 medical expenditures panel survey. *Journal of Occupational Rehabilitation, 14*(1), 1-11.

Fox, M. H., White, G. W., Rooney, C., & Rowland, J. L. (2007). Disaster preparedness and response for persons with mobility impairments: Results from the university of Kansas nobody left behind study. *Journal of Disability Policy Studies, 17*(4), 196-205.

Friedsam, H. (1961). Reactions of older persons to disaster-caused losses: A hypothesis of relative deprivation. *Gerontologist, 1*, 34-34-37.

Geis, D. (1997). Disaster resistant communities: A community-based approach to hazard mitigation. *The CUSEC Journal, Central United States Earthquake Consortium, 4*(1), 1-1-2.

Gignac, M. A. M., Cott, C. A., & Badley, E. M. (2003). Living with a chronic disabling illness and then some: Data from the 1998 ice storm. *Canadian Journal on Aging, 3*(22), 249-249-259.

Interagency Coordinating Council on Emergency Preparedness and Individuals with Disabilities. (2005-2006). *Individuals with disabilities in emergency preparedness executive order 13347 progress report July 2005-September 2006.* Retrieved from http://www.dhs.gov/xlibrary/assets/icc-0506-progressreport.pdf

Kaye, H. S. (1997). *Disability watch: The status of people with disabilities in the United States.* Volcano, CA: Volcano Press.

Lachlan, K. A., & Spence, P. R. (2007). Hazard and outrage: Developing a psychometric instrument in the aftermath of Katrina. *Journal of Applied Communication Research, 35*(1), 109-123.

Lin, V. W. (Ed.). (2003). *Spinal cord medicine: Principles and practice.* New York, NY: Demos.

Morrow, B. H. (1999). Identifying and mapping community vulnerability. *Disasters, 23*(1), 1-18.

Phifer, J. F., & Norris, F. H. (1989). Psychological symptoms in older adults following natural disaster: Nature, timing, duration, and course. *Journal of Gerontology, 44*(6), S207-S217.

Phillips, B. D., Morrow, B. H., & Fear, N. T. (2007). Social science research needs: Focus on vulnerable populations, forecasting, and warnings. *Natural Hazards Review, 8*(3), 61-68.

Rooney, C., & White, G. W. (2007). Narrative analysis of a disaster preparedness and emergency response survey from persons with mobility impairments. *Journal of Disability Policy Studies, 17*(4), 206-215.

Rosenthal, M. (Ed.). (1999). *Rehabilitation of the adult and child with traumatic brain injury.* Philadelphia, PA: FA Davis.

Spence, P. R., Lachlan, K., Burke, J. M., & Seeger, M. W. (2007). Media use and information needs of the disabled during a natural disaster. *Journal of the Health Care of the Poor and Underserved, 18*, 394-404.

Stone, J. (Ed.). (2005). *Culture and disability: Providing culturally competent services.* Thousand Oaks, CA: Sage.

Tucker, B. P. (1998). Deaf culture, cochlear implants, and elective disability. *Hastings Center Report, 28*(4), 6-14.

U.S. Census Bureau. (2008). *Number of Americans with a disability reaches 54.4 million.* Retrieved from http://www.census.gov/

U.S. Department of Homeland Security. (2005a). *Individuals with disabilities in emergency preparedness.* Retrieved from http://www.icdr.us/documents/AnnualReport05.pdf

U.S. Department of Homeland Security. (2005b). *National response plan.* Retrieved from http://www.dhs.gov/files/programs/editorial_0566.shtm

U.S. Department of Justice, Civil Rights Division, Disability Rights Section. (2008). *An ADA guide for local governments: Making community emergency preparedness and response programs accessible to people with disabilities.* Retrieved from http://www.ada.gov/emergencyprepguide.htm

Waterstone, M. E., & Stein, M. A. (2006). Emergency preparedness and disability. *Mental & Physical Disability Law Reporter, 30*(3), 338-339.

World Health Organization. (2001). *International classification of functioning, disability and health.* Geneva, Switzerland: World Health Organization.

Chapter Seven
Neighbors Helping Neighbors:
The Disability Community and Emergency Preparedness
Jessica C. Jagger

INTRODUCTION

Recent disasters in the United States have inspired advocacy efforts throughout the disability community. In Connecticut, Virginia, Texas, and New Mexico, people with disabilities and fellow advocates have developed and implemented projects that can serve as exemplars for all those interested in improving preparedness and ensuring better outcomes in times of disaster among people with disabilities. These projects have grown from grassroots personal endeavors and demonstration projects to nationally and internationally recognized and replicated exemplars. I will present the projects and the broader implications for advocates, self-advocates, social workers, and other helping professionals interested in fostering similar projects and leadership among the communities that they serve. I will begin with an introduction to the terminology, the experiences that provided the impetus for these projects, and a theoretical model that helps us to understand the change and growth that resulted. I will then discuss each of these projects, why they work, and how they could be replicated.

DEFINITIONS

For the purposes of this chapter, *disability* is defined as including physical, communication, cognitive, and/or psychiatric and mental health limitations that inhibit activities of daily living. The *disability community* is defined more broadly to include people with disabilities, including self-advocates, family members, friends, service providers and administrators, and other concerned citizens who share the goal of improving disaster preparedness for people with disabilities.

Physical disabilities reduce mobility, whether the loss of mobility is the result of illness, injury, or another disability (Centers for Disease Control and Prevention, 2007; U.S. Census Bureau, 2007). Communication disabilities include hearing, vision, and speech impairments as well as print and reading impairments. Cognitive disabilities include intellectual disabilities as well as traumatic brain injury and learning disabilities. Psychiatric disabilities include mental health diagnoses and mental illness as well as emotional/behavioral disabilities. While physical access and barrier issues are concerns of some individuals with the disability types listed above, other issues such as communication of information, respect, and understanding during disasters are concerns that are relevant to each of the disability types. For this reason, some of the most successful exemplars we will present take a cross-disability approach, providing disability-specific information, when necessary, and frequently drawing parallels across the disability community, whenever possible.

Emergency management is a broad term that encompasses mitigation, preparedness, response, and recovery (Federal Emergency Management Agency, 2004). *Mitigation* is the term for what we do to prevent an emergency and/or reduce its impact on us. *Preparedness* refers to what we plan to do when the emergency happens. *Response* refers to the work of those who assist during and immediately after the emergency, such as police, fire, and emergency medical services as well as shelter staff and volunteers. *Recovery* efforts are those that attempt to return people to their homes and restore survivors to the stability and quality of life present before the disaster. The emergency management community includes emergency managers or planners on the local, state, and federal levels in the United States as well as first responders such as police, firefighters, emergency medical technicians, shelter operators, other volunteer responders, and government officials.

THE CALL(S) TO ACTION

In this chapter, I will present efforts in the disability community to improve preparedness and to change the outcomes of future disasters. These efforts focus on the reality that, at some point, most of us will experience the impact of a natural or human-influenced disaster of a small or large scale. Many of these efforts have been inspired by lessons learned from recent disasters in the United States, including the terrorist attacks of September 11, Hurricane Katrina, and Hurricane Rita. The September 11, 2001 attacks in New York City, Washington, DC, and Pennsylvania propelled advocacy within the disability community, especially around issues of workplace preparedness. Hurricanes Katrina and Rita in August and September 2005 affected the entire Gulf region of the United States, with errors made in response and recovery that many believe could have been prevented or minimized through better management. In fact, there is a growing body of evidence supporting a paradigm shift toward inclusion of people with disabilities in emergency management, also driven in large part by the lessons learned from recent disasters (Deal, Fountain, Russell-Braoddus, & Stanley-Hermanns, 2006; Fox, White, Rooney, & Rowland, 2007; Rooney & White,

2007; Rowland, White, Fox, & Rooney, 2007). The hurricanes motivated many to take action on emergency preparedness, including the advocates and self - advocates responsible for the projects that I will discuss.

Crisis Response

According to Roberts (2005), a crisis situation or event can move an individual from equilibrium or a steady state to either a new equilibrium or to active crisis. Many social workers are familiar with fellow social worker Roberts' model of crisis intervention. If we think of this model at a community level, rather than at an individual one, we can see how recent disasters have inspired the movement of the disability community to a new equilibrium of better preparedness. The crises have raised awareness in the disability community as well as the emergency management community, and change has rippled through at the local, state, and federal levels. This change is manifested in trainings, conferences, advocacy, publications, policy changes, and awareness raising in various settings. Without the lessons learned from recent disasters, we may not have been able to make the progress achieved by these and other change efforts in recent years.

SELF-ADVOCATES PREPARING THEIR COMMUNITIES

Voice for Gap Kids

At a National Youth Leadership Forum not long after Hurricanes Katrina and Rita, youth with disabilities from the Gulf coast region shared their experiences of the response and recovery efforts. A young man in the audience heard the stories and began to think about what would happen if a disaster like Katrina or Rita struck his rural central Virginia community. Over the next four years, with the support of his mother, he developed and delivered trainings for people with disabilities and community members (Moore & Moore, n.d.). His training curriculum, "Disaster Preparedness for People with Disabilities," was delivered in four parts. On Part III alone, 3,440 staff hours were logged and 6,212 people participated, with a budget of $156 and in-kind donations (Moore & Moore, 2008). Students and teachers in several special education classrooms have participated, learning about preparedness by volunteering their time to pack emergency supplies in the go kits that were distributed at each of the trainings. Community members from across central Virginia have attended trainings and taken home their own go kits, beginning or improving their personal preparedness efforts.

Why Self-advocacy in Emergency Preparedness Works

This grassroots effort has reached thousands of people with disabilities as well as other community members in central Virginia as well as has been recognized as an outstanding volunteer effort by the governor. Central to the success of this project are the ties that this young man has to his county and to the disability community. He is able to clearly articulate the importance of emergency preparedness in his life and why it should be important to others with disabilities. His trainings incorporate his vast knowledge of emergency management and of disability issues, information he learned by spending time with emergency managers and people with disabilities and by reading resources available from the American Red Cross (2004), the U.S. Department of Homeland Security (2006), and the Federal Emergency Management Agency (2004). This project works because it is designed and delivered by a member of the disability community, embodying a mantra of the community: *nothing about us without us.*

Replicating Self-advocacy in Emergency Preparedness

Social workers in the community can play a role in replicating self-advocacy projects such as the service-learning project by Voice for Gap Kids. The importance of nurturing self-advocacy is well established in the literature (Beart, Hardy, & Buchan, 2004; Dearden-Phillips & Fountain, 2005; Geller, Fisher, Grudzinskas, & Manning, 1988; Hanna, 1978; Hess, Clapper, Hoekstra, & Gibison, 2001; Jurkowski, Jovanovic, & Rowitz, 2002; National Council on Disability, 2000; Stringfellow & Muscari, 2003; Traustadottir, 2006; Zirpoli, Hancox, Wieck, & Skarnulis, 1989). Social workers are often uniquely positioned and even obligated to foster self-advocacy skills among people with disabilities, given the multiple ways and settings in which we work with people with disabilities (Asch & Muddrick, 1995) and our profession's ethical commitment to self determination and social justice (National Association of Social Workers, 2008). For example, self-advocates may ask us questions and express interest in learning about emergency preparedness, and that interest can be supported. We also can ask self-advocates who are actively working on other disability issues what they know about emergency preparedness and help them to learn more if they are interested. With some training and proper support, self-advocacy efforts like this one can be replicated in any community. Many leaders in the self-advocacy movement have already begun similar efforts across the United States. Efforts like these have the potential to have a lasting impact when people with disabilities reach out to other people with disabilities and explain disaster preparedness.

INTRODUCING THE DISABILITY AND EMERGENCY MANAGEMENT COMMUNITIES

Lessons Learned: A Forum on Disaster Preparedness for People with Disabilities

In the months following Katrina, the Connecticut Developmental Disabilities Network (2007) planned a conference to discuss the lessons learned and improve community preparedness at the local level. Over 200 individuals attended the conference in December 2005, where speakers from the National Spinal Cord Injury Association, Louisiana Council on Developmental Disabilities, Commissioner of the Connecticut Department of Emergency Management and Homeland Security, and citizens with disabilities shared what they had learned from recent disasters and what they thought should be priorities for preparedness in the disability community. The conference included breakout sessions by region, inviting people with disabilities and their local emergency managers and first responders together into the same room for the first time. Several collaborations and long-term relationships took flight, and partnerships that began that day in 2005 continue today.

Why Introductions Work

For many in attendance at the conference, this was the first opportunity to do something about preparedness in the disability community. Citizens with disabilities and their emergency managers sat together and strategized about how to make sure that their community was as prepared as possible. The concept of including people with disabilities in the planning process as partners at the table with emergency management has been cited as an effective way to improve disaster outcomes for people with disabilities (Kailes, 2006; National Council on Disability, 2005).

Several trainings, publications, and preparedness tools were developed through partnerships forged at that conference, including local and regional trainings for first responders on disability awareness, regional trainings for people with disabilities on personal preparedness, the publication *A Guide for Including People with Disabilities in Emergency Preparedness Planning* from the Connecticut Developmental Disabilities Network (2007), and several tools for preparedness such as the *Disability Specific Disaster Preparedness Inventory* and a two-page issue brief for planners, *Including People with Disabilities in Disaster Plans: Important Considerations,* from the Network as well.

Replicating Introductions

Whether a large or small conference or an informal meeting, social workers can encourage community members with disabilities and emergency managers and responders to sit down together and learn about one another. The introduction of the two communities was central to the success of this effort and worked in Connecticut particularly well due to the timing, the publicity, and the format of the event. The conference was held within months of Katrina and Rita, while the issues of emergency management still captivated public attention. The event was publicized throughout networks and email listservs in both communities, and registration exceeded expectations. It was televised by the Connecticut Network television station, and lunch was served during the full-day event, which gave people an opportunity to network informally during the meal. These strategies can be replicated with small or large events that allow emergency managers and citizens with disabilities to explore what needs exist in their own community and then to develop a plan to meet those needs with the skills and resources that each has to offer.

LEARNING TO SPEAK EACH OTHER'S LANGUAGE AND LIVE IN EACH OTHER'S WORLD

Project REDD

Project REDD, from the Center on Disability and Development (2008) at Texas A&M University, has produced two handy tools that allow people with disabilities and emergency managers to understand one another's language. The acronym guide is a two-sided document with emergency management acronyms on one side in red ink and disability acronyms on the other side in black. This simple guide, printed on cardstock, can be placed in the hand of members of both communities to facilitate communication. The *Texas Guide to Supports and Services for Individuals with Disabilities and their Families Affected by Disasters* is a one-page laminated sheet of contact and service information on agencies and organizations serving people with disabilities. This abbreviated directory can be used in the response and recovery efforts by volunteers and professionals who are unfamiliar with disability service systems to locate aid for individuals in need of assistance.

Why Translation Works

These "translation" documents facilitate more effective communication between members of the disability and emergency management communities. Each community has its own jargon and acronyms that they use regularly, and the guides allow for a translation between what, at times, can seem like two different languages. The second guide puts practical and consolidated information into the hands of those responding to disasters. Both documents are formatted to be easy to use and handy during a disaster, when time is critical and communication can make a tremendous difference in the lives of citizens with disabilities.

Replicating Translation

The acronym guide and agency listing are available online, and anyone can access them through the Internet to learn what information to include when replicating them for another state or community. The two-sided format of both documents is manageable, and listings of service providers are already available in most communities and can simply be reformatted for this use.

Tips for First Responders

This handy, pocket-sized guide for first responders was developed by the Center for Development and Disability (2008) at the University of New Mexico. There are tips for responders on working with seniors, people with service animals, people with mobility impairments, people with autism, people who are deaf or hard of hearing, people who are blind or visually impaired, people with cognitive disabilities, people with multiple chemical sensitivities, and people who are mentally ill.

Why Tips Work

The *Tips* are portable and pocket-sized, attached to one another with a small ring that can be used to hang them in a convenient spot on a fire truck, ambulance, or police cruiser. They are concise and direct and broken down by functional needs, which makes them easy to review en route to an emergency situation. People with disabilities and first responders each had input in their design and development, and the tips have been well received. Over 80,000 copies have been disseminated by the Center on Development and Disability, and the input received from community members has been used to revise this publication, which is now in its third edition.

Replicating Tips

The tips are not specific to a geographic community, and they can be ordered for approximately five dollars per copy, depending upon the number ordered. They can also be viewed online at the website for the Center for Development and Disability.

Good to Go and How to Help Me

These two publications were developed by the Texas Center for Disability Studies at the University of Texas at Austin. The *Good to Go Hurricane Evacuation Kit* gives people with disabilities a guide and brief, critical safety tips for planning before, during, and after the emergency strikes (Texas Center for Disability Studies, 2008). Three short forms are included for the individual to fill out with her or his emergency support team, medication needs, and emergency medical and disability information. These forms capture critical information, such as support staff or family members to contact for assistance, equipment and other items needed during an evacuation, and other information on needs relating to the individual's disability.

The *How to Help Me . . .* sticky notes are two or three times larger than are most sticky notes, and they allow an individual to write down important information for the responders attempting to assist in an emergency. The individual can decide what information is most important for a responder to receive immediately and can then post that information in a location visible to the responders. These notes are temporary and disposable, which allows the individual to change them as needs and information change.

Why the Kit and Notes Work

These two items are manageable for people with disabilities and their families or support staff. They allow individuals to focus on conveying the most critical information and work together to provide sufficient structure and guidance as well as freedom to express unique needs. The kit is an 8 ½ x 11-inch magnetic folder that can be placed on the refrigerator, where many responders are trained to look for information such as the *Vial (or File) of Life*. The notes are disposable, so they can be changed as needs change, and they are sticky, so they can be posted anywhere that responders will be able to see them, including on assistive devices, in entryways, or near other emergency information.

Replicating the Kit and Notes

Kits and notes can be replicated and reprinted affordably using the information and forms that already have been developed and customizing them to a different community. The format should be simple and accessible, like the larger sticky notes and the consolidated kit. The kit is an excellent example of capitalizing on other efforts; the magnetic pocket folder can be hung on the refrigerator, where many first responders will attempt to look for information because they already know about the *Vial/File of Life* and other campaigns that promote keeping emergency information in that recognizable location. Kits and notes should also be designed to be easy to modify as needs change, so that out-of-date information can be removed and current information can replace it quickly and easily.

CONCLUSION

Learning from these Exemplars

Each of these projects has taken a unique approach to improving disaster preparedness for people with disabilities. Each project works in a unique way to give voice to a community often unheard as well as allows leaders to emerge. One project began with a simple attempt to bring the disability community and the emergency management community to the same table to strategize and collaborate. Others tried to facilitate the dialogue between the two communities by literally translating information and placing concise, practical tools in the hands of those who need them. All of these projects can serve as replicable models for other communities who wish to improve preparedness and outcomes for individuals with disabilities, their families, and their networks of support in times of disaster. Disasters, like disabilities, are a natural part of the human experience. When people work together to raise awareness and prepare for future disasters, the community is strengthened, inclusion thrives, and everyone prospers.

Social workers, advocates, self-advocates, and other helping professionals are uniquely situated to facilitate better communication between the disability and emergency management communities and to improve the preparedness, mitigation, response, and recovery processes. As Asch and Mudrick (1995) wrote in their entry in the *Encyclopedia of Social Work,* "[f]or as long as there has been an organized social work profession, social workers have been involved with people with a wide range of conditions defined as disabilities" (p. 752). Not all people with disabilities interact with social workers, but as a profession, we often serve people with many types of disabilities across diverse settings. We work in interdisciplinary teams and in interdisciplinary organizations with a unique understanding of the complexity of our clients' lives, including their social, behavioral, equipment, assistive technology, and medical support needs as well as their strengths and abilities. We are connected with the disability and social services networks, which allows us to access resources for our clients from a variety of sources and agencies. And although our time with clients is limited and easily usurped by numerous other priorities, we have a unique ability to view the individual as a whole in his or her environment in a way that physicians, nurses, therapists, teachers, and other medical or educational professionals may not.

Social workers are also often connected with the local government system, where emergency management begins and ends. We can access local emergency managers and emergency operations plans to learn what to expect in a time of disaster, which gives us the ability to better prepare our clients about what to expect. Some of us in municipal social services work in the same building or complex as the emergency management staff. Those of us who do not work in local government social services often know how to connect with the municipal social workers and can utilize these connections to ensure that people with disabilities are considered in emergency operations planning. The core function of our profession is helping people access basic needs, and disasters threaten access to food, clothing, and shelter for everyone in the affected area, especially those who may require additional assistance or accommodations to services planned for by emergency management. Equal access to any municipal services, including emergency preparedness and response services, is a right protected by Title II of the Americans with Disabilities Act (1990). We can also advocate for plans that address the needs of people with disabilities and that comply with the Act. Our expertise and the expertise of the self-advocates whom we support can be valuable to planners who want to comply but are unsure of how to plan for community members with disabilities.

These skills, abilities, and connections, along with exemplar projects like those discussed in this text, can be utilized to foster improved collaboration and get stronger, more inclusive communities better prepared for the challenges of natural and human-influenced disasters.

ACKNOWLEDGMENTS

The author would like to thank the individuals and organizations responsible for the projects discussed. Colleagues within the network of University Centers for Excellence in Developmental Disabilities have led the way on the issue of disability community preparedness, including the Center for Development and Disability at the University of New Mexico, the Center on Disability and Development at Texas A&M University, and the Texas Center for Disability Studies. Thanks also to colleagues at University of Connecticut Center on Developmental Disabilities, along with its DD Network partners, the Office of Protection and Advocacy for Persons with Disabilities and the Council on Developmental Disabilities, who sponsored the *Lessons Learned* forum. Finally, thank you to the Voice for Gap Kids project staff who have reached thousands with their trainings in central Virginia.

REFERENCES

American Red Cross. (2004, August). *Preparing for disaster for people with disabilities and special needs.* Retrieved from http://www.redcross.org/images/pdfs/prepared ness/A4497.pdf

Americans with Disabilities Act of 1990, Title II, Part A. Pub. L. No. 101-336, §2, 104 Stat. 328 (1991).

Asch, A., & Mudrick, N. R. (1995). Disability. In *Encyclopedia of social work* (19th ed., pp. 752-760). Washington, DC: NASW Press.

Beart, S., Hardy, G., & Buchan, L. (2004). Changing selves: A grounded theory account of belonging to a self-advocacy group for people with intellectual disabilities. *Journal of Applied Research in Intellectual Disabilities, 17,* 91-100.

Center for Development and Disability. (2008). *Tips for first responders field guide.* Retrieved from http://cdd.unm.edu/products/tipsforfirstresponders.htm

Center on Disability and Development. (2008). *Project REDD.* Retrieved from http://redd.tamu.edu/

Centers for Disease Control and Prevention. (2007). *National Center for Health Statistics: Disabilities/limitations.* Retrieved from http://www.cdc.gov/nchs/fastats/ disable.htm

Connecticut Developmental Disabilities Network. (2007). *Disaster preparedness for people with disabilities.* Retrieved from http://www.uconnucedd.org/Projects/DD Network /disasterpreparedness.html

Deal, B. J., Fountain, R. A., Russell-Braoddus, C. A., & Stanley-Hermanns, M. (2006). Challenges and opportunities of nursing care in special-needs shelters. *Disaster Management & Response, 4,* 100-105.

Dearden-Phillips, C., & Fountain, R. (2005). Real power? An examination of the involvement of people with learning disabilities in strategic service development in Cambridgeshire. *British Journal of Learning Disabilities, 33,* 200-204.

Federal Emergency Management Agency. (2004). *Are you ready? An in-depth guide to citizen preparedness.* Jessup, MD: Author.

Fox, M. H., White, G. W., Rooney, C., & Rowland, J. L. (2007). Disaster preparedness and response for persons with mobility impairments. *Journal of Disability Policy Studies, 17*(4), 196-203.

Geller, J., Fisher, W., Grudzinskas, A., & Manning, T. (1988). A national survey of consumer empowerment at the state level. *Psychiatric Services, 49*(4), 498-503.

Hanna, J. (1978). Advisor's role in self-advocacy groups. *American Rehabilitation, 4*(2), 31-32.

Hess, R., Clapper, C., Hoekstra, K., & Gibison, F., Jr. (2001). Empowerment effects of teaching leadership skills to adults with severe mental illness and their families. *Psychiatric Rehabilitation Journal, 24*(3), 257-265.

Jurkowski, E., Jovanovic, B., & Rowitz, L. (2002). Leadership/citizen participation: Perceived impact of advocacy activities by people with physical disabilities on access to health care, assistant care, and social services. *Journal of Health & Social Policy, 14*(4), 49-61.

Kailes, J. I. (2006). *Serving and protecting all by applying lessons learned: Including people with disabilities and seniors in disaster services.* Pomona, CA: Center for Disability Issues and the Health Professions.

Moore, T., & Moore, L. (2008, July). *Are you ready? Part III facts.* Retrieved from http://www.voiceforgapkids.com/pdf/PartIIIFacts.pdf

Moore, T., & Moore, L. (n.d.). *Voice for Gap Kids*. Retrieved from http://www.voiceforgapkids.com

National Association of Social Workers. (2008). *Code of ethics*. Retrieved from http://www.naswdc.org/pubs/code/code.asp

National Council on Disability. (2000). *From privileges to rights: People labeled with psychiatric disabilities speak for themselves*. Washington, DC: Author.

National Council on Disability. (2005, April 15). *Saving lives: Including people with disabilities in emergency planning*. Retrieved from http://www.ncd.gov/newsroom/publications/2005 /saving_lives.htm

Roberts, A. R. (Ed.). (2005). *Crisis intervention handbook: Assessment, treatment, and research* (3rd ed.). New York, NY: Oxford University Press.

Rooney, C., & White, G. W. (2007). Narrative analysis of a disaster preparedness and emergency response survey from persons with mobility impairments. *Journal of Disability Policy Studies, 17*(4), 206-215.

Rowland, J. L., White, G. W., Fox, M. H., & Rooney, C. (2007). Emergency response training practices for people with disabilities. *Journal of Disability Policy Studies, 17*(4), 216-222.

Stringfellow, J., & Muscari, K. (2003). A program of support for consumer participation in systems change. *Journal of Disability Policy Studies, 14*(3), 142-147.

Texas Center for Disability Studies. (2008). *Good to go*. Retrieved from http://tcds.edb.utexas.edu/GoodtoGo.html

Traustadottir, R. (2006). Learning about self-advocacy from life history: A case study from the United States. *British Journal of Learning Disabilities, 34*, 175-180.

U.S. Census Bureau. (2007). *2005 American Community Survey: S1801 Disability Characteristics*. Retrieved from http://factfinder.census.gov/servlet/STTable?_bm=y &-geo_id=01000US&-qr_name=ACS_2005_EST_G00_S1801&-ds_name=ACS_ 2005_EST_G00_&-_lang=en&-_caller=geoselect&-state=st&-format=

U.S. Department of Homeland Security. (2006). *Preparing makes sense for people with disabilities. Get ready now* [Brochure]. Washington, DC: Author.

Zirpoli, T. J., Hancox, D., Wieck, C., & Skarnulis, E. R. (1989). Partners in policy making: Empowering people. *Journal of the Association for Persons with Severe Handicaps, 14*(2), 163-167.

Part Three:
Notes from the Field

Chapter Eight
Mud and Mold:
Making Meaning of Adversity in New Orleans
Ronald E. Marks

On February 7, 2010, almost 4-1/2 years after Hurricane Katrina wreaked unspeakable havoc on New Orleans, flooded 80% of the city, and drained much of the life out of it, the New Orleans Saints football team defeated the Indianapolis Colts in the 44th Annual Super Bowl. For the two weeks leading up to that game, nothing else seemed to matter. New Orleans was beside itself with joy, and its citizens were exuberant. We had experienced a nightmare of biblical proportions, but now we were reveling in an American dream.

The city began to celebrate in the way that New Orleans knows best: parades. They broke out spontaneously. Former Saints quarterback Bobby Hebert followed up on a vow made by the late Buddy D, a much-loved sports announcer, that, if the Saints went to the Super Bowl, he would don a dress and parade through the city. Hebert was joined by hundreds of men wearing dresses and was greeted by screaming, joyful spectators. Life-sized replicas of pigs with colorful lights were hoisted three stories high in trees throughout the city, giving new meaning to the expression "When pigs fly . . . " The celebrations continued nonstop for those two weeks, and the city planned the largest parade ever to welcome the Saints back from the Super Bowl—win or lose.

When the Saints did win, there was no violence or rioting, as has been witnessed in other championship cities. People all over New Orleans and its suburbs joined in a demonstration of unity, unlike anything that the city has ever experienced. Strangers hugged, and any vestiges of racial tension dissolved. There was simply joy and even euphoria. In anticipation of the victory parade two days later, schools and universities closed, City Hall closed early, and the city came to a virtual standstill, all to welcome home its heroes.

It is nearly impossible to separate this joy from the aftermath of and recovery from Katrina. Perhaps it is even appropriate to ask to what extent the hurricane, which plunged people into such depths of despair, enabled and energized the exuberance that followed the Super Bowl.

Hurricane Katrina made landfall on August 29, 2005. Shortly after, I wrote to my fellow deans of schools of social work thanking them for their outpouring of support. The following is an excerpt from that letter:

Tuesday, September 6, 2005
5:00 pm

Dear Friends and Colleagues:

Eight days have passed since Hurricane Katrina found its way to our front door. Slowly, I am learning of the whereabouts of my faculty, staff, and students; yet, I still have not heard from many of them. Our communications have been disrupted; none of the cell phones with 504 area codes work, and the Tulane email server continues to be offline. All of our student records are inaccessible. Over the past 20 years, our lives and work have adapted to access to high-speed communications. This disaster underscores for me how devastating it feels to be isolated from those with whom we share our everyday lives.

I know that you are all painfully aware of what has transpired in our city and neighborhoods, from national news coverage. Although the coverage has been comprehensive, and attempts to convey the personal impact, when the stories happen in your own backyard the intensity and heartache are almost beyond comprehension. Millions of lives have been impacted. Millions of stories are yet to be told. Today, I learned of two of my colleagues who stayed behind. After the winds calmed, after the levee breached, after the city filled with water, they found a boat and began to look for ways to help. They paddled around the fairgrounds, where Jazz Fest is held, to Esplanade Avenue, a grand boulevard near the French Quarter. They came upon a nursing home where none of the residents had been evacuated, and none had had food or water for three days. For the next two days, they broke into homes to salvage water and food destined for spoilage and took it to the starving residents. In the next nursing home, they discovered that all the residents had drowned.

In the initial months following the storm, I was asked to speak at numerous venues outside of New Orleans. I found that my greatest challenge was conveying to these audiences the significance of this disaster to both the hundreds of thousands of individuals directly affected by it and the larger community comprised of families scattered throughout the United States who were indirectly affected by the displacement of and losses incurred by their loved ones. In every place that I spoke, I was warmly received. Yet, it was clear to me that words, no matter how descriptive or genuinely expressed, were not sufficient to tell the story. They were like two-dimensional photographs or postcards of the Grand Canyon that can never convey its majesty.

Several months later, I spoke at the University of Pennsylvania. By that point, I was bringing to the podium, as props, items that I carried with me every day in New Orleans. They included bandages, hydrogen peroxide, a facemask for protection against the mold, rubber gloves, and government-issued MREs (meals ready to eat).

The following spring, I was invited to be the graduation speaker at Boston College School of Social Work. I asked for the audience's indulgence, as if they were 500 of my personal critical-incident, stress-debriefing counselors. I asked that they allow my voice to represent the hundreds of thousands of Katrina survivors and to permit the stories of those survivors to wash over them, so that, together, we might derive some lessons.

I presented many of these lessons at the "Crisis as Opportunity" conference at Jerusalem University in Israel in January 2009. My presentation preceded the one by Brian Flynn, former Assistant Surgeon General of the United States Public Health Service, who was instrumental in developing critical policies related to disaster mental health. The two presentations complemented each other— Flynn's offering the view from 30,000 feet, while my view was from the trenches.

Today, five hurricane seasons have come and gone since Katrina's unwelcome visit to the Gulf Coast. For some, the approach of each of these seasons has been like growing up with an abusive, alcoholic parent. You live in fear, not knowing when he or she will come home drunk and abuse you. Evidence of this still-lingering trauma was particularly noticeable in September 2008, when Hurricane Gustav bore down on New Orleans. Many people could not shake off visions of four to five feet of water in their homes. Anticipating this, their preparation included frantic, even compulsive, attempts to protect everything below the Katrina water line, still visible in their mind's eye, if not physically on their houses, by moving their possessions to a higher place in their homes.

As one of the first to return to New Orleans after the storm, and one deeply engaged in the city's rebuilding, I participated in coalitions being organized to address the critical problems associated with our city's recovery. I met neighbors whom I had never met before and realized that, if ever there were a time to recognize that we could not solve our community's problems alone, this was it.

As dean of a school of social work, I was in a position that required balancing considerable charges: to rebuild the school and to plan for its eventual reopening as well as to reach out to our faculty, staff, and students who had evacuated to 30 or more states and who had enrolled in as many M.S.W. programs. With my wife, Carolyn, I was also trying to figure out how to rebuild our house, which had been inundated by the deluge. All of this, combined with the widespread sacrifices and suffering that I was witnessing, presented with an unprecedented number of challenges on an almost daily basis. There were so many that I feared I could not keep up with them.

Within the first six months after the storm, the School of Social Work at Tulane and its dedicated faculty partnered with several international aid organizations, many of which were providing service in the United States for the first time. With the faculty's combined expertise, we partnered with Save the Children to offer programs providing mental health services to children and families in temporary FEMA trailers, hurricane preparation for children in public schools, and training for students to work at shelters in the event of future need. We partnered with UNICEF to provide monitoring and evaluation of 12 projects being funded by the organization in the region. We also partnered with Mercy Corps and contracted for several projects, including the promotion of women's strengths in post-disaster community rebuilding, the enhancement of youth well-being, and the development of neighborhood capacity building. Working with the American Red Cross, we offered mental health training for first responders. We even organized a weekend-long communal grief ritual; complete with drums and a hastily built altar, in downtown New Orleans' Congo Square, with Sobonfu Some, an African healer from Burkina Faso.

In the immediate aftermath of the storm and continuing to the present time, Hurricane Katrina raised a number of human rights issues that the school addressed with its students and through engaging in academic dialogues with professional organizations. Faculty at the school addressed issues pertaining to the rights of poor and black Americans in relation to post-disaster reconstruction plans with regard to access to housing, education, and health care as well as the mistreatment of the local prison population during the flooding.

New Orleans received extensive media coverage after the storm. Locally and nationally, debates on such critical issues as whether New Orleans should be rebuilt and whether the flooding was due to negligence on the part of the Army Corps of Engineers captured the nation's interest. Politicians positioned themselves. Make no mistake: a disaster is always a political event. But I submit that, in the days immediately following the storm, a disaster of this magnitude calls for empathy, not for dispassionate analysis. In the midst of the disaster, there is an unparalleled intensity and intimacy that springs from the meaning and significance of human relationships. It was as if we had the uncanny opportunity to peer across an empty coffin with our name on it and see the quantity and quality of the flowers that were sent to our funeral by the people who care about us.

One question that was on everyone's mind in the days following Katrina was: Why did so many people, tens of thousands of them, not leave the city? There are several reasons for this. New Orleans has among the highest number of residents in the United States who grow up in their city and never leave it. There are families whose every relative lived within five blocks of each other. These were people who had no other place to go and who chose to stay. There are many others who had no choice because they did not have the resources to leave. Another significant population, thousands of elderly people whose social security checks were due to be delivered in two days, could not leave without those funds. It was this population of elderly, many frail and homebound, that represented a disproportionate number of those who died in the immediate aftermath of the storm.

In what follows, I share a few stories from the early days of this disaster.

Neighbors

By October, our neighbors were returning to the city. They would pull up to their houses, filled with hope. But it is difficult to imagine the havoc that four to eight feet of water can wreak in a home, especially when it sits for three weeks before being drained. Our neighbors would enter and, within minutes, emerge gagging and in despair. They described mold the size of pancakes on the ceilings, four-inch mushrooms growing from the furniture, and frogs in the living room. We sat on our front steps and watched National Guard troops marching past our house in full battle garb. Helicopters continued to hover overhead, as if they were in a war zone.

Looters

The days immediately after the storm, before the army and National Guard arrived, were pandemonium. One of my colleagues told me of a neighbor who had stayed in the city through the hurricane. Imagine the city without electricity: it's stiflingly hot, everyone is sweaty and dirty, night is dark as a swamp with no moon, neighborhoods are unprotected. My colleague's neighbor armed himself with a gun. His fears were realized, and when a looter tried to enter his home, he shot and killed him. In his delirium, he dragged the body to the corner of St. Charles Avenue, a street of stately mansions, and put a sign around his neck that read, "Who's next?" Weeks later, when the city had calmed down, this man was wracked with remorse, incredulous that he had been capable of such an act.

Hospitals and Helicopters

The wife of one of the crew members who was ripping out soggy plaster and drywall in our house came by one day and told us what had happened at Charity Hospital, where she was a nurse. After the hospital's generators failed, the medical staff found themselves in the incomprehensible position of having to make decisions regarding whom to save. She told us of a 16-year-old boy who had been in a car accident two days before the storm, and how they managed to keep him alive for four days with rotating shifts. He did not survive.

She also told of other dramatic scenes that unfolded, such as the one at Tulane Hospital after the backup generators failed. The hospital authorities called for helicopters to airlift the many critically ill patients who required more care than could be provided, given the failed generators. Three days later, the helicopters had still not arrived. Finally, a call was made to the family who runs the corporation that owns the hospital. They arranged for private helicopters. Upon their arrival, however, the governor commandeered them and demanded that they go to Charity Hospital. A fight ensued between Charity and Tulane hospitals regarding where the helicopters would land. The governor won this battle.

Refrigerators

One word was used more than any other in the first few weeks following the storm: surreal. We were living a reality that we were barely able to comprehend. If anything seemed surreal, it was the appearance, by November, of thousands of ruined refrigerators out on the streets. You couldn't go anywhere without encountering them. One columnist suggested that we change some street names to Amana Avenue, Kenmore Court, and Whirlpool Way.

Musicians Village

Almost everyone has now heard of the Ninth Ward, where a wall of water washed houses off their foundations. A full year after the storm, bodies were still being discovered in the rubble. Two years after the storm, it remained a community completely untouched, with one lone FEMA trailer occupied by one man. It was, essentially, an abandoned community, and many of the former residents continue to be dispersed to distant cities, with little hope of returning.

The Ninth Ward was home to many of New Orleans' greatest musicians. Fats Domino, for one, had to be rescued by boat from his home there. It is there that one of New Orleans' most well-known musicians, Harry Connick, Jr., initiated a project in partnership with Habitat for Humanity that would build housing for many of the city's musicians, who are a central part of the fabric of the city, enabling them to come home. Ironically, as these houses were being readied for their occupants, an unanticipated bureaucratic impasse arose. Most of the musicians had never established creditworthiness sufficient to secure a mortgage, even for the substantially discounted price of these homes. This was yet another insult (perhaps assault is a more apt word) to the recovery effort.

Rescue and Pets

One story illustrates how profound the impact of a poorly conceived government policy can be, in this case, pets being forbidden in rescue boats. Many residents who stayed during the storm found themselves trapped in their homes. Surrounded by rising water, they had to climb into their attics to escape. Some died there. Others, with family and pets, endured days of brutal heat. Many had no food or water. As the floodwaters continued to rise, the only escape was to cut a hole in their roof and climb onto their rooftop. Their pets came with them. After more days on the roof, again with no water and now with no shade from the burning sun, people were desperate for a rescue boat. When the rescue boats finally arrived, people were told that they had to leave their pets behind. It is not difficult to imagine the horror and suffering that this policy caused, especially after what these families had been through. They faced an unspeakably difficult decision involving whether their pets could survive without them or whether it was more humane to shoot them before they left. Five years later, that government policy has been changed.

Zoo Story

New Orleans's Audubon Zoo is a world-class facility. Almost all of its animals survived the storm, but many months were required get the zoo ready for the public. Finally, in the late fall, the zoo reopened. No one knew what to expect because so many families had not yet returned to the city. They had registered their children in schools that had been evacuated, and the city had become an odd and unsettling place, with empty playgrounds and no children on the streets. But the day that the zoo reopened, thousands of people showed up. It was a bright, warm, and sunny day. The vegetation at the zoo was beautiful. Even the animals sensed the difference and seemed happy to see the people return. As many entered the gates, they began crying. Do you know what the zoo did? They posted volunteers at the gates to welcome people with hugs! What a profound expression of smiling in the face of adversity!

Gestures of Good Will

And then there were stories of miraculous good will. When we evacuated, we took every photo album in the house. However, a friend of ours was out of town when the storm hit and couldn't save anything. She lived in Lakeview, a neighborhood almost completely destroyed by the floodwaters. She asked a neighbor to retrieve family photos, put them in the trunk of her car, and park the car in a high-rise garage downtown. Months later, when she went to get the car, she found the trunk empty. Her car had been looted, and she assumed that the photos had been tossed out. The heartache of losing her home, all her possessions, and her photographic memories was devastating. Later, she received a call from a stranger who had been trying to track her down for months. He had been walking through the parking lot in September and saw her photos scattered throughout the garage. He gently collected them, took them home, and carefully laid them out to dry. He found a high school diploma with her daughter's name on it and began trying to locate her. Her home phone no longer existed, of course, but he finally came upon an office number and found her. It was as if someone you thought had died had been brought back to life.

My Story

My wife, Carolyn, and I evacuated with enough clothes for two days. Little did we know that it would be virtually impossible to reenter the city for nearly a month. We were in a lovely home in Houston for four weeks. Nevertheless, every night that I crawled into bed I felt like I was in prison because I could not go home.

In early September, I secured a coveted pass to reenter the city to help survey the damage to the libraries at Tulane. Twenty miles outside the city, we ran into the first of the military barricades. It was bizarre to enter through the barricades, drive down an abandoned six-lane interstate, and approach a completely empty city. The closer we came to the city, the more rubble appeared. There were impassible neighborhoods still under six to eight feet of water and fallen trees everywhere. There were tanks and military transport trucks, and helicopters swarmed above. The night before, in Houston, Carolyn had purchased two pairs of rubber boots for each of us, one of which came up to the knee and the other which reached our hips. We thought that we would be adequately prepared. We drove to within a mile of our neighborhood where the water began and, still hopeful, pulled on our knee boots. Within 100 yards of the car the water lapped at the top of our boots. We returned to the car, changed to our hip boots and this time got less than a hundred yards farther. Although initially deterred, we were determined.

That night, we learned that a friend had a canoe in her backyard. We found it the next morning, but it was chained and locked. After an hour of working on removing the lock and carrying the canoe to the water line, we realized that we had no oars. This challenge proved less daunting than the lock, as all we had to do was collect two of the hundreds of fence boards strewn everywhere. We made our way to our neighborhood and discovered a bright orange "0" on our house underneath a large "X." The date was on the top, 9-13, with the "0" on the bottom, indicating zero bodies. My police officer neighbor had already spray-painted the "0" so that the army would not have to break down our front door to determine whether anyone was inside. There were other painted codes on our neighbor's homes: "1 cat RSQ," one cat rescued; "1 dog DOA," one dog dead on arrival.

Once we got into the house through a broken window, we found a nightmarish scene. All the furniture had floated into different rooms. Books and files were soaked. Our landscaped yard was submerged under six feet of black water. We stumbled around for an hour. Helicopters continued to hover within feet of the rooftop, searching for survivors, but the canoe docked at our front door was a signal that we had survived and had an escape route. We left with one antique child's rocker from my wife's family and paddled back to the car in silence. When we arrived, two special agents, dressed in black and carrying large machine guns, stood near the car. They asked if they could assist us. We were clearly exhausted, so they put down their guns and hoisted the canoe onto the car. They very much wanted to be helpful.

Each one of these stories is significant. Yet, even after hearing many such accounts, it is virtually impossible for those who were not there to fully comprehend the breadth and depth of the human suffering that took place. And many similar situations are ongoing. It was reasonable, for example, to think that, at the two-year mark, the city and most of its residents would have emerged from the crisis. But insurance companies were still not being forthright, and FEMA continued to be an unfathomable disaster. For example, FEMA continued to change the rules related to requiring homeowners to elevate their houses depending on the amount of damage due to the flood. At one point, homes that sustained 51% damage were required to be elevated. If they did not, the homeowners would no longer be eligible for federal flood insurance. This ruling changed twice, and each change required homeowners to renegotiate the settlement with their private insurers. Ultimately, FEMA dropped the elevation requirement altogether.

At the two-year period, marriages began to break up, suicides increased, the incidence of domestic violence and child abuse rose, and an unprecedented number of people began exhibiting classic post-traumatic stress symptoms.

While those with resources were rebuilding, those without sufficient resources were still living in distant cities, and the neighborhoods they once occupied remained empty. Expertise and commitment were needed to rebuild or, in many cases, to build for the first time, infrastructures that worked. For example, expertise was desperately needed to rebuild a damaged and broken school system. New Orleans' public school system was woefully inadequate prior to the storm, with many of its schools decrepit and unable to provide a meaningful educational experience. The extreme physical damage to so many of the district's school buildings provided the opportunity to address the physical/structural needs of the school district as well as served to bring into focus the extreme need to address the system of management that was so woefully lacking prior to the storm.

The city experienced labor shortages in numerous areas and industries. For example, in the aftermath of the storm, a massive infusion of federal money helped create and support an increase in construction jobs. This attracted a large number of new laborers (many undocumented) to the city. Similarly, significant needs existed in all aspects of the health care industry. The federal government responded to this daunting need in early 2008 and designated New Orleans a medically indigent city and offered one-time grants of up to $100,000 for physicians, social workers, and other health care workers to commit to work in New Orleans for three years. Young, educated professionals are now flocking to New Orleans from all over the United States, motivated by their desire to be civically engaged in something meaningful. Whereas most of the cities in the United States are experiencing a stagnant or spiraling downward housing market, New Orleans' housing market appears to be exempt from this.

For social workers, post-Katrina New Orleans presents an unforeseen opportunity to engage in ongoing activities related to economic development and to address the economic disparities that existed before the storm. Prominent among them is the controversy related to public housing and the desperate need for low-cost housing for the city's many poor families. New Orleans had one of the largest concentrations of public housing in the United States. At the center of this problem is the United States Department of Housing and Urban Development's plan to tear down public housing blocks and replace them with mixed-income housing. This has been and continues to be a highly charged issue. As the old public housing is removed, the building of new, modern housing lags behind. Although the new buildings are far more modern, current plans will not be able to provide an adequate number needed in relation to the demand. In the meantime, thousands of former residents who depended on Section 8 housing still cannot afford to return to the city.

This is the time to engage in the important debates related to the many social, health, and economic issues faced by the poor in New Orleans. These include those addressed above, related to education and housing, and others such as access to health care and public transportation. Social work has always understood the intransigent relationship between poverty, resource-poor communities, and the essential role that social work plays. In post-disaster New Orleans, this is more evident than it has ever been. In addition to the physical devastation suffered far and wide, there was another disaster. This disaster is the institutional damage, seen in the tales of the marginalized and disenfranchised; groups of critical concern to social work. The many institutions that make up the safety nets for these marginalized groups and individuals failed and poignantly pointed to the failures of the city, state, and federal government. New Orleans' experience with Hurricane Katrina focused our attention on class and race differences in the United States, how there were, in fact, two very different hurricane experiences, depending on your place in society.

During the fall term following Katrina, when Tulane's School of Social Work students were studying all over the country as visitors, we asked them to read *Man's Search for Meaning* by Victor Frankl. For those not familiar with this work, Dr. Frankl gives a moving account of his life amid the horrors of the Nazi death camps, which led him to develop his theory of logotherapy. In it, he stresses man's freedom to transcend suffering and to find a meaning to his life, regardless of his circumstances. It seems an appropriate work for this time. Frankl stated:

> We who lived in concentration camps can remember the men who walked through the huts comforting others, giving away their last piece of bread. They may have been few in number, but they offer sufficient proof that everything can be taken from a man but one thing: the last of the human freedoms—to choose one's attitude in any given set of circumstances, to choose one's own way.

In the same book, Frankl discusses human pain and likens it to gas in a chamber. No matter how much or how little there is, it expands to the fill the available boundaries. Thus, each person experiences his or her pain personally, and regardless of the extent of the loss, the pain is significant.

In New Orleans, there are many levels of loss, beginning with the staggering loss of life. Some lost their homes and possessions; some have rebuilt, some have torn their houses down, and some have elevated them as high as 12 feet above ground. Others have sold their gutted homes at a substantial economic loss. Still others experience survival guilt because they and their homes were spared. But, as Frankl said, pain, regardless of its nature, expands to fill the available space.

I contend that everyone has lost something because everyone has lost part of their community as they knew it. The lessons of this disaster are still surfacing, and they are both professional and personal.

What have I learned in the aftermath of Hurricane Katrina? Among many things:

- How to say thank you from the bottom of my heart like I've never done before.
- How trauma burns a new neural pathway in the brain—a very well-lubricated brain.
- How it feels like to share a deep "trauma bond" with 500,000 people.
- How adversity does not so much build character as reveal it.
- How important humor and laughing are, sometimes at ourselves. I was in a French Quarter nightclub a few months after the storm and heard a musician, taking a break between songs, blurt out: "We're all trying here in New Orleans to get back to abnormal." And once, when driving through one of our devastated neighborhoods, I came across a house that floated off its foundation and came to rest across the street. It was spray-painted with the phrase "Wicked witch of the east was here."
- That a small electric motor submerged under six feet of water for two weeks, if not plugged in while under water, will still work . . . at least until you burn it up whacking overgrown weeds in your neighbors' abandoned properties.
- That when I sweat so much that the earphones to my MP3 player don't work, it's time to take a break.
- About the tenuousness of the boundaries that define a civil society fractured by fear.
- About hope and resilience and how they work together to support healing.
- How buffering mechanisms, like suspending one's need for comfort and order, can help one cope.
- How we, as people, can never afford to be separate, and how we must not be now.

And I have certainly learned about patience. As Chris Rose, a former local newspaper columnist, once wrote, "New Orleans is the only place I know where patience is a higher form of currency than money."

Chapter Nine
Words of Wisdom Following the Tsunami: Lessons from Sri Lanka
Ahangamage Tudor Ariyaratne

This is a rendering of a speech by Dr. A. T. Ariyaratne, Founder and President of the Sarvodaya Shramadana Movement (Sarvodaya means "awakening of all," and Shramadana means "through the gift of effort and other resources") of Sri Lanka, presented on April 26, 2009, to an international meeting, "Five Years After the Tsunami: Lessons for Practitioners," held in Colombo, Sri Lanka.

My first involvement with organized relief in situations of disaster was in 1958. I was a young teacher and was dismayed by the man-made disaster that people called communal riots. This was in Colombo, the capital city of Sri Lanka. A few months later in the north central province of my country, several thousands of people were displaced by heavy floods and had to be provided with relief and resettlement services. From those times onward, up to today, we have been experiencing natural as well as man-made disasters, one after the other, causing heavy damage for living beings, including thousands of human beings, as well as destroying properties. Not only in Sri Lanka, but all over the world, disasters are taking place at an increasing rate, and governments as well as the United Nations and civil sector organizations have developed specialized institutions and trained personnel to deal with these disasters.

In his teachings, the Buddha identified five cosmic laws that bring about unstable and disastrous situations in nature and society. Violation of any of these natural laws can cause disasters. The first is the "Bija Niyama" cosmic law pertaining to the genetic order, which, if humans disturb, can cause heavy imbalances in nature, both with regard to plants and to other living beings, including humans. Similarly, if human beings, in their craze for economic development and the creation of wealth, disturb the natural working of the seasons, in turn disturbing the atmosphere and related factors, this also can cause disasters that affect everything on this planet. This second cosmic law is known as "Uthu Niyama," or the cosmic law pertaining to seasons. The third is "Kamma Niyama," or the cosmic law pertaining to humans' volitional actions and resulting consequences. When human beings act to gain selfish ends, by creating religious, communal, or political conflicts, this is a violation of the karmic law, resulting in untold damage to human societies and even resulting in genocidal violence and wars. The fourth cosmic law is "Citta Niyama," which is a disturbance that is brought about in the psychological sphere of human society, whereby humans with excessive greed, ill will, and egoism generate destructive mental energies and act in such a manner as to destroy human lives as well as the life support systems found in nature. This is the cosmic law related to consciousness or the mind. The final law is "Dhamma Niyama," which pertains to all natural phenomena, including floods, droughts, typhoons, earthquakes, and tsunamis, that can cause great disasters.

If a general theory for the origin of disasters could be traced in our culture, it would be the "Pancha Niyama Dhamma" (collectively, the five cosmic laws). All these cosmic laws are interrelated and generally work in harmony.

Over 50 years ago, the Sarvodaya movement in Sri Lanka did not have any such theoretical foundation on which we could work. All we did was to use our common sense, general intelligence, and general knowledge to engage ourselves in meeting the challenges brought about by disasters and to contribute our small share to redress the sufferings of the victims of disasters.

I vividly remember, in the latter part of 1967 and in early 1970, two major natural disasters that took place in our country, one in the northwestern coastal area and the other in the eastern province. The former was the result of an 18-foot tidal wave that swept across the coastal areas, destroying houses and inhabitants and displacing several hundred people. The latter was a cyclone that caused similar damage. At both times in both places, this happened during Christmas vacation, and the government not only had no disaster relief plans or experience responding to disaster, but they also could not send armed services, as they usually do, as most of them were on leave. I remember that, at that time, because Sarvodaya was already known to the people and to the government, we were called upon by the administrators to do whatever we could to help the people in the Mannar district and, later, in the Batticaloe district.

The first experience that I had, along with 300 of my university colleagues, who joined in batches, was to provide relief and to rehabilitate 300 families. I camped in the affected area for three months until the people could take over their own rehabilitation by themselves. When we first entered the area with 10 lorry loads of relief food and other material that we had collected from people from the 17 districts that were not affected, we found carcasses of a large number of animals, which had been there for 72 hours, giving off a terrible smell. We also found that the water reservoir that provided clean drinking water to the people was breached in its bund and was draining out. As we got down from the vehicles in which we came, the first thing that we decided to do was to repair the bund of the tank, clean up the area, and bury the dead animals. All this was done by getting the affected people themselves to participate in this work, which was ultimately going to benefit them.

In 1960s and 1970s, Sarvodaya gained lot of experience in responding to challenges of this nature, including floods, droughts, cyclones, typhoons, civil disturbances, and landslides, solely with people's resources and their participation.

As a result of the July 1983 communal riots, several hundred people were massacred, many more suffered serious injuries, and a large number were in refugee camps because their homes were burned down. Sadly, the political masters in our democratic country and the bureaucrats who served under them did not have in their governance agenda any plans or strategies to deal with emergency situations, man made or natural, or a budget, except for a small allocation for relief aid through the Social Services Department. They were not used to the idea of people's participation in their own welfare or development work because such voluntary services did not come within their purview of duties, which always involved privileges, promotions, per diems, perks, and so on. Voluntary work, even at a time of emergency, was not on their agenda.

These communal riots were the worst ever man-made disaster in Sri Lanka. The Sarvodaya Movement plunged into, in a very big way, relief and rehabilitation work, mobilizing thousands of volunteers and people's resources on a national scale. Sarvodaya became a countrywide operation in disaster management. I must admit, however, that there were a few senior government servants who gave us encouragement and help. But the major responsibilities were ours because the government had only the armed services to dispatch at times such as this. Our advantage was that, by being a village-level organization covering all districts, we could call upon the village Sarvodaya Shramadana Societies to send batches of volunteers to the needed areas.

It was the 1983 experience that guided us to formulate what is now widely known as the Sarvodaya 5R Programme, namely, Relief, Rehabilitation, Reconciliation, Reconstruction, and Reawakening. We have followed this method for over 25 years with great success. Other organizations, including government departments, also have developed their own 2R or 3R programs.

I consider the Tsunami 2004 disaster and the Sarvodaya involvement in it as the acid test for the Sarvodaya 5R Program, which is described below.

The first R is immediate Relief by way of providing clean drinking water, cooked food, first aid, medical relief, temporary shelter, sanitation facilities, and clothing as well as transporting the injured to hospitals, cleaning up the locality by disposing of dead animals and debris as well as burying or cremating the humans who are dead, with proper legal sanction and without violating their traditions and customs, and satisfying other basic needs.

The second R is Rehabilitation. While relief is carried out, it is essential to speak to the victims and to conduct oneself in such a manner as to build hope and confidence in them so that they can accept the fact that this disaster has occurred, whatever the causes that led to it, and now, as courageous human beings, face the reality of the situation. This is psychological rehabilitation, without which all other rehabilitation measures will not provide full benefit. They should be made participant beneficiaries rather than recipients of relief and rehabilitation services. While psychosocial healing goes on, activities such as organizing specialized services for infants, children, pregnant women, and the sick should be organized. It is also in this stage that families should be provided with accommodations in which their privacy can be maintained. Depending on the expected duration of the accommodation of refugees in temporary shelters, other services can be organized, such as a medical center under the direction of a visiting medical professional, a pre-school under a temporary teacher who herself may be a refugee, temporary classes for school-going children, a library, play material for children and youth, health education to prevent spread of disease, and immunization programs.

The Third R stands for Reconciliation. Earlier, I mentioned psychosocial healing. At this stage, it is essential to get the affected individuals to overcome their traumatic experiences. Each human being has to reconcile himself or herself with his or her own inner personality and with the outer environment and realities. If the disaster is man made, such as communal riots, Sarvodaya takes care to send mixed teams of youth, including Sinhala, Tamil, Muslim, Malay, Burgher, Buddhist, Hindu, Christian, and Islamic. The moment that the victims of violence see and talk to this mixed group, who serves all people without any sectarian bias, starts the process of removing the hatred and ill-will that they had for the perpetrators of violence. Therefore, we should remember that Reconciliation is a process that should start from the very beginning of disaster management.

The fourth R is Reconstruction. This can commence only with the political will of the government. The government has to make a firm decision about when they can commence the resettlement process. The government has to decide whether victims can be sent back to their villages or whether they will have find new lands in which they can resettle. In all the disaster situations that I have experienced, the government machinery moves very slowly in making decisions. To stall, they always give excuses such as security or ecological reasons or a lack of funds. I am not happy with excuses of this nature. I believe that these excuses are due to ignorance and an absolute lack of responsibility on the part of decision makers. Even after four years have passed, there are still Tsunami refugees in temporary shelters, and the excuses given remain the same.

When lands are allocated to refugees and plans drawn up with locations of dwellings, common buildings, facilities, and so on, we in the civil sector can assist government efforts by mobilizing the people whom I earlier called participant beneficiaries. If land allocations and water facilities are made available, it is our experience that, with some help from the outside, affected people can be put on a path of self-development. However, the reconstruction and resettlement stage needs help from the government and donor agencies.

The fifth R or stage is very special to the Sarvodaya way of self-development. We call it Reawakening because the victims were part of normal village communities before they faced the disaster. Now they have gone through the first four stages of the 5R process. At this stage, the village community has to be well organized, with programs meeting the basic needs of all sectors of people, from children to the elderly. They have to be helped to organize themselves as a society and to get a village executive committee elected to make all decisions pertaining to the development of the village, with or without outside help. Their final goals are to achieve economic self-sufficiency and political self-governance. The Sarvodaya objective is to transform our communities into what we call self-governing communities that can be networked horizontally using traditional value systems and modern communication technology.

The 2004 tsunami disaster affected eight districts in the coastal belt of Sri Lanka. Out of the hundreds of villages affected, there were 226 coastal villages where Sarvodaya was already active and where there were societies organized, as discussed above.

Within hours after the tsunami struck, Sarvodaya was able to mobilize the villages of the 17 districts that were not affected and to rush teams of volunteers with relief material that they collected to the affected 226 Sarvodaya villages in eight districts. They set up temporary camps and conducted the 5R program continuously for three months, not only for the affected people of those villages but also for at least five other villages close to them. When both local and foreign relief agencies arrived, Sarvodaya was already at work, which made it very easy for those organizations that preferred to work with Sarvodaya to carry out a successful disaster relief program. From around the world, many individuals and organizations supported us in cash and in kind. We completed the work that we undertook in four years and submitted regular reports and accounts to the government, the public, and our partners.

Several organizations continued to support Sarvodaya in her post-tsunami and normal community development programs. One such important partner was the American Jewish Joint Distribution Committee, which has been immensely supportive to Sarvodaya.

When disasters occur, several extraneous forces become activated, making the situation worse. It is important that relief workers understand these forces and act accordingly. I will provide three examples:

One: Amid the lawlessness and chaos of the July 1983 communal riots, we gave protection to 19 people who rushed into our Sarvodaya Centre. Suddenly, we had to rush out of the center to go to the Ratmalana Airport, to which several hundred refugees had been brought. Only my second daughter, Sadeeva, aged 9, was left at our center, along with some other children with whom she was playing. As we were leaving, I said to her, "Now you are in charge of the center. If anybody comes looking for Tamils, tell we have our Tamil brothers and sisters inside. If they intend to harm them, tell them that they should kill you first before they touch them." Actually, this had happened after we left, and Sadeeva spoke these exact words and continued to play. As children, they never understood the danger that they were in. The criminals who came greeted my daughter and left.

In times of disaster, criminals come to kill people and to loot their possessions. Deal with them without fear. "Fear is a dirty word," I said, when a previous head of state threatened me.

Two: When people are suffering from a disaster, most merchants and grocers behave as heartless exploiters and raise the prices of consumer goods. They see others' suffering as an opportunity to make money. I had this kind of experience umpteen times. Relief workers should be aware of this phenomenon and be prepared to take remedial measures.

Three: Immediately after doing our best in Colombo for the refugees during the 1983 riots, I drove up to Jaffna to see how those who were sent there by ship and plane were faring. During this visit, I saw an old respected Christian Bishop, with my Tamil colleagues, to get his cooperation for a reconciliation program. He kept me standing in front of him for one full hour while he continued to blame me in the most unchristian language, as if I caused the riots. He questioned the Tamil friends who were with me as to what they were doing with the Sinhalese. It was the same experience that I had with some Tamil political leaders who said that nothing could bring the two communities together. They said that the bridge could never be rebuilt and asked us to leave. But that is exactly what Sarvodaya is doing even to this day—rebuilding the bridge.

Remember that, at times of disasters, even sane individuals behave as if they were insane. So it is necessary to have immense patience and to exercise forgiveness and compassion.

What I have said thus far can be considered a kind of experiential wisdom. But in the present day, we need a more professional and scientific approach based on our wealth of experience dealing with disasters.

Our objective is to provide leaders with a means to create a different kind of social, political, and economic system, whereby almost all man-made and even natural disasters can be prevented or dramatically mitigated. We can learn from the election of President Barack Obama; ten years ago, no one would have dreamt of such a nonviolent transformation in political office. We can create a critical mass of non-violent consciousness in human society that will begin the necessary positive transformation, working toward freedom, peace, and the well-being of all—Sarvodaya.

Chapter Ten
Making the Voices of Victims Heard
Mihir R. Bhatt

I would like to argue that making vital voices of the victims of disasters heard in public and by decision-making bodies is a means for civil society to turn a crisis into an opportunity and for victims to gain greater control over their lives. I will do so by citing examples from All India Disaster Mitigation Institute's (AIDMI) activities in and around India and will follow with recommendations for organizations and professionals.

ALL INDIA DISASTER MITIGATION INSTITUTE (AIDMI)

AIDMI is a community-based action research, action planning, and action advocacy organization based in Ahmedabad, India. Established in 1995 in Gujarat, western India, it has a long tradition of social change work, and some of the key national civil society organizations of India started and are located in Gujarat. Now, AIDMI is spreading its work from Gujarat to five states in India as well as in Afghanistan, Myanmar, Sri Lanka, and beyond.

AIDMI was established in response to the repeated 1987-89 droughts in India. During its journey from a project to an autonomous organization, AIDMI has developed four security programs: (a) Food Security, (b) Water Security, (c) Livelihood Security, and (d) Habitat Security. The four jointly contribute to building human security or the achievement of victims' human rights.

AIDMI works toward bridging the system-wide gap between policy, practice, and research related to disaster risk mitigation. This bridging is focused mainly on the needs of the poor and excluded people who are at risk of being subjected to natural disasters. Its innovative approach for disaster risk reduction includes capturing and spreading new ideas based in practice, building the local capactiy of communities to do what they think will reduce risk, conducting research and sharing knowledge, holding policy round tables, and carrying out pilot projects that are likely to have a system-wide impact. The work process is implemented in four stages: Relief Phase, Rehabilitation Phase, Recovery Phase, and Risk Reduction Phase. Although AIDMI is only one organization, it works at many levels, with many types of partners, and in many ways. The most poor and vulnerable people are in the center of all actvities. AIDMI's work is inspired by Mahatma Gandhi's ideas and India's struggle for freedom.

The examples that I will present are taken from one year's activity of AIDMI, 2009-2010. This was a special year, as programs were growing in size and were spreading to locations beyond India to Maldives, Myanmar, and Afghanistan. Work expanded from relief and recovery within the system to more mitigation and preparedness projects for the poor and into climate risk (coastal areas of Tamil Nadu and flood areas of Bihar) and conflict risk (Maoist and Kashmir, Aceh in Indonesia).

PILOT PROJECTS: LEARNING BY DOING

AIDMI's pilots are operational projects that support the local initiatives of disaster victims. Below are some examples of how civil society can turn a crisis into an opportunity by making the vital voices of victims heard within the system.

Recovery by the Victims of Bihar Flooding

This project was designed and launched by community leaders. The worsening flood crises in South Asian countries over the past few years is responsible for an enormous loss of farm products, fertile land, and crops as well as significant destruction to the already-beleaguered infrastructure. In 2007, the northern part of the state of Bihar suffered the most adverse effects of the extensive flooding in northern India. AIDMI was invited into Bihar by two local community-based organizations and has supported initiatives of over 2,000 families in the worst-affected districts of Madhubani and Darbhanga by providing food, tarpaulin sheets, blankets, a community kitchen, and house repair support. AIDMI provided its Safer Schools Campaign to 60 schools in the state, with trainings on safety measures, technical support, and disaster risk reduction awareness as well as access to specially designed insurance packages that protect children 24 hours a day, seven days a week throughout the year. AIDMI listened to the demands of communities and mobilized resources to turn flood loss into safer development. What would have been a slow and painfully long recovery started turning into a rapid run toward development. Currently, under community leadership, AIDMI has started phase II activities for disaster risk reduction, covering livelihoods, shelter, risk transfer, school safety, and capacity-building initiatives. It has helped 278 families in livelihood relief, 500 in shelter support, and over 600 in risk-transfer initiatives. Listening to the community discussion on recovery helped AIDMI to design and define their activities. This approach was shared with the National Disaster Management Authority and National Human Rights Commission in India and encouraged the two authorities to listen to the communities when forming their policy.

Strengthening Disaster Response Capacity after the Myanmar Cyclone

Even in a country with strict government control, the victims of Cyclone Nargis in Myanmar played an active and vocal role in shaping some of the pilot projects for the recovery. In response to the Myanmar cyclone, AIDMI's Emergency Response Unit carried out an immediate damage and needs assessment whereby the victims reported what their needs were and turned these needs into demands. The team of AIDMI workers and community leaders visited the affected people in areas outside Yangon, through two local organizations, and identified the needs and opportunities for future action. All through the recovery effort, the team listened to the local organization and helped them to develop assessment forms as well as trained local volunteers to perform the assessment

Later, AIDMI was requested to take up two activities: (1) the support of in-kind donations based on sectoral needs and (2) the training of trainers for the local partners. The trainings have been conducted on various topics, including community-based disaster risk mitigation; proposal writing and budgeting; and community planning, implementation, monitoring, and evaluation. The result was a bottom-up and inside-driven recovery process in which the victims had an increasing say.

RESEARCH WITH COMMUNITIES

Bottom-up, system-wide views are best achieved by conducting research with communities of disaster victims. This gives the communities more say on what is researched as well as how, when, and for whom within the system. Following are two examples:

Afat Vimo Scheme (Disaster Insurance)

In India and South Asia, micro-insurance is increasingly viewed by the system as a tool that can prevent low-income families and individuals who experience a disaster or economic shock from descending into debt or poverty. The concept of *Afat Vimo* arose during community consultations on livelihood security following the 2001 Gujarat earthquake. At that time, only 2% of those surveyed had insurance of any kind. We asked the communities about ways to reduce risk and the type of insurance that they could use and afford. Based on what we learned from the community survey, AIDMI negotiated with Indian insurance providers to develop a simple, single insurance policy that would cover a wide range of disasters.

Two regulated Indian insurers currently underwrite *Afat Vimo:* The Life Insurance Corporation of India (LIC) covers life aspects, and the United India Insurance Company (UIC) provides general coverage. *Afat Vimo* is one of the most comprehensive products available in India. In a single policy, it covers five risks: (limited) losses of life, trade stock, livelihood assets, house, and house contents of policyholders, with an annual premium of around $4.50 and a total potential benefit of $1,560. The scheme covers damages or losses from a very wide range of disasters, including earthquakes, floods, fires, cyclones, lightning strikes, and landslides. Here, a crisis of severe and repeated losses by communities was turned into an opportunity to develop insurance coverage that is relevant, appropriate, and effective. This was done by using the voices of victims as client input in policy design. As a result, now the United Nations Development Programme (UNDP) in India is working with the National Disaster Management Authority to design a micro-insurance project for the government of India.

Regional Study: Micro-insurance Client Impact Evaluation

Even when they pay market price for relief goods, disaster victims are not often heard as clients of humanitarian services. AIDMI set out to listen to disaster victims in South Asia in regard to the impacts of disaster micro-insurance on their short- and long-term economic well-being. With international and local partners, the AIDMI is collecting and analyzing data from approximately 2,000 local community members as well as donors who invest in risk-reduction efforts worldwide. In this project, AIDMI was able to take the voices of victims to the global insurance policy level. As a result, at least two bilateral and two UN agencies are working on global insurance programs.

REVIEWS BY COMMUNITIES

Reviews and evaluations are good ways to capture voices of the victims as beneficiaries because they are given the opportunity to share their level of satisfaction, confirm results achieved, and analyze impact.

Impact Evaluation of Myrada Project in Karnataka

AIDMI set out to capture the voices of the communities who participated in the Japan International Cooperation Agency's bilateral project and who later faced floods. We wanted to know: What was the impact of the project on these communities? and What was the impact of the floods on the communities' benefits?

AIDMI carried out an impact evaluation of a watershed development project conjointly with two local non-government organizations (NGOs). The objective of the evaluation was to assess the impacts of the November 2009 floods in Karnataka on watershed development activities and on local implementation organizations in 26 project villages. By listening to the voices of flood victims, AIDMI was able to make a development project more disaster-risk sensitive. As a result, the Japan International Cooperation Agency is now integrating disaster risk reduction.

Local NGOs' Ratings

Following the Indian Ocean Tsunami of December 2004, the Disasters Emergency Committee (DEC), an umbrella organization comprising 13 of the largest global aid NGOs, raised an unprecedented millions of dollars for relief, recovery, and reconstruction work.

To draw lessons for future disaster preparedness and risk reduction, as well as to determine whether communities have become more resilient after aid work by DEC member agencies, AIDMI was contracted to conduct an impact assessment. The review covered member agencies' programs in Indonesia, Sri Lanka, and India and concentrated on examining aid impacts on communities and institutional capacity building in regard to reducing disaster risks and increasing preparedness for the future. Feedback on recovery work by international NGOs from communities helped improve global humanitarian financing mechanisms. As a result, DEC has now made it a standard practice to have community feedback on humanitarian response and disaster risk reduction after each appeal.

MUTUAL CAPACITY BUILDING BY VICTIMS

Disaster victims are in the best position to build the capacity of disaster victims. They know what is lost, what capacity remains, and what is needed from others. AIDMI tries to develop its capacity building based on this foundation.

Victims as Teachers

Learning from the voices of victims, and not only from the views of the experts, is uncommon in the field of disaster relief and recovery. In this regard, AIDMI gathered 60 community-level activists from six ongoing recoveries to come and learn from community leaders of the selected villages of Bhuj and Kutch in India, who have worked toward a full recovery for the past nine years. At a five-day South-South lateral learning initiative in Kutch, Gujarat, leading civil society organizations from 11 countries concluded that green and environmentally based livelihoods will suffer from the accelerated threats of natural disasters in coming years. Grassroots-level young leaders from nine states of India and their counterparts from Afghanistan, Nepal, Sri Lanka, Indonesia, Myanmar, Brazil, Peru, Philippines, and Maldives discussed these issues and recognized that this threat must be urgently addressed. Members representing NGOs, the media, research institutes, universities, UN bodies, national authorities, and trade unions argued that mitigation and preparedness measures must be integrated into development plans and adaptation measures. The participants, who demanded an effort to better capture the threats of disasters to green livelihoods, pointed out that basic human development programming must be more risk-sensitive to livelihoods and stated that green livelihoods—with lower carbon footprints—are more at risk from the adverse impacts of disasters than are other livelihoods.

Thus, voices of victims were heard by victims in other locations who drew lessons on ways to make their recovery safer, better, and faster.

Participants visited communities that had recovered from the double disaster of a drought and an earthquake in 2001 and reviewed policies that enable risk reduction, national and state level strategies that protect green livelihoods, and operational processes. The international participants admired the geographic and sectoral planning for risk reduction promoted in these communities by local civil society organizations such as the Rotary Club and Abhiyan, government authorities such as the Bhuj Area Development Authority, and the communities themselves. The role of integrated program and project proposals, democratic local structures and systems, and institutional relations that protect green livelihoods from disaster threats were studied. As a result, UNDP South-South conducted a follow-up process in Indonesia in 2009 and in the Philippines in late 2009 to build on the lateral learning processes in Asia.

ROUND TABLE WITH VICTIMS

One of the best strategies is to invite all stakeholders to a round table with victims to discuss and design ways to address bottlenecks and to bridge gaps.

Rights Holders Mapping Regional Humanitarian Issues

South Asia is a "theater for disaster." In the past decade alone, floods, cyclones, earthquakes, droughts, and a devastating tsunami destroyed hundreds of thousands of lives and livelihoods as well as left millions more homeless. In every disaster, humanitarian responders rushed to the scene to preserve human life and to reduce immediate suffering.

For many humanitarian agencies involved in disaster emergency response, rights protection has been a secondary and often neglected issue. It is the national government (not the humanitarian responder) that is charged with the responsibility to protect the rights of its citizens, especially when citizens are displaced. But when governments are unable or unwilling to act, humanitarian actors must step in to fill this "protection gap."

On April 9-10, 2009, AIDMI and the Brookings-Bern Project on Internal Displacement co-convened a two-day workshop on "Protecting and Promoting Rights in Natural Disasters in South Asia: Prevention and Response" in Chennai, India. A total of 37 delegates attended from India, Sri Lanka, Pakistan, Bangladesh, Maldives, Nepal, Myanmar, and the United States. Participants represented national and international NGOs, the International Committee of the Red Cross, civil society organizations, the UN, government agencies and ministries, the Indian military, the media, academic institutions, and environmental organizations. The workshop brought together diverse policymakers, activists, and practitioners in an open forum to discuss salient issues related to protecting and promoting rights in South Asia disasters.

This workshop was organized to raise regional awareness of the Inter-Agency Standing Committee Operational Guidelines on Human Rights and Natural Disasters and to share experiences and good practices in the South Asia region with respect to rights protection during disasters. The workshop also aimed to generate specific recommendations to strengthen policy and action for rights protection at the local, national, and regional levels. Voices of victims in South Asia were heard by their own government and civil society and taken to a global-level protection initiative to make it more victim focused than institution focused. As a follow-up, AIDMI, along with the UN, organized an event in Yogyakarta with the Brookings Institute and a local university in May 2010. AIDMI also held an Asia-wide event in Delhi in December 2010, with Cordaid and the National Institute of Disaster Management, to encourage the National Human Rights Commission of India to develop victims' rights to know the risks that they face before and after disasters.

CONCLUSIONS

The past two decades have seen substantial changes in the humanitarian response and management of disaster risks in South Asia. The countries of the subcontinent have experienced many rapid changes in the way that humanitarian responses are conducted as well as in the measures taken to identify, pool, and reduce risks. Disasters have increased in frequency as have their individual impacts but so has awareness and actions to address disasters within each country.

Although the task of disaster risk reduction is far from finished, millions of people are now better protected against natural hazards. Even as disasters have destroyed the shelters and livelihoods of communities across South Asia, an increasing number of people have been receiving public support to recover. The extent of these improvements varies across countries. Through extensive humanitarian and research projects across the region, I have observed that different factors affect disaster response capabilities in each country. But a common element in the growth of all these new measures, I have found, was truly listening to the voices of the victims—their needs and demands—and rethinking the earlier approaches to humanitarian crisis and disaster risk reduction. Listening to the voices of South Asia's disaster victims has been imperative, as the best opportunities are always rooted in a local reality, a constantly evolving set of determinants that necessitate continual redesigning and fine-tuning. Of course, we cannot yet be satisfied that these victims and vulnerable communities have a voice in policymaking that is fully and adequately heard. There is still a long way to go.

One central factor in making the humanitarian and disaster risk management changes substantial was the increased receptiveness to the voices of the victims by governments or through routes such as the media, civil society, and academia. Listening to these voices, in many cases, led to an increased openness to new ideas among practitioners. The ongoing changes to humanitarian policies, often initiated by national governments themselves but also by civil society, international organizations, and United Nations agencies, brought new space for innovations, fresh thinking, and experimentation.

Although changes have often been slow and policymakers hesitant, the newer policies have allowed for a greater scope of operations and for decentralized initiatives. This enabled field workers to undertake actions informed by the voices of the victims to reduce risks and improve recovery. No systematic study of these changes and their implications has yet been carried out by the global leaders in disaster risk reduction. I am sure, however, that such studies are on their way.

Drawing from its projects and initiatives, AIDMI offers a modest and limited but enriching set of examples on a wide range of actions that it has taken to make the vital voices of disaster victims and vulnerable communities it has worked with in past year heard. Based on our experience, the AIDMI can offer a look at what has worked in practice and suggest a framework for distilling the common elements across the various projects of the 2009-2010 period The lessons are complex and still emerging, and using them will certainly require some redesigning and fine-tuning, but they are certainly useful for the humanitarian system.

What we have learned is that the voices of disaster-affected communities must be heard in development, especially to protect the poor from risk. The more voices that are heard on this issue, the more likely we are to turn crisis into opportunity. Moreover, there must be a stronger commitment to gender initiatives so that more women participate in and direct disaster risk-reduction projects. This is not a new idea, but more action on this front, listening to the women and inviting them into a leadership position to speak up and speak out, helps turn crisis into opportunity. Disaster risk management and climate change adaptation cannot be separated and must overlap at a fundamental level. The voices of victims tell us how they overlap and what actions to take. Investments in micro-local projects are as important as macro-national initiatives, if not more so, and these micro-local projects enhance the shape of macro-national initiatives only when the voices of victims are heard. Administrative procedures must be opened to the voices of the victims, especially those who are already vulnerable, as they make governance more responsive.

What is most important, however, is that the experience of AIDMI shows that making the voices of the victims heard can work in India and in South Asia. If these and similar examples can be strengthened, expanded, and prioritized by national governments, UN agencies, and civil society in the coming half-decade, we may well be on our way to a safer South Asia.

Chapter Eleven
The Human Hand Behind Natural Disasters:
The Ugandan Experience

Benon Musinguzi

INTRODUCTION

The objective of this chapter is to show that most of the recent disasters that seem to be natural actually have a human hand behind them, that is, most of the time, human activities and behaviors initiate or intensify the disaster process.

A disaster is a natural or human-made hazard that has a strong and negative effect on the environment or on society. Disasters can be understood as the consequence of inappropriately managed risk.

Developing countries suffer the greatest costs when a disaster hits. Specifically, over 95% of all deaths caused by disasters occur in developing countries, and losses due to natural disasters are 20 times greater (as a percentage of GDP) in developing countries than in industrialized countries. Moreover, year after year, the destruction caused by natural disasters increases. In early 2000, over 10,000 people were killed by a cyclone in Orissa, India. The previous year, more than 1.5 million families in China lost their homes to floods.

At around the same time, the National Earthquake Information Centre in the United States reported that 2,900 people were killed in earthquakes in 1997 worldwide. In 1999, in Venezuela alone, it was estimated that up to 50,000 people died in floods and landslides, and an additional 200,000 people were left homeless as whole towns along the Caribbean coast were washed away. The increase in deaths from natural disasters and man-made disasters makes mitigation and prevention an urgent priority (Toepfer, 2005). In this regard, the UN's declaring October 10 as International Day for Natural Disaster Reduction recognizes the importance of disaster prevention, mitigation, and preparedness.

A clear distinction has been made between human-made and natural disasters that have occurred since the beginning of human history. Natural disasters, or "acts of God," according to conventional wisdom, are unpredictable and unpreventable, whereas human-made disasters, or "acts of man," are believed to be both predictable and preventable. Further, "acts of man" are perceived as more catastrophic and destructive than are "acts of God." These commonly accepted perceptions of "natural"' and "human-made" disasters, deserve a critical re-evaluation.

Many disasters, although triggered by natural events such as floods and earthquakes, are increasingly human-made and, hence, are both predictable and preventable. Likewise, certain human-made disasters cannot be so easily classified as "predictable" or "preventable" due to certain factors that render human beings incapable of rationally assessing the decisions that they make or foreseeing the consequences of their actions (Manion & Evan, 2001). This chapter will address these issues by looking at examples of "natural"' and "human-made" disasters in Uganda, including HIV/AIDS, floods, military conflicts, and others.

HIV/AIDS

Apart from the commonly known disasters such as floods, earthquakes, and tsunamis, the HIV/AIDS epidemic, both natural and human-made, is a major disaster in Africa that has killed millions of people. HIV/AIDS is a preventable illness, and, in Africa, about 98% of the infections are caused by heterosexual intercourse . When coordinated efforts to stop the epidemic were carried out, the scale of its destruction was dramatically reduced.

HIV/AIDS was first diagnosed in Uganda in 1982 along the shores of Lake Victoria. At the beginning of the epidemic, HIV/AIDS was mainly considered a health issue, so programs for combating it were based on health and medical science, and medical organizations were at the forefront of these efforts. However, the impact of HIV/AIDS on developmental institutions and their programs in Africa has forced health as well as non-health developmental agencies to approach the problem from a different angle. The HIV epidemic is now considered to have far-reaching implications for policy and programming for both government and international development agencies.

Throughout African history, few crises have presented such a threat to public health and to social and economic progress as does the HIV/AIDS epidemic. This becomes even more troubling when one considers that much of the suffering and the destitution caused by the disease could have been prevented.

Due to AIDS, decades of development have been lost in Africa, and the countries' efforts to reduce poverty and enhance living standards have been greatly undermined (Food and Agriculture Organization of the United Nations, 2002).

The Demographics of AIDS

It is difficult to downplay the effects of a disease that stands to kill more than half of the young adults in the countries with high HIV infection rates—most of them before they finish the work of caring for their children or providing for their elderly parents. By 2000, 18.8 million people around the world had died of

AIDS, 3.8 million of them children. Nearly twice that many, 34.3 million, were living with HIV, the virus that causes AIDS. It is estimated that, in 1999 alone, 5.4 million people were infected with HIV (Uganda AIDS Commission, 2003; World Health Organization, 2005). The national estimates of the HIV/AIDS epidemic in Uganda by December of 1999 suggested that the number of people living with HIV/AIDS was 1,438,000, of whom 1,294,200 were adults. Cumulative AIDS deaths in Uganda since 1982 have been estimated to be 838,000 adults. The overall mean age for adults with AIDS in Uganda is 32.2 years. Stratified by sex, the mean ages are 34.6 years and 31.3 years for males and females, respectively, and the male to female ratio is approximately 1:1.2 (Uganda AIDS Commission, 2003).

Socioeconomic Impact of HIV/AIDS

The age at which an individual contracts a long illness determines the extent of the impact of the illness on the household. Musinguzi's (2007) study of the socioeconomic impact of HIV/AIDS shows that those in the 15-64 age bracket were more likely than those in other age groups to suffer from AIDS-related illnesses (24.1%). This is the age bracket for individuals who are considered energetic, who have acquired skills, and who have young children and very old parents who may not fully care for themselves. Thus, their illness directly affects the economic and social welfare of their households and families (McGrath, Ankrah, Schumann, & Nkumbi 1993; Ndongko, 1996).

Additional detrimental effects of the AIDS epidemic are psychological distress as a result of the loss of dear ones, loss of incomes and savings, and fear of the unknown. Another major impact is on children; rates of both child mortality and child labor have increased as a result of the death of major income earners, and the educational possibilities of these children become constrained (Muller & Abbas, 1990; Preble, 1990). It has taken longer for the macro-economic impacts to be recognized, but in hard-hit countries such as Uganda, these impacts are becoming increasingly clear. It is also clear that the impacts will be felt for decades.

Politics, Coordination, and AIDS Reduction

Corruption, a human-made problem, has intensified the spread of HIV/AIDS and its effects. Funds (e.g., Global Fund for AIDS and Malaria) have been embezzled, leaving the poor vulnerable to HIV/AIDS infection and other consequences as well. Selfishness, greed, and hatred of our world leaders have combined with natural but preventable events to produce disasters that may be hard to categorize as either natural or human-made. Nevertheless, human-made efforts have helped to lessen the spread of AIDS. When it was first thought to be solely a medical problem to be addressed by medical means, there was no significant reduction in the infection rates or its impact.

A dramatic reduction occurred when politicians, including the President of Uganda, social workers, and religious workers got involved. There has been a dramatic reduction in infection rates, from 20% to its current rate of 6-7% of the population. These groups preached prevention in form of abstinence and faithfulness, and their message powerfully changed the trend of events.

FLOODS

Floods are one of the most frequent and widespread of all environmental hazards. According to the International Federation of Red Cross and Red Crescent Societies, between 1993 and 2002, flood disasters "affected more people across the globe—140 million per year on average—than all the other natural or technological disasters put together" ("Flooding in Uganda," 2007).
Several seemingly natural disasters have had a human hand. In Kampala, Uganda, we have had floods that have destroyed property and killed people not because the rains are "hurricane or tornado" force but simply due to poor town planning and building in wetlands, resulting in poor drainage. Massive flooding in Uganda affected some 300,000 people. Poor farmers in 16 districts in eastern and northern Uganda and the drought-prone Karamoja region suffered from the heaviest rains in decades, with the majority of families reporting crop losses of 90%. Continued flooding also meant that normal planting in September and October would be delayed, with no harvest until the next February.

Although floods could be categorized as natural disasters, they can be human-made or both. Despite the devastation, the Ugandan government has made no official estimate of the economic costs of the crisis. An officer in charge of Early Warning and Food Security at the Ministry of Agriculture of Uganda stated that, although early warning systems exist, they are not yet strongly developed, and the bill for disaster management remains in draft format.

MILITARY CONFLICTS

Uganda has experienced military conflicts over an extended period of time. The armed conflict that has affected Northern Uganda for nearly two decades has led to losses of human security, life, and assets. The conflict also has caused social upheaval, including dismantling of social safety nets, a marked drop in productivity, and the destruction of vital infrastructure, including health centers and schools. A combination of armed conflicts and other forms of disasters have weakened communities and institutions in the northern and northeastern regions as well as some areas in the western region of Uganda (United Nations Development Program, Uganda, 2008). The situation worsened until the whole of northern Uganda was a "no-go" zone. Social workers were involved only in helping the internally displaced people in their camps. It was not until 2007 that the government abandoned the military confrontations and moved to peace talks involving social workers, church leaders, and nongovernmental organizations. For the past two years, people have been slowly resettled into their homes.

This displacement of millions of people due to wars affects not only the displaced but also those found in the refuge zones. These wars cause epidemics and hunger. Additionally, wars in the neighboring Democratic Republic of Congo have produced waves of refugees into Uganda.

OTHER DISASTERS

Famine is another disaster that occasionally occurs in Uganda. Famine could be due to the long dry spells that occur at times, but, most often, it is due to poor planning. In some regions of Uganda, men do not participate in food production; instead they go to their drinking places early in the morning and remain there all day. This affects mass production and can lead to famine. Whenever there is a bumper harvest, most of the food is sold off, not stored, and the dry spell or floods find no stored food.

Windstorms are common in areas where there are no windbreakers. This is the situation in Uganda due to deforestation. Whenever winds occur, there is much destruction of property and even death.

Road accidents are another cause of disasters in Uganda. In most cases, they are the result of poorly managed vehicles, poor roads, or poor driving. The combination of the three factors has caused many vehicle-related deaths. Speeding, reckless driving, drinking and driving, and vehicles in poor mechanical condition remain the major causes of accidents.

CONCLUSION

It can be seen from these examples that there is not a clear boundary between natural and human-made disasters. What is true in most cases, however, is the presence of a human hand behind a disaster. Thus, our objective is to see social workers work in collaboration with governments, nongovernmental organizations, community-based organizations, village councils, academicians, and all other stakeholders to become more involved in the prevention of disasters.

REFERENCES

Flooding in Uganda: Can natural disasters be prevented? (2007). *IRIN: Humanitarian News and Analysis.* Retrieved from www.irinnews.org/ Report.aspx?ReportId=74765

Food and Agriculture Organization of the United Nations. (2002, February). *The Impact of HIV/AIDS on food security in Africa.* Paper presented at the Twenty-Second Regional Conference for Africa. Cairo, Egypt.

Manion, M., & Evan, W. (2001). Natural and human-made disasters. *International Journal of Risk Assessment and Management, 2*(1-2), 6-35.

McGrath, J. W., Ankrah, M., Schumann, D. A., & Nkumbi, S. (1993). AIDS and the urban family: Its impact in Kampala, Uganda. *AIDS Care, 5*(1), 55-70.

Muller, O., & Abbas, N. (1990). The impact of AIDS mortality on children's education in Kampala, Uganda. *AIDS Care, 2*(1), 77-80.

Musinguzi, B. (2007). *The socio-economic impact of HIV/AIDS on households in Bushenyi district, Uganda* (Unpublished doctoral dissertation). Makerere University, Uganda.

Ndongko, T. M. (1996). A preliminary study of the socio-economic impact of HIV/AIDS. *Africa Development, 21*(1), 39-55.

Preble E. (1990). Impact of HIV/AIDS on African children. *Social Science and Medicine, 31*(6), 671-680.

Toepfer, K. (2005, January 25). Environmental management for disaster reduction. *Environment and Poverty Times*, p. 1.

Uganda AIDS Commission. (2003). *AIDS in Africa during the nineties.* Kampala, Uganda: Ministry of Health.

United Nations Development Program, Uganda. (2008) *The Millennium Development Goals* (Special issue). Retrieved from www.undp.or.ug

World Health Organization. (2005, December). *AIDS epidemic update.* Geneva, Switzerland: WHO.

Part Four:
Psychosocial Interventions

Chapter Twelve
Cultural Sensitivity in Psychosocial Interventions Following a Disaster[1]:
A Tri-national Collaboration in Sri Lanka

Mooli Lahad, Yehuda Baruch, Yehuda Shacham, Shulamit Niv, Ruvie Rogel, Nitsa Nacasch, Lilach Rachamim, and Dmitry Leykin

BACKGROUND

In the early morning hours of Sunday, December 26, 2004, a massive earthquake, measuring 9.0, struck the west of northern Sumatra. Large tsunamis were generated that severely damaged coastal communities in countries around the Bay of Bengal and the Indian Ocean, including Indonesia, Thailand, Sri Lanka, and India (Liu et al., 2005). In Sri Lanka, one of the worst affected areas, the flood swamped widespread coastal regions in all directions and caused more than 40,000 casualties. Over 500,000 inhabitants of these regions were displaced from their homes and had to flee to 315 provisional refugee camps or to the homes of relatives (Ingram, 2005; Neuner, Schauer, Catani, Ruf, & Elbert, 2006; "Tsunami-hit Sri Lanka," 2005; World Health Organization, 2005). According to Mahoney, Chandra, Gambheera, Silva, and Suveendran (2006), "approximately one in every thirty Sri Lankans lost their homes and there was widespread destruction and damage to schools, hospitals, businesses and other infrastructure" (p. 593). According to Godavitarne, Udu-gama, Sreetharan, Preuss, and Krimgold (2006):

> An estimated 350,000 people lost their jobs, including fishermen, informal traders, and tourism workers. With a total population of about 20 million and a land area of 25,300 square miles, nearly everyone in the country was touched in some way. (p. S845)

PSYCHOLOGICAL IMPACT OF THE TSUNAMI

Natural disasters, including hurricanes, volcanic eruptions, earthquakes, tsunamis, and their aftermath, have a powerful impact on the community and may cause immediate and enduring psychological distress among adult and child populations (Ashraf, 2005; Frankenberg et al., 2008; Norris et al., 2002; Tuicomepee & Rornano, 2008). One of the common sequelae of exposure to natural disaster-induced trauma is posttraumatic stress disorder (PTSD). According to Neuner et al. (2006), 14% to 39% of the children within several affected districts in Sri Lanka had persistent PTSD symptoms about one month following exposure to the tsunami. Hollifield et al. (2008) estimated the prevalence of clinically significant PTSD, depression, and anxiety at 21%, 16%, and 30%, respectively, 20-21 months post-tsunami among adults in a coastal village in Sri Lanka. Other evidence estimates the prevalence of PTSD to be 52% in an adult population 15 months post-tsunami (Lommen, Sanders, Buck, & Arntz, 2009). Rachamim (2009) described the harsh reality in the refugee camps and the maladaptive behavioral responses in the aftermath of the disaster:

> Visiting those extremely crowded camps left a painful impression; people were crying about the loss of babies, children, husbands, wives and other loved ones. Victims frequently mentioned that not even a single photo was left for the memorial of the loved ones – as the sea had taken everything away. Some of the men who had lost their source of income spent their time drinking alcohol, and women were hanging around with their little frightened children who refused to leave their mothers even for a second. Male adolescents were lying around in tents, bored; some of them were drunk or depressed. Some of the refugees were working together with the volunteers in the reconstruction of schools, kindergartens and clinics. From time to time we arrived at camps that were empty and we were told that everybody had fled because of rumors of another tsunami on the way.

Rachamim (2009) also indicated that the affected islanders experienced prolonged displacement and were settled in inadequate housing, such as tents and rickety huts. Such living conditions exposed children and women to extreme potential assault and danger, and, frequently, "discreet" cases of rape, domestic violence, child molestation, and even child kidnapping were reported. Bereavement, as well as the loss of support systems, normal routines, and basic beliefs concerning safety, was a common reaction among many. Loss of close relatives and resources, displacement and inadequate housing, and lack of social and familial support are considered mediating factors for the development of chronic posttraumatic disturbances and interfere with the natural process of recovery following trauma (Foy, Madvig, Pynoos, & Camilleri, 1996; LaGreca, Vemberg, Silverman, & Prinstein, 1996; Lahad, 2008; Pynoos et al., 1993). These conditions put the tsunami victims at high risk for the development of chronic emotional effects, including PTSD, depression, and complicated grief.

The enduring civil war in Sri Lanka was another factor mediating chronic posttraumatic psychological distress. Since 1983, the longitudinal conflict between the government and the Tamil Tigers has caused massive and deadly destruction to the population of Sri Lanka (de Jong et al., 2002). It is plausible that an integral part of the posttraumatic psychological reactions observed was related to the ongoing threat induced by war and the accumulation of multiple stressors, rather than a direct consequence of the catastrophic tsunami itself (Baruch, 2009; Elbert et al., 2006).

IMPORTANCE OF MENTAL HEALTH SYSTEM PREPAREDNESS AND INTERVENTION

Past evidence suggests that availability of mental health services in the tsunami's affected areas reduced the occurrence of behavior problems among adolescents one year post-disaster (Tuicomepee & Rornano, 2008). The shortage of mental professionals in Sri Lanka was a difficulty mentioned by physical and mental health professionals, both local and foreign. In early 2005, the mental health system on the island consisted of approximately 60 psychiatrists and 19 psychologists, who were mainly situated in Colombo; child and adolescent psychiatry and psychology were practically non-existent, and the same professionals were responsible for adults as well as for children. Only three academic centers for mental health were available on the entire island (including one inaccessible center in the north; Baruch, 2009). The great magnitude of the trauma and an insufficient number of mental health experts raised the urgent need to train large numbers of people for the screening and treatment of even larger numbers of patients, with the following main aims: first, increasing the number of mental professionals in a relatively short time; second, disseminating treatment programs suitable for the treatment of posttraumatic distress that could be adopted by mental health professionals but also by nonprofessionals, including community leaders, family physicians, nurses, teachers, and religious leaders, such as Buddhist priests; and, finally, adapting Western mental assistance knowledge to the local culture to increase its applicability.

PAST EXPERIENCE IN CROSS-CULTURAL PSYCHOSOCIAL INTERVENTION

Prior crisis intervention and rehabilitation experience in natural and human-made disasters, such as the crisis intervention in Bosnia during the Balkan War, the earthquake in Turkey in 1999, and the Beslan school hostage crisis in 2004, led the various partners to choose the Community Stress Prevention Center (CSPC) as the leading organization to coordinate the international teams in conducting international cross-cultural psychosocial intervention in Sri Lanka. Past successful experience in using culturally sensitive methods, keeping in mind all cultural mediating factors, has set basic standards for intervention in foreign countries. One example of the use of the model "Train the Trainers" by the CSPC team occurred during the post-earthquake period in Turkey (Ayalon, 2003). This HANDS (Helpers Assisting Natural Disaster Survivors) project was designed for a period of one year. The CSPC team trained a core group of 20 local professionals in CSPC methods and the skills of trauma and recovery work, training them as master trainers. These master trainers, in turn, were encouraged to use the acquired knowledge and to adapt it to their culture and norms. They were obliged to pass this knowledge on to another 12 professionals each, who, in return, would eventually train at least 20-25 other local workers (e.g., teachers, nurses, community workers). Ultimately, this cascade model reached an approximate 4,500 people. Not surprisingly, Setiawan and Viora (2006), in their article on the post-tsunami disaster mental health preparedness plan in Indonesia, concluded: "The best form of disaster preparedness in mental health and psychosocial needs is to have a strong community mental health system" (p. 566). In addition, they recommended: "The preparedness planning (and thus the intervention) of any disaster management must include strengthening of existing mental health services, which should be based in the community" (p. 566).

ESTABLISHMENT PHASE

To Be Invited: Tri-national Trauma Response: Building Resiliency in Sri Lanka

The Tri-national Trauma Response: Building Psychosocial Resiliency Project was a collaboration between the CSPC, the Israel Trauma Coalition (ITC), the UJA Federation of New York's Trauma and Disaster Consortium, Israel's Ministry of Health, the American Jewish Joint Distribution Committee, and Sahanaya (National Council of Mental Health of Sri Lanka). The goal of the project, launched in response to the tsunami disaster, was to create and train a local cadre of trainers to strengthen the knowledge and skills of community-based providers and institutions to address psychosocial needs, to enhance resiliency, and to increase system capacity to support, treat, and train others. The agreement with the three Sri Lankan government ministries (Health, Education and Welfare, and Women's Empowerment) ensured funding for a one-week paid relief program for the master trainers for the first week of orientation, an additional four weeks of Master Training (MT), and future training time and training activities that the MT would provide.

In addition to specialized trauma training for mental health professionals, the project targeted strengthening system capacity through training health care providers such as doctors, nurses, and midwives, along with teachers and community and religious leaders, in skills that would enable them to recognize people at risk for serious disorders and help ensure that appropriate supports and interventions were available. To accomplish this aim, the Israeli/American team recognized the importance of creating partnerships with local experts and utilizing existing community assets and resources as well as the need for cultural adaptation and integration of Israeli and American methodologies to ensure applicability and continuity after the project had formally ended. It was agreed that a core group of professionals from Sahanaya would provide the anchor for long-term support and continued training activities, through the newly created district resource centers (DRCs; Hernandez, 2002). Overall, 12 members of the partner-organizations of the Israeli Trauma Coalition, 5 American institutes, 3 European NGOs, and members of the International School Psychology Trauma Task Force collaborated on this project.

FACT-FINDING TOUR

The first delegation that was sent for fact finding was in response to a direct request from the chief psychiatrist of Sri Lanka and in coordination with the Sri Lankan authorities (Ministries of Health, Education and Welfare, and Women's Empowerment). The aims of this team were to identify the local resources and to jointly define the expected need for help. The fact-finding delegation gained knowledge of the state, assessed needs, made an effort to understand the extent of the impact and the devastation, and defined an initial frame of work with local government and the Mental Health Organization. This could be described as a learning expedition rather than an action team, although some basic lectures were given (Baruch, 2009). Considering and following this open-minded approach, an organized and coherent process of joint thinking has the potential to assure fluent and well-concerted efforts for intervention and can lead to the initiation of a partnership.

IDENTIFYING PARTNERS, RESOURCES, AND ISSUES AT STAKE

De Silva (2006) noted that Buddhist priests in the affected areas provided immediate help and support to the survivors of the tsunami. As mentioned by Shacham (2009), such help was characterized by giving people shelter and daily occupation, "bringing smiles back to faces." Shacham mentioned meeting one Buddhist priest with whom he had a conversation (via an interpreter) immediately after the tsunami, while on the fact-finding tour, and compares the priest's deeds to psychological intervention. Sometimes after a major life event or crisis, people lose their physical, psychological, social, cultural, and historical sense of continuity; this impairs their ability to hold on to the belief that "yesterday predicts tomorrow" (see Omer & Alon, 1994). To rehabilitate their sense of coherence, one should find an appropriate way to bridge affected continuities or to strengthen existing unaffected resources (Lahad, 2009). The aforementioned priest managed to fill the psychological gap by opening the storage rooms and handing out rakes and brooms to the survivors, thus giving them practical tasks.

In this way, he fulfilled a primarily rehabilitating source of functional continuity.

It may be assumed that these acts of the priest affected other continuities, such as social interpersonal continuity (by making the survivors work together), emotional continuity (being active as a relief from various emotions), and the continuity of beliefs and self-esteem (by enabling them to do something for themselves). Shacham (2009) suggested that, even though Buddhist priests could not phrase their deeds in psychological terms, these deeds were important acute intervention actions. Moreover, establishing contact with the Buddhist priests served as an excellent source of partnership for the team in reaching broader sectors of the population. Baruch (2009) added that no work could have been accomplished without the cooperation of the Buddhist religious centers, which had the capacities and the willingness to assist. In support of this notion, De Silva (2006) stated, "Following their initial response, many priests and Buddhist organizations have been involved in further work, providing material help as well as psychological support and counseling" (p. 284). The respect that the Sri Lankan participants and the professional staff showed to the priests was widely commented on in team members' evaluation papers. Niv (2009) and Rogel (2009) mentioned local norms regarding the setting that should be arranged in the presence of the clergy members (i.e., setting a cloth upon the chair upon which the Buddhist priest would sit, making sure their meals were ready before noon).

FINDING PARTNERS AND A LEAD AGENCY

Baruch (2009) stated that a leading principle in working with foreign governments is that one should strive to have direct contact with the local government and not work independently or as an isolated, unconnected entity, as did some of the delegations or relief organizations. There were those who came and said, "Here we are; let us do what we can." Moreover, as stated by Van Rooyen and Leaning (2005):

> As more and more relief organizations arrive on the scene daily, coordination and communication become ever more crucial . . . International nongovernmental organizations, while often like-minded, tend to be fiercely independent. Several hundred diverse organizations have gathered in Indonesia and Sri Lanka, and it is difficult to coordinate their efforts. (p. 436)

Therefore, in the case of the project described, much effort was directed toward engaging, connecting, and collaborating with the local mental health organization and opinion leaders, making an effort to define together what had to be done to formulate a health program, rather than saying, "We know what to do."

Following the fact-finding tour, an appeal for a leading organization in the field of psychotrauma and rehabilitation outside Sri Lanka was launched to invite them to participate in the project, and an agreement was signed between the project managers and the relevant Sri Lankan government offices, which stated that all participants would be released from their other work obligations for the purposes of the training course. They would continue to receive wages while on the course and would be given the opportunity to train others upon their return from the training on work time (Chemtob & Dutch, 2006). Shacham (2009) noted that, in this project, the fact that the local partner had a proper location for training made the planning and execution of the training much easier. Moreover, a training space can be better utilized when the local partner has similar aims as the training bodies.

MAIN CONSIDERATIONS BEFORE LAUNCHING
AN INTERNATIONAL PROJECT

Cultural Sensitivity

In many cases, we find ourselves teaching people things that they know intuitively or in different terminology. As such, it is of utmost importance to establish a dialogue with the target population in a foreign country where we plan to intervene. To do that, we have to understand the culture and its norms (Rogel, 2009). Cross, Bazron, Dennis, and Isaacs (as cited in Saldaña, 2001) introduced the term *cultural competency* as:

> A set of congruent behaviors, attitudes, and policies that come together in a system, agency, or among professionals that enable teams to work effectively in cross-cultural situations. Cultural competency is the acceptance and respect for difference, a continuous self-assessment regarding culture, an attention to the dynamics of difference, the ongoing development of cultural knowledge, and the resources and flexibility within service models to meet the needs of minority populations. (p. 3)

Operationally, *cultural competence* is defined as "the integration and transformation of knowledge about individuals and groups of people into specific standards, policies, practices, and attitudes used in appropriate cultural settings to increase the quality of services; thereby producing better outcomes" (Davis, as cited in Saldaña, 2001, p. 3). In a practical guide for mental health service providers, Saldaña (2001) presents the essential components of cultural competence development: knowledge, skills, and attributes. As previously mentioned, interveners must gain considerable knowledge of culture (i.e., history, traditions, values, family systems, artistic expressions, specific rituals of passage). They must explore the history of the culture's rituals and norms about "getting help," that is, knowledge of the help-seeking behaviors of the population: Are the people ready to be helped? What are the ways in which they express mental disorders and/or grief? Are they ready to be helped by foreigners or locals? What are their attitudes toward doctors, medicine, and other helping professions? As part of this project, the delegation met many dignitaries to hear their views on the concept of preparedness, intervention, and psychosocial projects. Listening, discussing, and debating various aspects of the training course was a learning experience for both sides and involved a process of clarifying terms and inclinations.

One good example of the difficulties involved was the process of clarifying the local rituals of bereavement. The delegation expressed a strong wish to meet with a local anthropologist to learn about perceptions of death and customs of grief. It took several discussions and one presentation by a local expert to understand that there was a grave misunderstanding and that the lecture given by the local expert was based on "Western psychological perceptions of death."

Another example of misunderstanding involves issues raised by local experts, to which different cultures relate in different ways. The preliminary discussion between the international staff and the local staff identified women's empowerment as an issue that should be raised during the training. Some of the international female staff members were very sensitive about the issue, and it was decided to incorporate it into the training, especially because the Ministry for Women's Affairs was one of the training partners. Consequently, in one session, the issue of women's status in Sri Lanka was raised, but discussion ended in failure. Nobody in the group was willing to speak about the issue, even though the staff tried its best to engage the participants. Eventually, during the last ten minutes of the session, the young unmarried women started to talk. The little that was said made it clear that it is impossible to have a discussion on such a sensitive topic in a big group that includes both genders and people of different marital statuses. It was also clear that topics discussed in an informal way are not always suitable for the curriculum of the large group. Some conclusions, in retrospect, are that professional values may be in conflict with trainee needs and that the way power relationships within communities or institutions affect different cultures should be studied. At times, the same words may have different connotations in different cultures. Still another rather sensitive issue concerned joint training for trainees coming from a Tamil background (the minority opposition group in Sri Lanka). The issue never arose in the groups, but an important part of the staff preparation involved sensitivity to any difficulty which might arise.

Coming from different countries and cultures as well as having unfamiliar languages, distinctive socioeconomic backgrounds, and diverse values and views, as well as aiming to bequeath theoretical knowledge, skills, and methods to locals, required the trainer to adapt training ideas to a language that would be familiar and understandable for locals. Hence, prior to any overseas intervention, it is important to study the local culture. One very accessible resource is the Internet. Through the Internet, it is possible to access articles on the culture, the population, the spoken languages, policies, customs, and other issues that may assist in the preparation process and help to avoid conflicts and misunderstandings.

Cultural conceptual frameworks are paramount for psychosocial intervention projects. Saldaña (2001) stated that communication is the most fundamental function of any therapeutic session, and verbal and non-verbal ways of self-expression are formed by the culture in which we were raised. Additionally, she noted that styles of communication vary among people from different backgrounds and referred to issues involving personal space, gesturing, facial expression, silence, eye contact, interruptions, and turn-taking behavior. In conversations with project participants and professionals, the concept of PTSD was repeatedly questioned, as it seemed like a Western model for understanding responses to trauma. For example, very early on, we noticed that the Singhalese did not have a word for depression. Most of the Sri Lankan patients and people did not understand the meaning of the word, but they would come up with some other manifestation for the word, mostly describing the somatization accompanying the distress. The same applies to the word resiliency and many others. Thus, teaching and evaluation should take all of these factors into consideration when looking at course content.

Considering participants' backgrounds when teaching specific techniques is also a key principle. For example, in the Buddhist religion and culture, meditation and mindfulness are part of regular practice. Hence, using the word meditation for the purpose of relaxation was inappropriate, so we used only the word relaxation so as not to offend the religious participants (Chemtob & Dutch, 2006). The following sections present our practical considerations on these matters.

Personal Space

Before conducting warm-up exercises that involve touching, the issue of personal space should be considered. Moreover, the presence of possible physical contact between participants, or between males and females, may be problematic in relation to religion, marital status, attitudes, or customs. We found, however, that participants of both genders willingly participated in such exercises.

Silence and Feedback

When somebody is not responding to you, is it because they do not understand? Is it because they are not interested in what you are saying? Or is it simply due to their culture? Frequently asking those questions, we found that the main problem that we had with silence was when we had to select participants for the Master Training Program based on their classroom performance evaluations. If somebody had been sitting quietly during lectures for the whole week session, what would that mean as far as their performance and ability? Because this was found in most cases to be part of the culture, we had to respect that silence and use other evaluation methods, such as incorporating local trainers' evaluations or sociograms.

Gesturing

While comprehending the lecture's information, participants were nodding their heads, which looked like a cross between a nod and shake. This head-wobble gesture was the source of much confusion and wonderment, leaving the lecturers uncertain as to whether participants did or did not understand them or agreed or disagreed with what they were saying. It was found that direct questions about their attitude while they were gesturing (Does it mean yes or no?) helped to clarify the gestures and their meaning.

Developing the Curriculum

The selection of teaching materials for the orientation seminars and, later on, for the MT course, was based on various criteria: the foremost was the use of a subject/model or a method that was already in use in non-Western cultures and that local experts were able to adapt to local needs and norms. The other criterion was that the model would be an evidence-based treatment that had proved to be effective through a rigorous scientific process.

The first batch of training subjects for the Orientation Course was based mostly on the discussions held in Sri Lanka and on CSPC experiences around the world. Based on the evaluation and feedback compiled after the orientation courses, the most appropriate skills, methods, and protocols were selected to be taught in the MT course. During the first week, the training team identified areas and topics that were perceived as most suitable and useful for the trainees. Among them were a desensitization protocol, parents' counseling meetings, play therapy with children, debriefings, prolonged exposure protocol, non-pharmacological techniques to treat PTSD and stress symptoms, uses of warm-ups, storytelling and drama, and art forms to express feelings and ideas as well as training techniques. These topics were expanded on in the following three weeks of training, based on written and oral feedback given by the MT trainees and the teaching staff. Thus, some of the experts recruited for the training were approached based on the ongoing needs assessment, and the curriculum was adjusted accordingly.

In the middle of October 2005, at the end of the orientation training, a debate broke out among the staff regarding the importance of theory versus skills and where to put more emphasis in the future MT course. One opinion was that, although theory was important, local needs involved providing practical tools, even in the form of a "cookbook." Another opinion was in favor of grounding the material in theory. One of the training staff commented that, after working in the refugee camps for over a month, there was a feeling that skills in working with children were needed much more than were theory lectures. Others argued that, even though trainees needed more skills, future MTs must have certain knowledge so that, in the future, they would be able to understand what they teach (Lahad, 2005). Van Peski (2006) stated that, in addition to knowledge or skills, a major focus for the training should be the further development and consolidation of the level of perceived self-esteem of the trainees. The debate culminated with an overall agreement in favor of skills and methods in the face-to-face teaching, and theory and knowledge provided in a written form.

Training a Multi-Disciplinary Team

One of the major considerations in planning the training was the group composition. The facts that there were so few psychosocial staff available in Sri Lanka, that the needs following the tsunami were enormous, and that our resources were limited led us to consider multidisciplinary training. However, such training had never existed in Sri Lanka. Medical staff had never trained with educational staff or community staff and vice versa. This was not only an historical issue but also a matter of background, mentality, and professional perception. The solution was to create training that would address several needs, including the need for a common language, to create a network of trainers, and to provide specific training for each professional group. Thus, the training was based on joint sessions and then specific training. As it turned out, this was one of the achievements of the training, leading to recognition of the various partners in the community and their cooperation with each other.

Training Delivery

Another issue was how to teach. Would we focus mostly on knowledge (i.e., giving lectures)? How were we going to get enough proficiency in such a short time, considering that the subjects were very new for most participants? The solution was to focus on experiential learning, supported by lectures and printed materials, simulations, and role-play. Hands-on methods followed almost every subject that was taught, and for the MT course, simulated teaching by the participants as well as home assignments to train others and an independent study project that they had to plan and deliver all proved effective. Finally, because most of the participants did not have teaching skills, but the expectation was that, following the MT course, the participants would teach, a module on teaching skills was added to every week of the MT course, and simulations of teaching by participants, followed by feedback from fellow trainees and the trainers, became part of the training.

Lost in Translation

Trainers often said they felt wary that translators were improperly elaborating on lecture material or leaving out crucial information. A brief sentence uttered by a teacher sometimes became a "paragraph" when translated into Singhala, and a long series of English sentences were often shortened to a few words.

Stoller (2006), a creative arts therapist from the United States, described her experience of working with translators:

It is challenging. One has to remember to stop for translation . . . and then you are never completely sure if the translation was accurate or if part of your meaning is lost. I realized that as a teacher and trainer I am used to a lot of give and take with the audience. That is harder to achieve with the translation lag, but not impossible. I got more comfortable working with translation in the second week when we repeated the same courses for the second group of Master Trainers. (p. 18)

Although there were many cultural differences and issues that arose from the orientation and MT courses, these issues were attended to by professional staff. Janaki Pethiyagoda, a senior MT (personal communication, December 14, 2008), noted that the training personnel were very sensitive to the cultural aspects. She stated, "In Sri Lankan culture, people do not get used to sitting next to a Buddhist priest, so they (the trainers) would come and ask the dos and the don'ts." She mentioned that the trainers were constantly asking about proper clothing and other cultural aspects and not just when it was necessary. The strong intention of the trainer team to adapt culturally is reflected in her closing statement: "They just wanted to know everything about what happens in Sri Lanka."

Compiling and Translating the Teaching Material

Upon the arrival of each expert team, the relevant teaching materials (e.g., handouts, power-point slides, DVDs, CDs) were prepared, shared via email communication, revised, and passed on to the local translators, either in printed or handwritten form for forward-backward translation. However, as an increasing number of materials arrived, the translating team (consisting of several local professionals) became overloaded and functioned less effectively. Thus, it took an increasingly long amount of time to get all the material done. However, by the end of the project, the entire curriculum had been translated into Singhala. An important lesson learned is that, when working in several locations, it is crucial to establish a solid means of information transmission, such as a stable Internet connection, which enables transmission of materials to specific teaching centers on time.

Accommodating Local Experts in the Teaching

One very important area in which we did not succeed much, but still feel that it should be part of such a project, is the accommodation of local experts in the teaching. We failed to find an anthropologist to teach rituals of grief and bereavement or an expert in the use of traditional methods of post-trauma healing. We resolved this need by calling upon the local professional staff (psychologists and psychiatrists) to be our interpreters. Most of them have been trained in the West or in Western institutes in Sri Lanka and thus were able to provide a bridge between Western terminology and local terms and habits. Further, because they speak the local language and could "feel the waves," they provided us with first-hand feedback and insights into the culture, the adequacy of the delivery of materials, and gaps in knowledge and skills that needed either clarification or more exercise.

Efforts to Keep the Teaching Continuity Among the Various Teaching Staff

Conducting multicultural training with an international training team that could be composed of different nationalities, as in the Sri Lankan experience (Israeli, American, Dutch, and Turk personnel) requires similar work with each team member (Rogel, 2009). For the orientation phase, the first team that went out comprised mostly CSPC and a few other Israeli experts, namely psychiatrists, from the Ministry of Health (MOH), whose focus was to reduce strain and to ensure that the team had a common language. Thereafter, a brief introduction was given to each new member arriving on site, and one or two senior members from CSPC were always present to ensure a smooth introduction and continuity of the program. Every evening, the team met for discussion and debriefing by heads of teams. This was helpful in maintaining the team's mental and physical welfare as well as team integration over the week of training. Team members shared an apartment, and common meals or outings were encouraged. The spirit of pioneering and volunteerism was very much part of the general atmosphere. The leaders of the local mental health team were also invited to the evening sessions, during which cultural and evaluation issues, as well as practicalities such as translation of material and interpreters, were discussed. Individual reports on the teaching and the training are vital and provide a wide range of personal views of the project. These reports equip the future professional team coming on site with essential information and feedback.

SPECIAL TEACHING FOCUS

Teaching Preventive Methods

During this psychosocial resiliency-building project, crisis management-related theoretical subjects and therapeutic methods were taught through lectures and exercises. The terms and the concepts were not only translated but also had to be suited to the local situation, for example, the building of the local DRC. The DRC was an attempt to bring together the local authority, representatives of the ministries on a district level, and the NGOs. One of its tasks was to facilitate the dissemination and local facilitation of the newly acquired knowledge and skills, which were included among the targets of the project and depended upon cultural adaptation.

Art has healing effects insofar as it is natural to many cultures when attempting to make sense of events and in tribal rituals of healing. Originally, one of our local senior partners advised us to avoid using the arts, stating that participants would not cooperate nor would they find it helpful and could even find it childish and inappropriate. We believe that this was a reflection of an unspoken expectation by a local expert that Western psychotherapy is cognitive and scientifically bound and that art therapies are not serious enough. This is one example in which what outsiders (the trainers) consider "serious work" led to a misrepresentation of reality. In fact, the art-form activities (drawing, dictionary of emotions, playing, dramatizing, and storytelling as well as the use of therapeutic cards) were found to be natural to the group, easily adopted, and effective in releasing tension and stress as well as a gentle way to disclose and work through painful memories. These art-form therapeutic methods were commonly used in the many field projects that the trainees implemented in their own sites.

Basic PH: The Integrative Model of Coping

The most adaptable model that has been taught in many places around the globe and was found to be sensitive to cultural diversity is the BASIC Ph model (Ayalon, 2003). Introduced and developed by Lahad (1992), this multidimensional approach using an available set of coping mechanisms and channels and serving individuals and communities during times of crisis, aroused great discussion among the participants. Stoller (2006) described her experience with the use of BASIC Ph in the training:

> It has been wonderfully encouraging to see the participants become 'fluent' in BASIC Ph. All seem able to apply the concepts to assessment and interventions and are really beginning to speak a 'new language' and see their communities and work places through new eyes; focusing on coping resources. (p. 9)

She also noted that the basic concepts of the multidimensional model were integrated easily into drama play (i.e., enacting the Little Red Riding Hood story, using different sources of coping). Regarding the *Little Red Riding Hood* enactment, it is important to mention that, due to cultural gaps, some participants were not familiar with the fairy tale and found it difficult to comprehend the task. However, with the assistance of the participants who did know the story, and who were nominated as team leaders, it became easier to complete the exercises.

Teaching Psychotrauma Subjects: Prolonged Exposure (PE), PE for Children, and Eye Movement Desensitization Reprocessing (EMDR)

Child Treatment Methods

After assessing the local situation, Rachamim (2009) found that there were no trained psychosocial relief professionals specializing in work with children and adolescents. Consequently, she decided to find and recruit local community workers and leaders who could be trained to support the survivors in the camps. Extensive training workshops were conducted by a few Israeli specialists, focusing on identifying children and parents suffering from posttraumatic stress and teaching basic intervention methods for posttraumatic symptoms. Shaded spots were placed in several camps, where the trained local teams encouraged children and mothers to play and draw together. After building rapport, the children and parents were encouraged to share their concerns. Mothers or other caretakers, such as grandparents and adult siblings, approached the local volunteers and talked about sleeping problems, clinging children who refused to go to school, and numerous suicidal attempts of child and adult survivors. Psychoeducation about trauma and its aftermath is one of the core elements in trauma-focused interventions (Foa, Keane, Friedman, & Cohen, 2009).

To provide essential knowledge about posttraumatic reactions and symptoms to caretakers and children, as well as to identify children who were suffering from posttraumatic symptoms, a story-based intervention was used. Together with a local translator, a short story was written about a child named Janaka who experienced a natural disaster and described his reactions to the trauma (physical, behavioral, and emotional reactions, such as separation fear, frightening dreams, and startle responses). The trained community workers sat together with the mothers, other caretakers, and children in the shady places and read the story. Several mothers who were reluctant to discuss these matters with their children, so as to protect the child from further distress, were encouraged to do so. They were educated about essential factors in the normal healing process following trauma and ways to discuss the events with the child. Throughout the telling of the story, children and caretakers shared some of their unexpressed emotions and experiences through recounting and drawings. Through the story, as discussed below, children were able to describe their psychological reactions to the traumatic events.

Taking into account the development of communication skills, especially in terms of descriptions of events that are far from the child's understanding (e.g., descriptions of complex emotions), props such as stories and drawings may facilitate communication by allowing the child to show and recount the traumatic memory and thus compensate for the lack of words to describe the traumatic event and the related emotions. The use of stories and drawings facilitated children's recall and their recounting of the traumatic events. The volunteers helped children and their caretakers to appraise and interpret their experiences and to correct misconceptions of the event itself as well as the posttraumatic symptoms, behaviors, and emotions of the child and his or her caregivers. Other interventions, such as culturally accepted forms of relaxation techniques (e.g., meditation), were used daily, and methods of desensitization were practiced with groups of children and caretakers (e.g., gradual exposure to school, to the beach) to confront their fears and to gradually return to daily routines.

Prolonged Exposure

Over the last 20 years, several effective cognitive behavioral therapy (CBT) programs for PTSD have been developed, extensively studied, and been found to be effective. One such program is prolonged exposure therapy (PE; Foa et al., 2009). PE is a specific exposure therapy protocol that has elicited empirical evidence of its effectiveness with a wide range of trauma. It is a relatively short treatment (9-15 sessions, once or twice a week), divided into four parts (breathing retraining, psychoeducation, imaginal exposure, and in vivo exposure). During the past six years, a model of training and dissemination of PE to non-CBT clinicians in different countries has emerged. In the face of the tsunami, the need for an effective time-limited treatment for trauma casualties became urgent. To address these needs, the task of the third master trainings was to focus on CBT for PTSD, depression, and panic disorders. The decision to use PE was based on its extensive ongoing research and its recorded effectiveness, as demonstrated in behavioral studies (Bradley, Greene, Russ, Dutra, & Westen, 2005).

During the three-day workshop, participants from the health subgroup received training in basic CBT, assessment and psychopathology of PTSD, and specific PE therapy components such as imaginal exposure and in-vivo exposure. Cultural adaption of these components was essential and was done through videotapes and small-group practice. For instance, during in vivo exposure to trauma reminders in life, the patient builds a hierarchical list of reminders (e.g., palm tree, sand, beach, sea) and gradually exposes him or herself to those situations, until there is a noticeable decrease in anxiety (e.g., being 2 km from the sea, gradually getting closer, watching the sea, sitting on the beach, and eventually swimming in the sea). The factors that facilitated teaching included the use of an English manual protocol, videotaped session demonstration, commitment from the trainees, team support, and team preparedness.

Nacasch (2009) noted that cultural aspects have considerable influence on the content of emotional behaviors. For instance, issues of shame, reluctance to express emotions, and a high prevalence rate of suicide were discussed as they were reflected in role-plays followed by treatment adaptation for these issues. Another concern was the time limitation for conducting PE treatments in Sri Lanka, as the general practitioners' session is limited in time and lasts about 20 minutes per patient, while a regular PE session lasts approximately 90 minutes. Although the entire protocol, as studied in empirical research (Bryant, Moulds, Guthrie, Dang, & Nixon, 2003), could not be accomplished, it was decided that using only parts of the protocol in the clinical work might still be beneficial to the patient.

Nacasch (2009) also found numerous difficulties in using CBT in Sri Lanka due to the limited words used for emotions in the Sinhalese vernacular, resulting in difficulties in labeling emotions and, thus, confusion in identifying thoughts as independent from emotions. The use of role-play revealed sources of trauma and distress that were not related to the tsunami but rather to rape in the refugee camps, domestic violence, and ongoing terrorism. In her continuous support for the Sri Lanka team, Nacasch found, through e-mail based supervision with a participant, evidence for the extensive use of this protocol, mostly for mood and anxiety disorders.

In the child psychotrauma training, a PE workshop for child and adolescent therapists was conducted by Rachamim (2009). The PE program for the treatment of children and adolescents (Foa, Creshman, & Gilboa-Schechtman, 2008) is based on the PE program for adults. Several adaptations to the adult protocol were made to create a developmentally sensitive program. These adaptations included stories conveying knowledge about psychological reactions to trauma and recounting the trauma memory by symbolic means such as drawing and playing. In the training workshop, the treatment methods were adapted by Rachamim to fit group interventions that took into account the massive number of victims and to fit systemic guidance (e.g., ways of recognizing post-trauma in the classroom, talking with children about trauma and death). Finally, given the high prevalence of child abuse, special emphasis was accorded to the treatment of sexual assault. Supervision that was conducted several months after training revealed that the trainees used the methods learned in the treatment of children and found them highly helpful in reducing posttraumatic symptoms in the children and adolescents.

EMDR

Another method that was taught as a separate psychotrauma protocol was EMDR, which is also considered effective for PTSD symptom reduction and, because it involves little verbal communication, can be adapted to take into account cultural issues (Maxfield & Hyer, 2002; Rodriguez et al., 1998; Spierings, 2005). During the two EMDR five-day training periods, 25 (out of 28) doctors, psychiatrists, psychologists, and social workers became familiar with the therapeutic method and were trained in EMDR practice using the standard translated EMDR protocol, consisting of level I (trauma therapy) and level II (cognitive interweave; Maxfield, 2007). One of the course translators stated that, despite major differences in background profession and English proficiency, the practical sessions allowed application of the learned techniques and clarification of any queries raised, and trainees acquired the necessary knowledge of EMDR as therapy (S. Amarasuriya, personal communication, 2009).

Arts Therapies

Art Therapies and Techniques

The use of art as a healing process is as old as mankind. However, when using art-form therapy, one should be very careful about which art to introduce first. Stoller (2006) noted that, because sewing is a traditional art form in Sri Lanka, working with fabrics might be comfortable for them. Thus, she opted to introduce the many ways of using fabric on an introductory day, when, following the experiential workshop, the participants were engaged in discussion of the goals of art therapy groups comprised of children, adolescents, adults, the elderly, the mentally ill, the developmentally disabled, learning disabled children, traumatized children and adults, and those who are grieving. During the quilt-making activity, the conversation flowed, and various issues were raised concerning women's affairs and status as well as concerns that were previously seen as Western psychosomatic problems, including eating disorders, which are becoming more common in Sri Lanka. A two-year follow up with MTs revealed that the majority of them referred to the powerful impact of such therapy. Art therapy training, composed of drama-therapy, biblio-therapy, dance, movement, and music therapy, was in such demand that further courses were held in these subjects after the MT was completed. Rogel (2009) noted that, although participants enjoyed the art activities, such activities should follow after learning about the most common art forms in a given culture along with participants' styles, attitudes, and strengths.

TRAINING IN TEACHING SKILLS

Up until now, we were focusing on the establishment and delivery of the training, with all of its cultural concerns. However, an important challenge lies in the management and maintenance of the trainers' teams and their well-being, as discussed below.

The Multi-national Training Team

Ground Representative

The complexity of working in a faraway land, with expert teams arriving for intensive and short visits, calls for the establishment of a ground post in the target state. We found that having an on-the-ground representative of the project team sent from one of the organizations, who would be stationed in Sri Lanka, was an indispensable component of the project's success. We therefore had a representative living in Sri Lanka for nine months, who developed a proficient understanding of local norms and eased the adjustment of every team of experts arriving each month. She was our liaison and helped mitigate relations between the foreign and local teams as well as took care of the expert team's needs for accommodation, for preparation of the teaching materials (locating translators), and even for their out-of-work entertainment.

Management

The international steering committee was meeting on nearly a biweekly basis, using conference calls to discuss general and specific management issues as well as to approve training priorities and to suggest the experts to deliver it. This helped to maintain the delicate balance to defuse tensions so that, when the teams met on the ground, the team's leader, the teaching setup, and the schedule were all clear. Building a trusting atmosphere among the steering committee of such a diverse group was a key component of the project's success.

Leadership

The issue of leading the various teams, and of leadership in general, was crucial to the success of such a project. Trainers coming from different organizations, from different countries, and from rival professions might have led to clashes within the group. The leader had to deal not only with the curriculum and training but also with the social and other aspects of well-being among team members during after-work hours, as the team lived together and spent many hours after work in the same space and in a foreign environment. We addressed this issue by appointing leaders who were experienced in leading international teams, by transferring leadership from one training week to another, with an overlap of 1 to 2 days with the previous leader, by holding evening discussion groups, by caring for the team's need for entertainment in the evenings and on the weekends, and by maintaining an open dialogue between participants. However, this is still a delicate and important issue that requires a lot of attention.

ACCOMPLISHMENTS AND THE VOICE
OF THE TRAINEES

Over the course of approximately one year (September 2005 to June 2006), the project accomplished its main objectives, holding four week-long basic orientation courses and teaching 245 professionals from a variety of disciplines (health, 104; community and welfare, 79; and education, 62) the fundamental concepts, methods, and applied skills of trauma recovery and resiliency. Participants included four spiritual leaders, police officers/superintendents, doctors, nurses, public health inspectors, medical officers, psychiatrists, psychologists, welfare workers, probation officers, school principals, teachers and counselors, and community leaders.

Candidates for the orientation courses were referred by various organizations and ministries from Kalutara, Galle, and Matara as well as from the eastern

Batticaloa provinces. Sixty-six people who attended these orientation courses
tested through formal test evaluation but were selected and chosen mainly by
instructor ratings to become MTs and participate in four one-week sessions of
intensive training. These MTs, comprised three groups (health, community, and
education), working together with 14 Sahanya staff members, had four additional weeks of training. The new trainers adapted the class materials to the local
norms and culture through an independent study project.

The project was supported by Israeli and American tutoring efforts involving the sending of relevant teaching manuals and protocols to the Sri Lankan
coordinator in advance of each training session for the laborious process of
translation. Finally, all 80 trainers received feedback and supervision on their
project, later reporting 664 training lecture hours, 438 hours of workshops, and
712 hours of hands-on exercises. Additionally, two EMDR courses (level I and
level II) were held for 28 clinicians, and three expressive art courses (art, drama,
music, and movement) were held over the three months, with more than 50 participants (psychiatric nurses, special education teachers, school counselors, and
social workers).

General Feedback

Focus groups, trainers' reports, and follow-up interviews were the main sources
of gaining knowledge about participants' experience in the training (Chemtob &
Dutch, 2006; Stoller, 2006). Some participants commented that they had gained
knowledge from the education and that the activities were beneficial. Others
mentioned that they were glad to receive formal education on psychosocial issues and schools of thought and methodologies as well as noted that the training
had enhanced both their professional and personal lives. They also stated that
they had been unaware of PTSD but that they now knew a lot about it. Other
participants stated that the knowledge that they had gained regarding child psychiatry also helped them build their family lives as well as upgrade their knowledge and increase their confidence in their disaster-management skills.

Sustainability (The Outcome of the Independent Study Projects)

Previous research has suggested that systematic follow-up is required for the
success of many interventions (Nikapota, 2006). Lahad (2009) noted that, in the
follow-up study one year after training, when the funds had already been used
and the intensive training was already over (apart from the ongoing training on
art therapies), the MTs were asked what was left after all the experts were gone.
We were gratified to learn that over 18 master trainers who had completed the
orientation programs had initiated 25 in the local community, using 27 of the
acquired methods and techniques (e.g., BASIC PH model, communication skills,
art therapy, pacing and leading). The various projects were directed toward
school principals, teachers, schoolchildren, and students. Support and treatment
were also given to physical and mental health patients, parents, and elderly peo-

ple in the community. As a result of this training, the MTs created their own professional network. Thus, they can call upon a psychiatrist, a general practitioner, a teacher, or a supervisor and combine what they learn. Lahad (2009) noted the extent of the projects, that some were still ongoing.

Some of the obstacles mentioned by the master trainers concerned practicalities such as a shortage of time, transportation, funds, art materials, and so forth. However, the closing of the Sahanaya branch in Kaluthra was seen as major obstacle because it was the master trainers' main resource center. The closure, due to lack of funds, added to other "normal" obstacles to implementing a new idea in the field, including reluctant cooperation responses from the community and fluctuating numbers of participants in the activities. Some of the master trainers found that difficulty in assuring continuity and lack of training in counseling were also hindrances in their practice. As for support by the training team, follow-up in-depth interviews held in December 2008 with Sri Lankan participants indicated that the new trainers constantly stayed in touch with the Israeli and the American expert teams. In the email communication (by now, a technology that is more readily available), the Sri Lankan team addressed their questions, concerns, or ideas and, in turn, received detailed advice from overseas. When a program or project was about to be developed, the Sri Lankan team found it helpful to refer to the experts in regard to details about target population, goals, and other features of the future projects (I. Wijesundera, J. Pethiyagoda, December 14, 2008, personal communication).

CONCLUSIONS AND RECOMMENDATIONS

Looking back on this rewarding process, one should not overlook the harsh reality and the painstaking process that it takes to respond to a disaster in a different culture. In the current situation, there was a mixture of several components that demanded fast training of local trainers: a tragedy with the loss of thousands of people and some quarter of a million who were injured and/or were made homeless, causing social, physical, and economic devastation, combined with the fact that there were very few mental health professionals and very little psychosocial training, along with a huge demand for support. But the greatest challenge, from our point of view, was that the disaster took place in a non-Western country, necessitating the calling of outside professional help to assist in the aftermath of the disaster while also using professional trainers from a diversity of the cultures. One very important implication is that alignment with the local leadership, both religious and ministerial, is crucial to the success of the operation and to its sustainability in the long run.

Our conclusion is that effective multidisciplinary intervention in such conditions must be organized with great care. It must focus on genuine and deep-rooted community needs and aim to increase the availability psychosocial support. However, for the "imported" knowledge and skills to reach the local population, there must be culturally sensitive mutual learning, a focus on existing sources of coping, local sources of information, and a profound respect for the local culture's traditional ways of healing.

Our final conclusion concerns the sustainability of such foreign intervention. For the recently trained trainers to be able to implement the various knowledge and skills and to work through the many challenges of such an endeavor, it is crucial to support these trainers on an ongoing basis, maintaining supervision through electronic means of communication such as instant messaging and email discussion forums. Whenever possible, a follow-up update and encouragement of the local trainers to publish their observations and experience are recommended as vital for the sustainability the locally accumulated knowledge. Last but not least, a long-term evaluation process should accompany such projects, serving as feedback and as a monitoring mechanism.

We would like to conclude this chapter with the Confucian proverb that codifies the message of our work in Sri Lanka: "You can't prevent the birds of sorrow from hovering above your heads, you can only prevent them from building nests in your hair."

REFERENCES

Ayalon, O. (2003). The HANDS Project: Helpers Assisting Natural Disaster Survivors. *Community Stress Prevention Centre, 5,* 127-135.

Ashraf, H. (2005). Tsunami wreaks mental health havoc. *Bulletin of the World Health Organization, 83,* 405-406.

Baruch, Y. (2009). *Mental health assistance in national emergencies: Initial phase* [Unpublished PowerPoint slides]. Paper presented at the International Conference on Crisis as an Opportunity: Organizational and Professional Responses to Disaster, Ben-Gurion University of the Negev, Beer-Sheva, Israel.

Bradley, R., Greene, J. Russ, E., Dutra, L., & Westen, D. (2005). A multidimensional meta-analysis of psychotherapy for PTSD. *American Journal of Psychiatry, 162,* 214-227.

Bryant, R. A., Moulds, M. L., Guthrie, R. M., Dang, S. T., & Nixon, R. D. (2003). Imaginal exposure alone and imaginal exposure with cognitive restructuring in treatment of posttraumatic stress disorder. *Journal of Consulting and Clinical Psychology, 71,* 706-712.

Chemtob, C. M., & Dutch, H. (2006). *Bi-national trauma response: Building psychosocial resiliency in Sri Lanka* (Evaluation report). New York, NY: UJA Fed NY.

De Jong, K., Mulhern, M., Ford, N., Simpson, I., Swan, A., & Van Der Kam, S. (2002). Psychological trauma of the civil war in Sri Lanka. *Lancet, 359,* 1517-1518.

De Silva, P. (2006). The tsunami and its aftermath in Sri Lanka: Explorations of a Buddhist perspective. *International Review of Psychiatry, 18,* 281-287.

Elbert, T., Huschka, B., Schauer, E., Schauer, M., Hirth, M., Rockstroh, B., et al. (2006). *Trauma-related impairment in children: An epidemiological survey in Sri Lankan provinces affected by two decades of civil war and unrest.* Manuscript submitted for publication.

Foa, E., Creshman, K., & Gilboa-Schechtman, E. (2008). *Emotional processing of traumatic experiences in adolescence: The efficacy of prolonged exposure treatment.* New York, NY: Oxford University Press.

Foa, E. B., Keane, T. M., Friedman, M. J., & Cohen, J. A. (2009). *Effective treatments for PTSD: Practice guidelines from the International Society for Traumatic Stress Studies.* New York, NY: Guilford Press.

Foy, D. W., Madvig, B. T., Pynoos, R. S., & Camilleri, A. J. (1996). Etiologic factors in the development of posttraumatic stress disorder in children and adolescents. *Journal of School Psychology, 34,* 133-145.

Frankenberg, E., Friedman, J., Gillespie, T., Ingwersen, N., Pynoos, R., Rifai, L., et al. (2008). Mental health in Sumatra after the tsunami. *American Journal of Public Health, 98,* 1671-1677. doi:10.2105/AJPH.2007.120915

Godavitarne, C., Udu-gama, N., Sreetharan, M., Preuss, J., & Krimgold, F. (2006). Social and political prerequisites for recovery in Sri Lanka after the December 2004 Indian Ocean Tsunami. *Earthquake Spectra, 22,* S845-S861.

Hernandez, D. (2002, Fall). DRC: District resource center defined. *Insights.* Retrieved from http://www.openinc.org/newsletters/Insights_2002Fall. pdf

Hollifield, M., Hewage, C., Gunawardena, C. N., Kochuwakku, P., Bopagoda, K., & Weerarathnege, K. (2008). Symptoms and coping in Sri Lanka 20-21 months after the 2004 tsunami. *The British Journal of Psychiatry, 192,* 39-44.

Ingram, D. (2005). Commonwealth update. *Round Table*. doi:10.1080/00358530500103068

LaGreca, A. M., Vemberg, E. M., Silverman, W. K., & Prinstein, M. J. (1996). Symptoms of posttraumatic stress in children after Hurricane Andrew: A prospective study. *Journal of Consult Clinical Psychology, 64*, 712-723.

Lahad, M. (1992). BASIC Ph: The story of coping resources. In S. Jennings (Ed.), *Drama therapy: Theory and Practice* (Vol. 2, pp. 150-163). New York, NY: Routledge.

Lahad, M. (2005, October 10). *1ˢᵗ report to JDC & UJA Fed NY on the progress of the Tri National Project* (Unpublished manuscript).

Lahad, M. (2008) Post-traumatic responses in disasters: A community perspective. In K. Gow & D. Paton (Eds.). *Resilience: The phoenix of natural disasters* (pp. 33-46). New York, NY: Nova Science.

Lahad, M. (2009). *Lessons learnt from the tri-national project in Sri Lanka following the 2004 tsunami: Focusing on culturally sensitive issues of mental health and psychosocial support and the management of such a project.* Paper presented at the International Conference on Crisis as an Opportunity: Organizational and Professional Responses to Disaster, Ben-Gurion University of the Negev, Beer-Sheva, Israel.

Liu, P., Lynett, P., Fernando, H., Jaffe, B., Fritz, H., Higman, B., et al. (2005). Observations by the international tsunami survey team in Sri Lanka. *Science, 308*, 1595. Retrieved from Psychology and Behavioral Sciences Collection database. doi:10.1126/science.1110730

Lommen, M. J. J., Sanders, A. J. M. L., Buck, N., & Arntz, A. (2009). Psychosocial predictors of chronic post-traumatic stress disorder in Sri Lankan tsunami survivors. *Behaviour Research and Therapy, 47*, 60-65.

Mahoney, J., Chandra, V., Gambheera, H., Silva, T., & Suveendran, T. (2006). Responding to the mental health and psychosocial needs of the people of Sri Lanka in disasters. *International Review of Psychiatry, 18*, 593-597. doi:10.1080/09540260601129206

Maxfield, L. (2007). Current status and future directions for EMDR research. *Journal of EMDR Practice and Research, 1*, 6-14.

Maxfield, L., & Hyer, L. (2002). The relationship between efficacy and methodology in studies investigating EMDR treatment of PTSD. *Journal of Clinical Psychology, 58*(1), 23-41.

Nacasch, N. (2009). *Training mental health professionals of a different culture: dissemination of prolonged exposure therapy in Sri Lanka after the tsunami* [Unpublished PowerPoint slides]. Paper presented at the International Conference on Crisis as an Opportunity: Organizational and Professional Responses to Disaster, Ben-Gurion University of the Negev, Beer-Sheva, Israel.

Neuner, F., Schauer, E., Catani, C., Ruf, M., & Elbert, T. (2006), Post-tsunami stress: A study of posttraumatic stress disorder in children living in three severely affected regions in Sri Lanka. *Journal of Traumatic Stress, 19*, 339–347.

Nikapota, A. (2006). After the tsunami: A story from Sri Lanka. *International Review of Psychiatry, 18*, 275-279.

Niv, S. (2009). *Working model for educators and community workers* [Unpublished PowerPoint slides]. Paper presented at the International Conference on Crisis as an Opportunity: Organizational and Professional Responses to Disaster, Ben-Gurion University of the Negev, Beer-Sheva, Israel.

Norris, F. H., Friedman, M. J., Watson, P. J., Byrne, C. M., Diaz, E., & Kaniasty, K. (2002). 60,000 disaster victims speak: Part I. An empirical review of the empirical literature, 1981-2001. *Psychiatry: Interpersonal & Biological Processes, 65*, 207-239.

Omer, H., & Alon, N. (1994). The continuity principle: A unified approach to disaster and trauma. *American Journal of Community Psychology, 22*, 273-287.

Pynoos, R. S., Goenjian, A., Tashjian, M., Karakashian, M., Manjikian, R., Manoukian, G., et al. (1993). Post-traumatic stress reactions in children after the 1988 Armenian earthquake. *British Journal of Psychiatry, 163*, 239-247.

Rachamim, L. (2009). *Using western methods of child treatment with Sri Lankan Children* [Unpublished PowerPoint slides]. Paper presented at the International Conference on Crisis as an Opportunity: Organizational and Professional Responses to Disaster, Ben-Gurion University of the Negev, Beer-Sheva, Israel.

Rodriguez, G., Luber, M., Hofmann, A., Marquis, P., Sprowls, C., & Snyker, E. (1998, July). *EMDR in the world: Training and practice in different cultures.* Paper presented at the annual meeting of the EMDR International Association, Baltimore, MD.

Rogel, R. (2009). *Cultural aspects and dilemmas in direction multi-national project* [Unpublished PowerPoint slides]. Paper presented at the International Conference on Crisis as an Opportunity: Organizational and Professional Responses to Disaster, Ben-Gurion University of the Negev, Beer-Sheva, Israel.

Saldaña, D. (2001). *Cultural competency: A practical guide for mental health service providers.* Austin, TX: Hogg Foundation for Mental Health, University of Texas at Austin.

Setiawan, G., & Viora, E. (2006). Disaster mental health preparedness plan in Indonesia. *International Review of Psychiatry, 18*, 563-566. doi:10.1080/09540260601037920

Shacham, Y. (2009). *Challenges in extending help cross culturally* [Unpublished Power-Point slides]. Paper presented at the International Conference on Crisis as an Opportunity: Organizational and Professional Responses to Disaster, Ben-Gurion University of the Negev, Beer-Sheva, Israel.

Spierings, J. J. (2005). *Adapting EMDR to work effectively with clients from other cultures.* Paper presented at the annual meeting of the EMDR Europe Association, Brussels, Belgium.

Stoller, E. (2006). *With art as our bridge: An international approach to art therapy training* (Unpublished manuscript).

Tsunami-hit Sri Lanka faces huge challenges. (2005). *Asia Monitor: South Asia Monitor, 11*, 1-7. Retrieved from EBSCOhost.

Tuicomepee, A., & Rornano, J. (2008). Thai adolescent survivors 1 year after the 2004 tsunami: A mixed methods study. *Journal of Counseling Psychology, 55*, 308-320. doi:10.1637/0012-0167.55.3.308

Van Peski, C. (2006, January). *CSPC crisis intervention training, Colombo, Sri Lanka.* Kiriat Shmona, Israel: CSPC.

Van Rooyen, M., & Leaning, J. (2005). After the tsunami: Facing the public health challenges. *New England Journal of Medicine, 352*, 435-438.

World Health Organization. (2005). *Sri Lanka tsunami situation report: 03.02.2005.* Retrieved from http://www.searo.who.int/-en/Section1257/Section2263/Section2310/Section2311/Section2312_12301.htm

NOTE

1. This project was made possible due to the generous donation of the JDC NY and the UJA Federation of New York. We wish to personally thank Ms. Shelley Horowitz, whose devotion made this project real.

Chapter Thirteen
Psychological Outcomes of the 2001 World Trade Center Attack
James Halpern and Mary Tramontin

They who can give up essential liberty to obtain a little temporary safety deserve neither liberty nor safety.
Benjamin Franklin, 1775

This chapter considers the immediate and long-term psychological consequences of the September 11th, 2001 World Trade Center (WTC) attack. Clinical observations, research findings, and reflections derived from the vantage point of nearly a decade post event are offered.

Trauma's impact, formally recognized by mental health professionals with inclusion of posttraumatic stress disorder (PTSD) in the *Diagnostic and Statistical Manual of Mental Disorders (DSM)* in 1980, has increasingly been studied, leading to significant findings regarding prevention, mitigation, and treatment. Disaster research points to recovery over time for most, especially when buoyed by an accommodating, positive recovery environment.

Immediate, common reactions following exposure to severe stress and resembling PTSD are now considered normative. One may have a heightened startle response, be generally anxious, or have problems sleeping. Re-experiencing, especially when cues are present, may occur. Such reactions fade, gradually becoming less frequent and intense. The traumatic event becomes a normal memory and does not possess the immediacy of the original experience. Stress, even extreme stress, does not equal debilitation (Shalev, 2004). Was this the case following the WTC attack?

TERRORISM-CAUSED DISASTER

A terrorism-caused disaster has defining characteristics. Terrorism is meant to be traumatizing (Silke, 2003) and to produce psychological effects far beyond the immediate physical damage: "Terrorism can be thought of as a psychological assault that challenges the society's sense of safety, security and cohesion"

(Hamaoka, Shigemura, & Hall, 2004, p. 533). Everly and Mitchell (2001) go so far as to call it "psychological warfare."

Hence, terrorism-caused disasters induce dread and foreboding and erode a basic sense of safety and order. Demoralization and emotional distress ensue in the general population, even in the absence of direct or proximal exposure. Emotional contagion is salient, and individuals and communities have to contend with a persistent if subliminal sense of arousal and vigilance. As Beutler, Reyes, Franco, and Housley (2007) stated:

> The fear generated by terrorist attacks extends into the most basic reaches of the human mind, activating systems that have been fundamental to our survival but long unused, and this may cause reactions that undermine one's emotional and mental well-being. (p. 33)

Terrorist acts are especially difficult to integrate because they violate basic assumptions through their intentionality, shock value, and choice of noncombatants as victims. In the aftermath, one feels that such events can happen anytime, anyplace, to anyone. With no advance warning, they are unfamiliar and unpredictable, and the inherent element of surprise serves to perpetuate and reinforce the basic fight-or-flight response.

WTC Attack Characteristics

Disasters differ with regard to scope, intensity, and duration. These all serve to determine the size of the event, which is highly correlated with disaster's psychological impact. Scope refers to the number of people, families, and structures affected. Intensity is related to scope but is not the same thing. Intensity serves to "up" the psychological ante: Events small in scope but intense, such as those that include loss of life, carry more psychological consequence. Duration refers to the length of time that people are affected, so that events of prolonged or uncertain duration are particularly difficult with which to cope. Survivors and the community not only have to deal with the consequences of the event but also remain anxious about what will happen next.

The events of 9/11 can be distinguished from what Americans had previously experienced. The magnitude of the WTC attack is reflected in terms of the number of lives lost, physical space affected, number of helping agencies involved, and long-term recovery efforts. The attack was also distinguished by its cause; it was a deliberate and conscious attempt to destroy people, property, and spirit. In this attack, the expectation that the worst was not over persisted, even as recovery efforts took place. In other disasters, there are some lingering effects related to the actual event. With earthquakes, there are aftershocks, while, with hurricanes, there can be tidal waves or flooding. Still, the perception is mostly that the "big" event has passed. In such a perspective, the work that remains is arduous, long, and stressful but is viewed as a bounded recovery phenomenon. In the case of the September 11th attack, however, intelligence and security agencies predicted that there would be additional attacks "with a 100% degree of certainty." The scope of terrorist acts was expanded to include biochemical and nuclear threats. As a result, a heightened sense of vulnerability existed and still persists.

PSYCHOLOGICAL REACTIONS: WTC RESEARCH

Disasters have an intense, acute beginning and a collective impact; involve significant disruption of biopsychosocial resources; affect those who are victims, who bear witness, or who come to help; and include a spectrum of losses. Reactions evolve through the stages of a disaster's lifecycle, and short-term reactions can be quite different from long-term ones. The most common psychological aftereffect is a heightened sense of distress and arousal (Norris et al., 2002).

As Neria, Jung Suh, and Marshall (2004) point out, in the days following the attack, the New York City mental health community braced itself for an anticipated increase in the need for mental health support and treatment. There were good reasons for this, even though there is little data on the psychological sequelae of terrorist acts in urban communities. Norris et al. (2002) found that disaster's effects are most extreme when at least two of the following conditions are met: (1) salient property damage, (2) extreme financial problems for a community, (3) causation by human intention, and (4) injuries and threat to, or loss of, life. Terrorist acts combine these risk factors.

Galea, Ahern, Resnick, and Vlahov (2006) believe that all residents of New York were potentially exposed and could possibly develop psychological symptoms. Consistent with other surveys, a persistent, concentric pattern of PTSD and depression was discovered. Both invariant and changing variables were predictive of PTSD, including being directly affected, being Latino, being female, peri-event emotional reactions, ongoing traumas, and ongoing stressors. Additionally, low social support was a central determinant. Daily life stressors, not just other traumatic events, were independently predictive, thus strengthening a stress-vulnerability model of PTSD and pointing to a possible preventive strategy of focusing efforts to mitigate post-disaster stressors. The same survey also showed significant increases in tobacco, alcohol, and marijuana use (Vlahov et al., 2004).

Silver et al. (2006) discovered that psychological aftereffects for people were multiply determined and that there were important influences beyond exposure or loss that were predictive. The authors stated:

[T]o understand fully how trauma affects human functioning, we need to consider the unique roles of individual differences (e.g., coping responses, previous experience with trauma), and social interactions (e.g., social constraints, conflict, social support) in mediating the relations between specific events and subsequent outcomes. (p. 46)

Gross (2006) focused on uniformed workers who were at Ground Zero for the nine-month recovery period and discovered significant rates of PTSD, major depressive disorder (MDD), and generalized anxiety disorder (GAD). More than a quarter of respondents had sought mental health services. Workers all experienced traumatic exposures, and the risk factors of having experienced 9/11-related loss and peri-event emotional reactions were identified.

Neria, Gross, and Marshall (2006) studied the impact on a lower socioeconomic group located in upper Manhattan. In general, the researchers concluded that this poorer population had higher rates of all disorders found post disaster, including PTSD, MDD, GAD, and panic disorder.

Gould, Munfakh, and Kleinman (2004) focused on teenagers' mental health and found that the majority did not exhibit "untoward psychological consequences from the attack." For the smaller number who experienced more severe reactions, initial numbing was associated with negative psychological outcomes. The teenagers assessed sought more assistance from informal (e.g., teachers) rather than formal (e.g., hotlines) sources, at least in the immediate aftermath, underscoring that schools may be the best setting for dispensing services during a post-disaster period.

Regarding children, Hoven, Mandell, Duarte, Wu, and Giordano (2006) reported findings from the New York City public school system, which is the largest in the United States. Children were "exposed" to the attack in several ways: directly due to their proximity to Ground Zero, through family members who were WTC evacuees, through television coverage, and through family member's involvement in the recovery efforts. Those with exposure had increased rates of probable disorders, and the vulnerability of children via exposure through indirect ways is a notable finding.

A novel feature of these studies, consistent with one of the more unique features of terrorism, that of widespread impact, is that they investigated "remote exposure" (Stewart, 2004). The psychological effects of a major national trauma are not limited to those who experience it directly, and the degree of response is not predicted simply by objective measures of exposure or loss. Outcomes are the products of a variety of factors. Disasters are "like motion pictures," not snapshots; effects are not linear, and how people fare relates to the nature of their lives, circumstances, and the set of continuing adversities that follow (Norris, Donahue, Watson, Hamblen, & Marshall, 2006).

The research captures the fact that initial distress was high, that there are those individuals who suffered chronic negative mental health consequences, that proximity and loss were not always the key determinants of how people fared, and that certain populations had increased vulnerability or susceptibility to the event. WTC research suggests that the *psychological* aftermath of this event was not very different from other significant disasters. However, in the next section, we look further at unique outcomes of the WTC attack.

UNDERAPPRECIATED TRAUMATIC CONSEQUENCES

Two sources of continuing trauma generated from the WTC catastrophe that often are not cited are the physical illnesses of recovery workers, residents, and others who were exposed to toxic chemicals in the air from the WTC site and the wars in Afghanistan and Iraq.

Danger in the Air at Ground Zero

The collapse of the WTC towers released a massive cloud of dust across the landscape that consisted of cement dust, glass fibers, asbestos, lead, hydrochloric acid, PCBs, pesticides, and polychlorinated dioxins and furans (Herbert et al., 2009). On the scene, first responders were highly exposed. In the following days, rain caused the toxic mix to settle and reduce the risk to the population at large. However, a diverse range of professionals such as operating engineers, sanitation workers, laborers, railway tunnel cleaners, ironworkers, telecommunications workers, and staff of the Office of the Chief Medical Examiner had sustained exposure as their cleaning efforts progressed over months and unearthed the toxic debris.

A 2009 study demonstrated the toll from unsafe air surrounding the site. Of the almost 10,000 responders who worked at the WTC site, 69% reported that, since September 11, 2001, they either had developed a new respiratory condition or found a previously existing one noticeably worsened (Herbert et al., 2009); 48% sought medical help for acute bronchitis.

In the aftermath of September 11th, a significant portion of those who had responded became very ill. A unique outcome of the WTC attack in terms of its psychological toll is the reality that many affected continue to suffer disaster-associated physical conditions. Such physical health problems have significant mental health consequences. Symptoms of illness can serve as reminders or "triggers" back to 9/11 involvement. In addition, little is known about the spectrum of illnesses that can be connected to exposure to these toxins. This fearful uncertainty may contribute to increases in somatization, helplessness or depression, and anxiety or panic as well as to potentially drastic lifestyle changes in response to a perceived foreshortened future. Intergenerational and community impact must also be considered. Spouses who must care for their sickened partners, and children who must deal with enduring health effects of their once seemingly immortal parents, will have to contend with profound stress and loss. These outcomes are magnified by the uneven commitment to provide healthcare for those affected. The undermining of the resilience of individuals, families, and their communities should be considered when looking at the long-term impact of the WTC attack. Will helpers be as selfless in their service in the future?

The Trauma of War

The United States' engagement in war should be considered as another trau-matic outcome, one that distinguishes it from other disasters and highlights the social psychological impact of terrorism. Operation Enduring Freedom in Af-ghanistan, clearly, was caused directly by the WTC attack. In addition, it has often been asserted that the war in Iraq may well not have occurred had it not been for the impetus of September 11th. President Bush, Vice President Cheney, and other government officials consistently referenced September 11th in their case for war (BBC News, 2004). It was asserted that, while the Hussein Iraqi government may not have planned and executed the WTC attack, they were im-plicit (Russert, 2002).

An equal, if not greater, part of the movement toward war connecting Iraq to the September 11th attacks stemmed from not only trying to assert links be-tween the plot and Saddam Hussein but also from evoking the tragedy as proof that the United States had entered a new era of foreign policy necessities. In the lead-up to war, then-Vice President Cheney explained:

> The world before 9/11 looks different than the world after 9/11, especially in terms of how we think about national security and what's needed to defend America . . . We believe that, especially since September 11th, we have to con-sider action that may, in fact—I suppose you can call it pre-emptive—we've talked about it in the past—to head off an attack against the United States. (Russert, 2002)

Severe trauma ruptures world views and cherished beliefs. A national event such as the WTC attack can affect the psychology of an entire country at a broad level. When examining the cost of this event, one must consider that a long-term impact was the creation of a climate that made war possible. To date, there have been 4,432 military service men and women killed in Iraq and 1,455 in Afghani-stan (iCasualties, 2011a, 2011b). In addition there have been over 32,000 U.S. soldiers wounded in both wars combined. Estimates of Iraqi casualties are highly controversial but range between 151,000 (Boseley, 2008) and close to 1,300,000 (Susman, 2007).

Bearing in mind the concept of ripple effect, the scope of the psychological damage is immense; there are soldiers suffering terribly who will never be re-corded as casualties or listed among the wounded because their scars are not physical. Milliken, Auchterlonie, and Hoge (2007) found that the overall mental health risk for active duty troops was 17% as they returned from Iraq but rose to 27% on average of six months later; the risk for National Guard members and reservists rose from 17.5% to 35.5% when troops were screened 3 to 6 months after returning home. A heavy burden is shouldered by families—relations, par-ents, children, and spouses—who may find that, even if their loved ones return seemingly untouched, they are deeply changed, transformed by their combat experiences and often haunted by what they have seen.

THE MENTAL HEALTH RESPONSE TO THE WTC ATTACK

Numerous organizations and individuals participated in the mental health response to the terrorist attack of September 11th. These included local and national Red Cross volunteers, psychologists from the New York State Disaster Response Network (DRN), Disaster Psychiatry Outreach (DPO), city and state mental health employees, school counselors and psychologists, hospital social workers, crisis counselors organized by employers and insurance companies, FDNY and NYPD counselors, private practitioners, peer counselors, members of the clergy, and Doctors without Borders.

Within weeks after the attack, the presidential declaration of a disaster in New York City and 10 surrounding counties made the entire region eligible for FEMA programs, including the Crisis Counseling Assistance and Training Program designed to provide supplemental funding to states for short-term crisis counseling services after national disasters. More than $137 million was spent on Project Liberty, as it was named, which served about 1.5 million people, thereby making it the largest federally funded disaster mental health program in history (Donahue, Lanzara, Felton, Essock, & Carpinello, 2006). Crisis counseling was provided by about 5,000 professionals and paraprofessionals working through about 200 agencies (Naturale, 2006). The primary goal of Project Liberty (and most early disaster mental health interventions) was to provide counseling that enables survivors to return to a pre-disaster level of functioning.

One of the many challenges to mounting an effective DMH response was the extraordinary range of clientele. In every disaster there are typically "primary" victims and "secondary or indirect" victims—those with close ties to the primary victims (National Institute of Mental Health [NIMH], 2002). The ripple effect from a terror attack can be so great that there is a danger that someone who needs care might be overlooked. Tens of thousands of men and women worked through the recovery efforts at Ground Zero, recovering more than 30,000 body parts, at extraordinary personal costs. All these workers had family and friends (indirect victims) who were also affected by the disaster through its impact on their loved one.

Mental health services were offered at shelters, in hospitals, over the phone on the Missing Person's Hotline (later called the Police Hotline when it was clear that all those missing had perished), at the New York City Armory and later at Family Assistance Centers, where responders, victims, and survivors went to obtain information and services. In response to the loss of 343 firefighters in one day, the FDNY Counseling Services Unit (CSU) expanded services by assigning 42 clinicians to 62 firehouses, making the scope of their "firehouse clinician project" unprecedented (Greene, Kane, Christ, Lynch, & Corrigan, 2006). CSU also provided support in the homes of bereaved widows and their children. Mental health workers were deployed to airports to mitigate anxiety, at hotels where bereaved family members gathered, on boats where survivors were escorted to Ground Zero to see where their loved ones had perished, in lobbies as residents moved back into their apartment buildings, and at many funerals and memorials. Teams of crisis counselors were deployed by employee assistance programs, both in the private and public sector, to support employees in offices and workplaces. Mental health support was available at St. Paul's Chapel and at the "Big White Tent," where recovery workers went for their breaks.

Some survivors needed continued care and referral to traditional providers. Most treatment was and continues to be provided by private practitioners located throughout the New York metropolitan area. In the summer of 2002, the American Red Cross and the September 11 Fund in New York City initiated a joint long-term psychiatric benefit program for an estimated 150,000 eligible families, including relatives of the deceased or seriously injured, rescue and recovery workers or volunteers, displaced residents, those who lost their jobs, evacuees from the Twin Towers and nearby buildings, and children attending schools in the area and their families. Funds for mental health support continue to be available to those who meet these requirements and are still in need. Clients come from all socioeconomic classes as well as from urban, suburban, and rural areas in New York.

EARLY AND INTERMEDIATE INTERVENTIONS

NIMH (2002) defines Psychological First Aid (PFA) as:

> Pragmatically oriented interventions with survivors or emergency responders targeting acute stress reactions and immediate needs. The goals of PFA include the establishment of safety (objective and subjective), stress-related symptom reduction, restoration of rest and sleep, linkage to critical resources, and connection to social support. (p. 26)

Because the great majority of survivors recover from trauma and disaster without professional help (e.g., Litz & Gray, 2004), the best early interventions should not interfere with natural recovery. PFA is an approach that sets the stage for this (Brewin, 2003) and removes obstacles to its progression. The practice of PFA was not widely known or taught at the time of the WTC attack. However, many clinicians did have the good sense to practice PFA in many of the settings described above. There is now an explicit consensus about the usefulness of PFA as the intervention of choice in the immediate aftermath of disaster. The elements and practice of PFA can be found in recent trainings described by the National Child Traumatic Stress Network and National Center for PTSD (2006) and the American Red Cross (2006) and are summarized by Halpern and Tramontin (2007).

Intermediate interventions are those that occurred several weeks after the WTC attack. They included elements of PFA but were increasingly psychoeducational and cognitive-behavioral in nature. Interventions included trauma exposure and focused on affecting thought and action. Intermediate, supportive counseling helped to alleviate distress, identify coping strategies, facilitate social connections, and provide pragmatic resources. After even a few weeks, many of those affected were better able to begin to reflect upon their experiences and problem-solve as well as were receptive to psychoeducation and stress management. Psychoeducation in the aftermath the WTC attack focused on providing information about a range of biopsychosocial processes, including common reactions to disaster, stages of reactions to disaster, symptoms, resilience, treatment, effective and ineffective coping strategies, the stages of loss and other information about grief, and ways that parents can help children. Psychoeducation as an intermediate intervention is one of the least controversial and most recommended in disaster mental health (Litz & Gray, 2004; Miller, 2002; Raphael & Wooding, 2004).

SCREENING AND LONG-TERM TREATMENT

Screening survivors involves monitoring a large population to determine which individuals need or will need treatment.

Specific screening methodologies used for individuals or groups considered to be at high risk for chronic PTSD and other serious mental health outcomes following mass violence and disasters should be evaluated to ensure that their use is both safe and effective. (NIMH, 2002, p. 8)

Survivors of mass violence and disaster that should be considered for possible follow-up include those:

- who have acute stress disorder or other clinically significant symptoms;
- who are bereaved;
- who have a preexisting psychiatric disorder;
- who require medical or surgical attention;
- whose exposure to the incident is particularly intense and of long duration.

As noted earlier, money from the American Red Cross and the September 11 Fund allowed thousands of survivors to obtain long-term treatment. Evidence-informed best practice for long-term treatment of PTSD involves a combination of cognitive and exposure therapies (Brewin, 2003). Survivors whose symptoms did not dissipate months after the attack were eligible to receive treatment, but the extent to which such treatment was effective has not been fully researched. One potential concern with the long-term care offered post 9/11 is that most practitioners do not appear to treat PTSD according to evidence-based best practice guidelines (Halpern & Freeman, 2008).

The mental health response to the WTC attack took place in one of the most exceptionally resource-rich environments in the nation and in the world, replete with means at all levels: financial, cultural, medical, and psychiatric. New York City is a sophisticated setting in terms of mental health. The response from the professional community to the attacks was "exceptional . . . these 'mass drives' of 'psychological first aid' . . . were conducted with the utmost dose of respect and sensitivity. It appears that these attempts effectively minimized eternal traps

for potential stigmatization, marginalization and medicalization of help-seekers"
(Kaniasty, 2006, p. 532).

GAPS IN THE MENTAL HEALTH RESPONSE
TO THE WTC ATTACK

We noted that perhaps the most significant and serious psychological sequelae
from the attack occurred long after the event. We still do not know the full extent of the physical and emotional trauma to those who became ill from Ground
Zero carcinogens. We also cannot yet calculate the full extent of the physical
and emotional trauma resulting from the wars in Iraq and Afghanistan. Could
the mental health community have done more in the way of prevention and
mitigation with regard to these traumatic stressors? It is hard to see how we
could have done less.

We might have done better in communicating the health dangers of working
at the recovery site and in ensuring that masks and other equipment were worn
by everyone at the site. Workers were passionately mission driven, casting aside
precautionary measures designed to ensure their own well-being. As mental
health professionals, we might have done better at supporting the practice of
health and safety measures among responders, perhaps as a way to encourage
self-care and self-regulation. In this way, we may have helped in reducing the
denial of the real risks that they were facing and lessening the stigma likely associated with working more cautiously at the site.

Trauma induces fear and often a desire for revenge. This was certainly the
case after the attack on the WTC. As the nation prepared for war, the mental
health community was relatively silent. Most were bystanders as the cycle of
violence and trauma unfolded. Thousands of mental health professionals were
active and generous in their support for survivors, but we need to ask ourselves
if we did enough to educate the public and those in positions of power regarding
the psychological dynamics of the purposively induced mass-mediated fear en-
gendered by terrorism. Perhaps we need to consider whether we could become a
voice for a more calm, rational, and humane solution to social and political
problems. In the aftermath of a terrorist-caused disaster that is significant in
scope, intensity, and duration and that induces significant hypervigilance and
hyperarousal, we must *actively* work to prevent the "trajectory of a culture of
posttraumatic conditioning" (Embry, 2007, p. 172).

SOME FINAL THOUGHTS

New Yorkers showed higher rates of anxiety, depression, and substance abuse,
with those closer to the event or directly affected showing the highest rates.
Those in distress were cared for with PFA, intermediate interventions, and a
variety of long-term treatments. In addition to the increased rate of symptoms,
the appraisal of risk and safety were also altered after the attacks of 9/11. New

Yorkers did not feel safe on subways, airlines, driving over bridges, or entering tall buildings. For years, city residents were hypervigilant, bracing for what was said to be a certain next attack. The Department of Homeland Security registered the "threat level" as High or Orange for New York City and has not lowered it. As Brandon and Silke (2007) noted, "A preparedness strategy that focuses on fear is likely to produce either habituation to alerts and threats or adaptation and a chronic state of anxiety that depletes individual and community resources" (p. 186).

The appraisal of a specific danger was skewed and maximized unrealistically, and many suffered due to this misappraisal (Marshall et al., 2007). Much post-trauma counseling is intended to teach survivors that a danger has passed and, in moving forward, to be able to discriminate between what truly is a threat and what is safe so that they do not overgeneralize from their traumatic experiences. In the days, months, and years following the WTC attack, there seems to have been as much misappraisal of safety as there was of danger. The air around ground zero was reported to be safe. It was not, and thousands became ill with resultant physical and psychological trauma. Our political leaders led a nation inflamed by patriotism, born out of profound shock, alarm, and sorrow, into a conflict in which we were promised safety if we invaded Iraq and killed Saddam Hussein. A very significant psychological impact of 9/11 was the penetrating fear that contributed to a war resulting in hundreds of thousand of fatalities and injuries and accompanying decades of psychological trauma. The mental health community possesses much knowledge about managing the human fear response to threat—even that from terrorism—and the poor consequences that derive from fear-based decision making. As such, we believe that the mental health community needs to examine our roles and responsibilities in addressing and preventing these kinds of mass casualty events.

REFERENCES

American Psychiatric Association. (1994). *Diagnostic and statistical manual of mental disorders* (4th ed.). Washington, DC: Author.

American Red Cross. (2006). *Psychological first aid: Helping people in times of stress.* Washington, DC: Author.

BBC News. (2004, October 5). *In quotes: US policy in Iraq.* Retrieved from http://news.bbc.co.uk/1/hi/world/americas/3433613.stm

Beutler, L. E., Reyes, G., Franco, Z., & Housley, J. (2007). The need for proficient mental health professionals in the study of terrorism. In B. Bongar, L. M. Brown, L. E. Beutler, J. N. Breckenridge & P. G. Zimbardo (Eds.), *Psychology of terrorism* (pp. 32-55). New York, NY: Oxford University Press.

Boseley, S. (2008). 151,000 civilians killed since Iraq invasion. *The Guardian.* Retrieved from http://www.guardian.co.uk/world/2008/jan/10/iraq.iraqtime line

Brandon, S., & Silke, A. (2007). Near- and long-term psychological effects of exposure to terrorist attacks. In B. Bongar, L. M. Brown, L. E. Beutler, J. N. Breckenridge & P. G. Zimbardo (Eds.), *Psychology of terrorism* (pp. 175-193). New York, NY: Oxford University Press.

Brewin, C. R. (2003). *Posttraumatic stress disorder: Myth or malady?* New Haven, CT: Yale University Press.

Donahue, S., Lanzara, C. B., Felton, C. J., Essock, S. M., & Carpinello, S. (2006). Project Liberty: New York's crisis counseling program created in the aftermath of September 11, 2001. *Psychiatric Services, 57*(9), 1253-1258.

Embry, D. D. (2007). Psychological weapons of mass disruption through vicarious classical conditioning. In B. Bongar, L. M. Brown, L. E. Beutler, J. N. Breckenridge & P. G. Zimbardo (Eds.), *Psychology of terrorism* (pp. 164-174). New York, NY: Oxford University Press.

Everly, G. S., & Mitchell, J. T. (2001). America under attack: The "10 commandments" of responding to mass terror attacks. *International Journal of Emergency Mental Health, 3*(3), 133-135.

Galea, S., Ahern, J., Resnick, H., & Vlahov, D. (2006). Post-traumatic stress symptoms in the general population after a disaster: Implications for public health. In Y. Neria, R. Gross & R. Marshall (Eds.), *9/11: Mental health in the wake of terrorist attacks* (pp. 19-44). Cambridge, UK: Cambridge University Press.

Gould, M. S., Munfakh, J. L. H., & Kleinman, M. (2004). Impact of the September 11th terrorist attacks on teenagers' mental health. *Applied Developmental Science, 8*(3), 158-169.

Greene, P., Kane, D., Christ, G., Lynch, S., & Corrigan, M. (2006). *FDNY crisis counseling: Innovative responses to 9/11 firefighters, families and communities.* Hoboken, NJ: John Wiley & Sons.

Gross, R. (2006, November). *PTSD and other psychological sequelae among WTC clean up and recovery workers.* Paper presented at the International Society for Traumatic Stress Studies 22nd Annual Meeting, Los Angeles, CA.

Halpern, J. & Freeman, P. (2008, November). *Treating returning veterans: Are practitioners using evidence based best practice.* Paper presented at the International Society for Traumatic Stress Studies 24th Annual Meeting, Chicago, IL.

Halpern, J., & Tramontin, M. (2007). *Disaster mental health: Theory and practice.* Belmont, CA: Thomson Brooks/Cole.

Hamaoka, D. A., Shigemura, J., & Hall, M. J. (2004). Mental health's role in combating terror. *Journal of Mental Health, 13*(6), 531-535.

Herbert, R., Moline, J., Skloot, Q., Metzger, K., Baron, S., Luft, B., Markowitz, S., Udasin, I., Harrison, D., Stiene, D., Todd, A., Enright, P., Stellman, J. M., Landrigan, P. J., & Levin, S. M. (2006). The World Trade Center disaster and the health of workers: Five-year assessment of a unique medical screening program. *Environmental Health Perspectives, 117*(5). Retrieved from http://www.ehponline.org/members/2006/9592/9592.html

Hoven, C. W., Mandell, D. J., Duarte, C. S., Wu, P., & Giordano, V. (2006). An epidemiological response to disasters: The post-9/11 psychological needs assessment of New York City public school students. In Y. Neria, R. Gross & R. Marshall (Eds.), *9/11: Mental health in the wake of terrorist attacks* (pp. 71-94). Cambridge, UK: Cambridge University Press.

iCasualties. (2011a, January 11). *Iraq coalition casualty count.* Retrieved from http://icasualties.org/Iraq/index.aspx

iCasualties. (2011b, January 11). *Operation Enduring Freedom.* Retrieved from http://icasualties.org/oef/

Kaniasty, K. (2006). Searching for points of convergence: A commentary on prior research on disasters and some community programs initiated in response to September 11, 2001. In Y. Neria, R. Gross & R. Marshall (Eds.), *9/11: Mental health in the wake of terrorist attacks* (pp. 529-542). Cambridge, UK: Cambridge University Press.

Litz, B. T., & Gray, M. J. (2004). Early intervention for trauma in adults: A framework for first aid and secondary prevention. In B. T. Litz (Ed.), *Early intervention for trauma and traumatic loss* (pp. 87-111). New York, NY: Guilford Press.

Marshall, R. D., Bryant, R. A., Amsel, L., Suh, E. J., Cook, J. M., & Neria, Y. (2007). The psychology of ongoing threat: Relative risk appraisal, the September 11 attacks, and terrorism-related fears. *The American Psychologist, 62*(4),304-316.

Miller, L. (2002). Psychological interventions for terroristic trauma: Symptoms, syndromes, and treatment strategies. *Psychotherapy: Theory/Research/Practice/ Training, 39,* 283-296.

Milliken, C. S., Auchterlonie, J. L., & Hoge, C. W. (2007). Longitudinal assessment of mental health problems among active and reserve component soldiers returning from the Iraq war. *JAMA, 298,* 2141-2148.

National Child Traumatic Stress Network and National Center for PTSD. (2006). *Psychological first aid: Field operations guide* (2nd ed.). Retrieved from www.nctsn.org and www.ncptsd.va.gov

National Institute of Mental Health. (2002). *Mental health and mass violence: Evidence-based early psychological intervention for victims/survivors of mass violence. A workshop to reach consensus on best practices* (NIH Publication No. 02-5138). Washington, DC: U.S. Government Printing Office.

Naturale, A. J. (2006). Outreach strategies: An experiential description of the outreach methodologies used in the September 11, 2001, disaster response in New York. In E. C. Ritchie, P. J. Watson & M. J. Friedman (Eds.), *Interventions following mass violence and disasters* (pp. 365-383). New York, NY: Guilford Press,

Neria, Y., Gross, R., & Marshall, R. (2006). *9/11: Mental health in the wake of terrorist attacks.* Cambridge, UK: Cambridge University Press.

Neria, Y., Jung Suh, E., & Marshall, R. D. (2004). The professional response to the aftermath of September 11, 2001, in New York City. In B. T. Litz (Ed.), *Early inter-*

vention for trauma and traumatic loss (pp. 201-215). New York, NY: Guilford Press.

Norris, F. H., Donahue, S. A., Watson, P. J., Hamblen, J. L., & Marshall, R. D. (2006). A psychometric analysis of Project Liberty's Adult Enhanced Services Referral tool. *Psychiatric Services, 57,* 1328-1334.

Norris, F. H., Friedman, M. J., Watson, P. J., Byrne, C. M., Diaz, E., & Kaniasty, K. (2002). 60,000 disaster victims speak: Part I, an empirical review of the empirical literature, 1981–2001. *Psychiatry: Interpersonal & Biological Processes, 65,* 207-239.

Raphael, B., & Wooding, S. (2004). Early mental health interventions for traumatic loss in adults. In B. T. Litz (Ed.), *Early intervention for trauma and traumatic loss* (pp. 147-178). New York, NY: Guilford Press.

Russert, T. (Moderator). (2002, September 8). *Meet the Press.* New York, NY: NBC News.

Shalev, A. (2004). Further lessons from 9/11: Does stress equal trauma? *Psychiatry, 67*(2), 174-176.

Silke, A. (Ed). (2003). *Terrorists, victims and society: Psychological perspectives on terrorism and its consequences.* West Sussex, UK: John Wiley & Sons.

Silver, R. C., Holman, E. A., McIntosh, D. N., Poulin, M., Gil-Rivas, V., & Pizarro, J. (2006). Coping with a national trauma: A nationwide longitudinal study of responses to the terrorist attacks of September 11. In Y. Neria, R. Gross & R. Marshall (Eds.), *9/11: Mental health in the wake of terrorist attacks* (pp. 45-70). Cambridge, UK: Cambridge University Press.

Stewart, S. H. (2004). Psychological impact of the events and aftermath of September 11, 2001, terrorist attacks. *Cognitive Behaviour Therapy, 33*(2), 49-50.

Susman, T. (2007, September 14). Poll: Civilian death toll in Iraq may top 1 million. *Los Angeles Times.* Retrieved from http://www.latimes.com/news/nationworld/world/la-fg-iraq14sep14,0,6134240. story

Vlahov, D., Galea, S., Ahern, J., Resnick, H., Boscarino, J., Gold, J., et al. (2004). Consumption of cigarettes, alcohol, and marijuana among New York City residents six months after the September 11 terrorist attacks. *American Journal of Drug and Alcohol Abuse, 30*(2), 385-407.

Chapter Fourteen
Social Work Students During Wartime: "False Effect" of Professional Self-efficacy?

Shira Hantman and Miriam Ben-Oz

For six weeks during the summer of 2006, villages, towns, and cities in Northern Israel suffered the deadly effects of unprecedented daily heavy missile attacks. Many families desiring to escape the fire found relief in a refugee camp set up by private donations. The camp, popularly known as "Tent City," on the Nitzanim beach, was originally the site of rock concerts and summer festivals. The camp accommodated 7,000 men, women, and children and provided food, laundry, first aid, and entertainment facilities. Initially, the management of the camp was composed of the director and a number of volunteers, all with backgrounds in education. However, by the second week, many emotional and social problems cropped up that they were not equipped to handle. Problems resulting from the protracted emotional strain involved in leaving homes, family, and friends unprotected as well as interfamily tensions resulting from war and financial difficulties created feelings of distress, fear, confusion, and guilt. Consequently, the director put out a call for volunteers from the helping professions. Among those answering this call were 70 students, mostly social work students, from Tel Hai College. Students found themselves confronted with problems and situations, some of which were beyond their scope of knowledge and training. A faculty member was assigned to supervise students' interventions.

THE PROJECT

Students acted as case managers, working in conjunction with the few volunteer psychologists on site and local social services. This proved to be a problem because the local social services were under fire, and their social workers were occupied with those civilians who stayed behind.

Because there was no adequate professional infrastructure on hand, students provided necessary services, while a number of faculty members provided ad hoc support and supervision.

The literature points to the importance of immediate intervention at a time of crisis. The goal of crisis intervention is to help traumatized persons confront the reality of what happened, deal with the crisis, and go beyond the pain and emotional trauma toward new strength and opportunities for growth and change. The challenge for crisis intervention programs is to provide effective crisis support and assistance as soon as possible following the event and to make available resources and services to meet the needs of traumatized persons by providing direct assistance or referrals to other agencies.

Crisis intervention aims to meet the specific needs of the population. There are some critical elements to crisis intervention services that are necessary in all situations; these include psychological first aid, needs assessment, and empathic support.

Immediate crisis intervention, or "psychological first aid," involves establishing rapport, conducting short-term assessment and service delivery, and averting a potential state of crisis. The immediacy of the response is critical to ensure the safety of the traumatized person and his or her family. Time may be extremely important due to impending danger to the traumatized person or the family. Immediate crisis intervention includes caring for the medical, physical, mental health, and personal needs of the traumatized person as well as providing information to the traumatized person about local resources or services.

Students applied social work intervention techniques aimed to move the client from victim to survivor. This was accomplished by utilizing common social work skills such as empathic action, active listening to personal stories, active understanding of pain and anxiety, and active validation of personal feelings as well as by making meaning of uncertainty, ambiguity, and fear and managing emotions by emphasizing strengths and resources and by alleviating emotional distress. Further, the students worked to augment a sense of personal safety by normalizing and acknowledging the refugee's condition and feelings. Additionally, students took action to resolve concrete problems concerning social or medical service provision, medications, money, and clothes for families who fled their home in a hurry. In some instances, referrals to other agencies or organizations were implemented.

A number of prerequisites were needed to implement the above intervention:

1. Trained and experienced professionals
2. Skilled social workers to provide student supervision
3. Systematic need assessment and follow-up of high-risk population

Because there was no adequate professional infrastructure on hand, the students provided the necessary service, while a number of faculty members provided supervision. A needs assessment questionnaire was created to assist the students in their work. In sum, students treated 140 referrals for those dealing with financial difficulties, health problems to family violence, child abuse, homesickness, and fear and anxiety related to the situation at home.

The aim of this chapter is to describe the effects of this unique experience of beginning social work students in "Tent City" who took on the role of practitioners in a "pseudo-professional" intervention. We will explain the effects that this unusual experience had on the developmental process of their professional identity, which resulted in a sense of false professional self-efficacy.

RETURN TO LEARNING

The academic year that opened less than two months following the end of the war was marked by an attempt to return to business as usual. Classes commenced and students were assigned to their field placements. Shortly after the first signs of unrest appeared. Students who had volunteered in "Tent City" voiced dissatisfaction with their supervisors, reporting confusion regarding their field placement role.

In an attempt to understand these voices, students were gathered for a series of three focus group discussions (Morgan, 1998). They were asked to talk about their wartime experiences and share present feelings and thoughts. The atmosphere was lively and nostalgic as students remembered their contribution to their clients in the camp and how well they were received by them. They spoke of the excitement that they felt while providing professional help to their clients, the appreciation that their clients showed them, and the experience of working with other professionals and being treated as peers. "We didn't even think what was going to happen next year. In a state of war you create a 'war routine' and give no thought to what will happen after the war . . . we felt that the present situation would last forever."

As the conversation moved closer to the present day, a flow of emotions reflecting confusion and anger emerged, and a very different voice was heard. The feeling of personal responsibility that they felt toward their clients in "Tent City" was replaced with a feeling of insignificance in their field placements. These feelings were reflected in the focus group in statements such as "I've returned to a place that makes me feel small;" "I feel that, in my field placement, my wings have been clipped." It would be expected that the return to the structured environment of field placement and supervision would provide a sense of security and relief. However, here, too, students reported feeling trapped in the supervisory relationship. "I feel that I'm constantly under observation." Further, they complained that, because of the constant criticism of supervisors, they were afraid to try any new interventions. The personal responsibility and self-efficacy experienced during their wartime experience was replaced with a feeling of professional and personal insignificance.

Listening to them raised the question: "What is the transformation that took place in the students' self-perceived professional identity following their experience as volunteer workers in 'Tent City' and their subsequent return to a student's role?" Is it possible to relate this extreme transformation that students underwent to their professional development stage?

Related to Ronnestad and Skovholt's (2003) professional development model, these second-year trainees who had experienced one year of supervised fieldwork were actually toward the end of the Beginning Student Phase, preparing to enter Advanced Student Phase. However, their experience in "Tent City" created a "false effect" of professional self-efficacy. This was enhanced by positive and enthusiastic feedback from clients and peers as well, creating the illusion of a fully developed and competent professional identity characteristic of a far more advanced stage (i.e., Novice Professional Phase).

The model emphasizes the essential role that self-efficacy plays in understanding professional development. The role of self-referent thought in guiding human action and change has been found relevant to understanding and predicting career relevant behaviors, in general (Hackett, 1995; Multen, Brown, & Lent, 1991), and social work students' behaviors, in particular. Given that self-efficacy predicts career interests, occupational consideration, and career choice, one would expect those enrolling in a social work program to have confidence in doing the work that they have chosen (Holden, Meenaghan, Anastas, & Metrey, 2002).

SELF-EFFICACY IN PERCEIVED PROFESSIONAL IDENTITY

One explanation for the incongruity between the feelings of control and empowerment that students reported in "Tent City" in contrast to a sense of powerlessness in their field placements, may be found in the theory of self-efficacy. Albert Bandura (1997), the undisputed architect of self-efficacy theory and research, defines perceived self-efficacy as the belief in one's ability to organize and carry out actions needed to produce desired results. This is a subjective phenomenon in that people can possess a high degree of talent or skill but not see themselves as able to apply their capabilities consistently or across a variety of situations. Beliefs about self-efficacy affect a multitude of diverse factors: the decisions that people make, the amount of effort they put forth, their perseverance and resilience in the face of adversity, their tendency to think in ways that are self-hindering or self-aiding, and the amount of stress and depression that they experience in response to difficulties (Bandura, 1997).

Due to its flexibility, self-efficacy theory is well suited to the design of professional training (Petrovich, 2004), giving emphasis to pragmatic, situation-specific, client-focused interventions and a focus on empowerment. Self-efficacy has been used as an outcome in a number of evaluations of social work education (Holden et al., 2002). The students in this study reported a sense of power and omnipotence: "I felt as if I was saving the world"; "I felt I had reached the peak." At "Tent City," students were looked to as the sole providers of immediate solutions and services, intensifying their commitment toward their clients.

Self-efficacy also has been found to provide an important stimulus for and to be a byproduct of incidental learning as opposed to formal or intentional learning. Incidental learning is unintentional or unplanned learning that results from indirect activities. It happens in many ways: through observation, repetition, social interaction, and problem solving (Rogers, 1997); by watching or talking to colleagues or experts (Van Tillaart, Van den Berg, & Warmerdam, 1998); or from being forced to accept or adapt to situations (English, 1999). This "natural" way of learning (Rogers, 1997) has characteristics of what is considered most effective in formal learning situations: it is situated, contextual, and social. "Tent City" had the characteristics of an incidental learning environment created by the wartime situation; the environment was ambiguous and uncertain. The learning opportunity arose as a result of the war, and students were sent to do a job that was initially vague. Their role was defined by the immediate needs of the refugee population and interpreted by a group of social work students who had just completed one year of fieldwork, equivalent to a Beginning Student Phase.

Incidental learning can result in improved competence, changed attitudes, and growth in interpersonal skills, self-confidence, and self-awareness (McFerrin, 1999; Ross-Gordon & Dowling, 1995). Students encountered a situation in which they were on their own and were expected to provide immediate answers. Using the limited skills that they had acquired during their prior fieldwork experience, they functioned as professional social workers with confidence and earnestness. Students expressed feelings of elation and enthusiasm: "I felt there something special that I had never experienced before"; "I felt like a real social worker." This feeling of exultation expressed by the students became an objective in itself, and although it was an unintended consequence of the learning situation, it was as important to the learner as the original objectives (McFerrin, 1999). This became the source of the students' motivation and perception of self-efficacy.

Research has demonstrated that self-efficacy is derived from four types of experiences: those in which one observes valued role models; successfully practices a skill or behavior; receives encouragement and support from valued others; and learns to keep one's emotions and physiological arousal at a self-supporting versus a harmful level (Bandura, 1997).

The first type of experience, also described as vicarious experience, is defined as "learning mediated through model attainments" (Bandura, 1997, p. 86). This is an important source of self-efficacy information for the learner. Petty and Cacioppo (1986) recommend the observation of persons successfully handling difficult situations as one of the most effective approaches to acquiring practice skills. The students, in the Beginning Student Phase, were in dire need of the support and encouragement of more advanced members of the profession. They fed on the support of the volunteers from different backgrounds, mostly experienced psychologists who inadvertently became their role models. Being accepted as peers and treated as professional equals reinforced the feeling: "I realized that I had chosen the right profession."

Moreover, in lieu of the infrequent visits of their supervisors and other social workers, they also became their own role models. Self-modeling can be especially effective when other methods have failed (Dowrick, 1983). Surprisingly, in some studies, self-observation of illusory skillfulness, with mistakes edited out, improved performance just as effectively as self-observation of actual skillfulness. This suggests that the enhancement of belief in one's capabilities, rather than an actual improvement in one's skill, may be the influential factor (Ganzales & Dowrick, as cited in Bandura, 1997). It is possible that observing oneself performing successfully allows learners to be their own source of reinforcement, motivating continued effort and self-imitation of successful performance.

The second type of experience from which self-efficacy has been found to be derived is successful practice or enactive mastery. Enactive mastery is defined as the "experience of overcoming obstacles through perseverant effort" (Bandura, 1997, p.80). This is the most powerful source of efficacy information, exceeding the impact of cognitive simulation, tutorial instruction, or modeling. Mastery experience is subjective in that the sense of self-efficacy comes from the learner's interpretation of a performance as reasonably successful. The support and attention that students provided the refugees were met with a positive response, boosting confidence in their social work skills and feelings of being needed. This is congruent with the development model in that students in the early stages of development give advice based on personal experience, especially in this situation, where the students themselves were also refugees.

The third source is verbal persuasion from significant models. This has been found to be a weaker source of self-efficacy, with less research support (Petrovich, 2004). Certain conditions are important for verbal persuasion to have an impact in educational settings. The effectiveness of feedback will depend on how it is delivered and who the sender is. Students described the atmosphere at "Tent City" as one of mutual assistance and appreciation: "Everyone was willing to lend a hand"; "I received immediate and positive feedback from my clients and the other volunteers."

The fourth source is the ability to engage in demanding activities by attending to their emotional and physical states. Mood and physiological states affect judgments about personal efficacy, and past experiences of vigilant self-monitoring of arousal lead to the same response in similar situations. How people will interpret the arousal will vary depending on their perceptions of the situation. Affective states might also bias attention and affect self-efficacy; a negative mood tends to induce thoughts of past failings, while a positive mood induces thoughts of past accomplishments (Bandura, 1997). Paradoxically, working with the refugees, and feeling needed and appreciated, helped alleviate feelings of personal anxiety and fear resulting from the state of war. One student, whose brother was serving on the front, dreamt that her brother was killed. When encouraged to seek help for herself, she responded, "these people here need me and that is more important now than my own fears." She remained until the camp was dismantled when fighting was terminated.

In essence, these students experienced a condensed version of the Novice Professional Phase, skipping over the Advanced Student Phase, which normally would have been spread out over an entire academic year. The Novice Professional Phase is the first period after graduation, when the young professional initially experiences a sensation of freedom and enthusiasm. In other words, a sense of competency was achieved not through internalizing the socialization process but rather by self-modeling, incidental learning, self-mastery, and modeling. With this fragile self-image, the students began their third academic year.

THE AFTERMATH

Upon return to fieldwork placements, students were thrown back into what essentially was the real-time phase of their professional development, i.e., the Advanced Student Phase. Still under the illusion of the "false effect" of the Novice Phase, students expected to be treated by their supervisors as peers rather than trainees. However, this illusion was soon shattered as students were required to adhere to the Advanced Student Phase expectations of their supervisors.

It is not surprising that the supervisory relationship exacerbated students' frustration because, at this phase, experiences in supervision have particular significance. In this encounter, students' aspiration to be autonomous, based on their war experience, contributed to their ambivalence toward supervision. The supervisor, on his part, treated them as students entering the Advanced Phase. The students reported supervisors' disregarding their war experience, treating them as ordinary students, while they felt professional competency, bordering on heroism. The gap between students' self-perception and supervisors' disregard became a source of mutual resentment and frustration. Unlike their war experience, students were now expected to follow the clinical teaching curriculum in regard to their clients. They were no longer free to make independent decisions.

The encounter with systematic supervision emphasized the students' lack of understanding of the complexity and difficulty of the professional tasks in which they were engaged. The more the students were aware of the gap between themselves and their supervisors, the less they were able to perceive them as senior practitioners to whom they may look up.

CONCLUSIONS

The aim of this chapter was to discuss the implications of an inconsistent professional socialization process on the professional identity of social work students, with special emphasis on the creation of professional self-efficacy. We had a unique opportunity to see this inconsistent professional socialization process in the "Tent City" experience. This resulted in the creation of a sense of false professional self-efficacy that showed us how much a real-time emergency situation that calls for student involvement could be detrimental to the student's professional development process.

An explanation was provided through the professional development model (Hess, 1985; Ronnestad & Skovholt, 2003) and self-efficacy theory (Petrovich, 2004). At "Tent City," students reported a sense of power and omnipotence by watching or talking to colleagues or experts in a setting that had the characteristics of an incidental-learning environment. This resulted in a feeling of improved competence, changed attitudes, and growth in interpersonal skills, self-confidence, and self-awareness. Using the limited skills that they had acquired during their fieldwork experience, they functioned as "pseudo-professional" social workers. Further, learning mediated through model attainments also was experienced. Becoming their own role models was found to be especially effective when they had observed persons who successfully handled difficult situations in the absence of supervisors and other social workers. The positive response that students received from clients further strengthened their sense of mastery.

In sum, the overall experience in "Tent City" seemed to have a very positive effect on the students' professional development, enhancing their self-efficacy and confidence. However, two months later, students reported a sense of powerlessness and insignificance in their field placements. These feelings were related to the transformation that students underwent in regard to their professional developmental stage. This experience moved them forward, skipping a phase without proper preparation. Because difficulties were encountered upon return to the normative process, we may assume the importance of adhering to a consistent professional development process.

Therefore, we recommend maintaining a portion of consistency using supervisors in unique opportunities. As was demonstrated in "Tent City," a lack of supervision caused harm to the students' professional identity. The importance of the reliable presence of the supervisor will facilitate maintaining the process of identity construction and consolidation of the professional identity. This process occurs through identification with the supervisor as an internalized role model.

In retrospect, it is clear to us that, as their teachers who are responsible for students' professional training, we should have been aware of the significance of this event in terms of the professional developmental process. In view of the stressful environment in which we live, where war and terror are a part of our everyday existence, it would be useful to keep in mind the risk that we take when involving our students in pseudo-professional volunteer work.

REFERENCES

Bandura, A. (1997). *Self-efficacy: The exercise of control.* New York, NY: W. H. Freeman.

Dowrick, P. W. (1983). Self-modelling. In P. W. Dowrick and S. J. Biggs (Eds.), *Using video: Psychological and social applications* (pp. 105-124). London, UK: Wiley.

English, L. M. (1999). Learning from changes in religious leadership: A study of informal and incidental learning at the parish level. *International Journal of Lifelong Education, 18*(5), 385-394.

Hackett, G. (1995). Self-efficacy in career choice and development. In A. Bandura (Ed.), *Self-efficacy in changing societies* (pp. 232-258). New York, NY: Cambridge University Press.

Hess, A. K. (1986). Growth in supervision: Stage of supervisee and supervisor development. In N. J. Kaslow (Ed.), *Supervision and training: Models, dilemmas & challenges* (pp. 51-67). New York, NY: Haworth Press.

Holden, G., Meenaghan, T., Anastas, J., & Metrey, G. (2002). Outcomes of social work education: The case for social work self-efficacy. *Journal of Social Work Education, 38*(1), 115-133.

McFerrin, K. M. (1999). Incidental learning in a higher education asynchronous online distance education course. In J. D. Price et al. (Eds.), *SITE 99: Society for Information Technology & Teacher Education International Conference Proceedings.* Charlottesville, VA: Association for the Advancement of Computing in Education.

Morgan, D. L. (1998). *Focus group kit: Vol. 2. Planning focus groups.* London, UK: Sage.

Multen, K. D., Brown, S. D., & Lent, R. W. (1991). Relation of self-efficacy beliefs to academic outcomes: A meta-analytic investigation. *Journal of Counseling Psychology, 38*(1), 30-38.

Petrovich, A. (2004). Teaching notes: Using self-efficacy theory in social work teaching. *Journal of Social Work Education, 40*(3), 429-443.

Petty, R. E., & Cacioppo, J. T. (1986). The elaboration likelihood model of persuasion. In L. Berkowitz (Ed.), *Advances in experimental social psychology, Vol. 19* (pp. 123-205). New York, NY: Academic Press.

Rogers, A. (1997). Learning: Can we change the discourse? *Adult Learning, 8*(5), 116-117.

Ronnestad, M. H., & Skovholt, T. M. (2003). The journey of the counselor and therapist: Research findings and perspectives on professional development. *Journal of Career Development, 30*(1), 5-44.

Ross-Gordon, J. M., & Dowling, W. D. (1995). Adult learning in the context of African-American women's voluntary organizations. *International Journal of Lifelong Education, 14*(4), 306-319.

Van den Tillaart, H., Van den Berg, S., & Warmerdam, J. (1998). *Work and learning in micro-enterprises in the printing industry.* Thessaloniki, Greece: European Centre for the Development of Vocational Training.

Chapter Fifteen
Shared Traumatic Reality:
Social Work Students and Clients in an Area Under Attack
Nehami Baum

Terrorist attacks in Israel invariably affect the entire country. Whether the attack is in Tel-Aviv, Haifa or Jerusalem, Beer Sheva, Eilat, or Sderot, or in the Northern communities, the reverberations are felt by everyone, sometimes more strongly, sometimes less so. But no one here really escapes the unsettling sense of danger and the feeling of threat that the attacks evoke or the grief for the injured and dead and their families. The literature on the effects of 9/11 indicates that the trauma of terror can extend very far from the geographic target (Galea et al., 2002; Schlenger et al., 2002; Schuster et al., 2001). Given Israel's tiny size (it is a 7-hour drive from the northern to southern tip and less than a 1-hour drive at the narrowest point east to west), the impact of terrorist attacks is felt very intensely, even as everyone continues to go about their daily lives as normally as possible (Bleich, Gelkopf, & Solomon, 2003; Somer, Maguen, Or-Chen, & Litz, 2007).

Researchers and practitioners in the field of mental health have become familiar with the term "shared traumatic reality" (Baum, 2010). This term was introduced into the professional discourse after the first Gulf War to refer to a shared exposure to a collective trauma (Keinan-Kon, 1998; Kretsch, Benyakar, Baruch, & Roth, 1997). After 9/11 the term became highly apt and widely used (Altman & Davis, 2003; Saakvitne, 2002; Tosone, 2006; Tosone & Bialkin, 2003; Tosone et al., 2003). The two chief components of the phenomenon are that the clinician and client are exposed to the same traumatic event and that the clinician is exposed to the event twice over: once personally as a member of the collective that was attacked and again professionally, through the work with his or her clients, whether or not the clients were actually caught in an attack and whether or not they sustained any personal injury or losses.

This chapter focuses on the impact of shared traumatic reality on a particular group of social work students in Israel and the means they used to cope with it. The inspiration and material for this chapter came from my own students.

Some of these students had lost a friend, a neighbor, or some other person whom they knew in a terrorist attack and who was part of the fabric of their lives. The chapter will not focus on students who lost members of their immediate family but rather those who lost someone with whom they were in close "psychological proximity." To the best of my knowledge, this term was coined by Ayalon and Lahad (1995) to refer to situations of "being personally acquainted with victims ([that is] relatives, friends, acquaintances) or identifying with them because they are of the same age, sex, or social status" (p. 305). The focus on these students is important because their particular plight has not received the recognition that it merits.

The literature on the impact of loss following a terrorist attack can be roughly divided into that which focuses on the mental health professionals (Adams, Boscarino, & Figley, 2006; Adams, Figley, & Boscarino, 2008; Boscarino, Figley, & Adams, 2004; Cohen, Gagin, & Peled-Avram, 2006; Dekel, Hantman, Ginzburg, & Solomon, 2007; Eidelson, D'Alessio, & Eidelson, 2003; Lev-Wiesel, Goldblatt, Eisikovits, & Admi, 2008; Shamai & Ron, 2009) and that which focuses on the general public (Bleich et al. 2003; Galea et al., 2002; Schlenger et al., 2002; Schuster et al., 2001; Somer et al., 2007).

Four studies in the literature focused on mental health professionals. Two of them, written in the wake of 9/11, simply stated that some practitioners lost first-degree relatives in the attack but did not elaborate on their responses or how the loss affected their practice (Pulido, 2007; Seeley, 2003). Two others, by Shamai (2005) and Shamai and Ron (2009), examined the impact of terrorist attacks on social workers in Israel. Two of Shamai's interviews were with social workers who had lost their husbands in an attack some years earlier. These social workers stated that their experience made them more sensitive to the feelings of clients who had suffered a similar loss. Shamai and Ron, who did a mixed-methods study, found that, of the 406 social work participants, 74 (18.2%) had lost a non-first-degree relative. Interestingly, their analyses showed no increase in emotional distress among them or any impact of the loss on their professional experience.

The findings of Shamai and Ron (2009) are unexpected. Studies of the general public in both the United States and Israel show that the loss or injury of a relative or friend is a predictor of augmented posttraumatic symptomatology (Bleich et al., 2003). Warren, Lee, and Saunders (2003) compared medical professionals who knew someone who was killed in a terrorist attack with those who dealt with the dead and injured during the attack and found similarly heightened levels of distress. Unfortunately, these studies do not distinguish between first-degree relatives and other close individuals.

The grief and disruption that follow the loss of a child, spouse, or parent are likely to be vastly more intense than the grief and disruption following the loss of a more distant relative or friend. By combining the two in research, however, we blur the evidence of the impact that the latter loss can have and delegitimize the grief of those who sustain it. While there is ample legitimization of the grief of mental health professionals who lose a first-degree relative in a terrorist attack, the grief that follows upon the loss of someone with psychological proximity tends to be disenfranchised. The term "disenfranchised grief" was coined by Doka (1989) to refer to the grief that persons suffer following a bereavement that is not socially recognized, that cannot be mourned in public, and for which they receive no social support.

The social work students whom I studied suffered from "disenfranchised grief" following the loss of a relative outside the immediate nuclear family or of a friend, neighbor, or other person in their "psychological proximity." The Jewish religion has well-elaborated rituals for easing the mourning of the immediate family of someone who has died. These rituals, observed by almost all Jews, are designed to cushion the shock of the loss, to provide the bereaved family members with a constant presence of company and support, to enable them to talk about the dead, and to free them from their mundane duties and responsibilities so that they can begin to absorb and work through their loss. Their pain is recognized and given a place. Friends and more distant family partake of the rituals to provide the immediate family with the warmth and support that they need to soften their ordeal. In this process, their own loss usually takes a secondary place.

In the larger social sphere, Israeli society deals with the losses incurred in terrorist attacks in a similar way. From the moment of the death, they are offered mental health assistance. This offer is soon followed by regular monetary compensation. Here, too, little, if any, attention is paid to the more distant relatives and friends of the deceased, who are left to cope with their loss on their own. In good measure, this attitude is aimed at enabling normal life to resume as soon as possible.

The lack of attention and recognition is an added burden on mental health professionals in times of terror. As the literature points out, in times of trauma, mental health professionals are generally expected to put their own problems aside while tending to the needs of others, including, but not only, the injured and bereaved (Figley, 1995). Being part of a traumatized community, as well as mental health professionals, local caregivers feel responsible and somehow obliged to demonstrate their psychological fitness through help giving (Myers & Wee, 2002; Ostodic, 1999). Where the practitioner has suffered the loss of a person who was meaningful to him or her, fulfilling professional obligations sometimes becomes an intolerable challenge.

The following section will present the impact of shared traumatic reality on social work students in Israel who lost a friend, a neighbor, or some other person whom they knew in a terror attack and who was part of the fabric of their lives. As background, I am a social work instructor at a school of social work in Israel, where I taught undergraduate courses in intervention methods. As it is taught at the university, the course in intervention methods accompanies the students' practical field training and places considerable emphasis on methods of individual intervention. It is a highly interactive course, in which instruction plays only a small part. Students are expected not only to participate actively in class discussions but also to share personal experiences that have a bearing on their fieldwork and supervision. Personal experience, as understood in such courses, refers not only to external events but also to the student's feelings, thoughts, and behaviors. Accordingly, I generally start every class by asking whether anyone wants to bring up any personal matter before I proceed with the day's course content.

For the most part, students brought up issues involving interpersonal processes that arose with their clients and in supervision as well as ethical issues. The start of the 2002 spring semester, in March, was accompanied by a sharp rise in the number and deadliness of the terrorist attacks in Israel. Inevitably, some of the matters that the students brought up that semester involved these terrorist attacks. In addition, the students approached me in the corridor before or after class and asked to speak to me in private about the way in which the attacks were affecting their fieldwork.

What follows is based on accounts made in class or to me personally by four students who had lost a meaningful person in a terrorist attack. The four students may be briefly identified (with names changed) as follows: (1) Netta, a 28-year-old mother of a toddler and pregnant with her second child when the son of her child's babysitter was killed; (2) Yael, a 27-year-old student whose 17-year-old nephew had been killed in a terrorist attack in Jerusalem; (3) Anat, 26 years old, who lost her best friend and her friend's fiancé in a terrorist attack in Jerusalem shortly before their wedding, in which she, Anat, was to accompany her friend throughout the preparations and ceremonies; and (4) Nirit, a 23-year-old student when her best friend's brother was killed in a terrorist attack at the religious boarding school that he attended.

Broadly speaking, four interrelated issues arose in the students' discussions and accounts: (1) the conflict between personal needs and professional needs; (2) doubts about professional competence; (3) ways of and the legitimacy of carving out personal space at the expense of fulfilling one's professional responsibilities, and (4) doing fieldwork under terror.

CONFLICT BETWEEN PERSONAL NEEDS
AND PROFESSIONAL NEEDS

Three of the students who had sustained a meaningful loss asked: "How can I make space for others when I can barely contain my own feelings?" The clearest example of both the question and the emotional turmoil that gave rise to it is provided by Netta. In response to my opening question on the first day of the semester, Netta raised her hand and asked, "What does a therapist do with personal matters that weigh on them when they have to treat others?" The question was provoked by the emotional flooding that she experienced in the wake of the death of the son of her child's babysitter. Netta told me after class that this death was terrible for her, not only because the child's babysitter was like a mother to her, which gave the loss of her son something of the force of the loss of a close relative, but even more because this was the first time that someone she knew had died when she herself was a mother. The death touched her to the very core. It terrified her and undermined her faith in God. It can be conjectured that her great distress stemmed not only from grief but also from the fact that the son's death brought home to her the vulnerability of her own child and the fragility of her own family's wholeness at a time when the ongoing terror had raised the sense of imminent threat among all Israelis. Similar anxiety and pain made Anat, who had lost her best friends in a Jerusalem explosion, wonder, "I don't know if I can contain other people's pain."

Of the four students who had sustained a meaningful loss, Nirit was the only one who did not raise this question. She did not speak about the difficulty of containing her personal feelings or ask how she could make space for others. She expressed no personal grief, horror, or inner turmoil and did not speak of any difficulties in functioning. As will be shown in greater detail under the following categories, instead of allowing herself to feel the pain and the turmoil that naturally follow upon a close loss, she wrapped herself in the social worker role.

DOUBTS ABOUT PROFESSIONAL COMPETENCE

Three of the students who had sustained a meaningful personal loss expressed intensified, terror-related doubts about their professional competence. The intensified doubts were rooted in the difficulties that they had in containing their feelings and the concomitant uncertainty that they felt about their ability to contain the feelings of their fieldwork clients. These doubts were expressed with particular clarity by Yael. Sharing her response to the death of her nephew three months earlier, she told the class that, following his death, she found it difficult to return to the rehabilitation facility where she was doing her fieldwork. This was a facility that treated trauma casualties, including, although not only, victims of terrorist attacks. For her, this meant that, at work, she had to help people who had suffered losses, much as she had. "When I got to the hospital where I do my fieldwork," she said, "I wasn't sure that I was at all capable of working and meeting people who had suffered losses." Her doubts, like those of two of the other students who had sustained a personal loss, were intensified by the emotional vulnerability that she felt in its wake. In addition, because her fieldwork was with trauma casualties, she may have experienced the fear, common in trauma, that she would not be able to cope with any reminders of the traumatic experience.

Nirit, who distanced herself from any emotions that she might have felt in the wake of her best friend's brother's death, did not express any direct doubts about her ability to fulfill the obligations to the clients. Instead, she expressed concern with the negative image of the social worker. She opened her account to the class by expressing outrage at what she termed the "unprofessional conduct of the hospital social worker" who had phoned her friend's parents after their son's death. According to Nirit, the "social worker" had told the family to come to the hospital, a two-hour drive from their home, in the middle of the night, even though it turned out that their son had not been injured but killed. She spoke angrily and in great detail about the "social worker's" "nerve" and "lack of professionalism," even though she had no way of knowing whether the person who phoned was actually a social worker and not, for example, a clerk or other hospital worker. To be sure, the expression of anger at hospital staff by bereaved persons is quite common, a way for them to deflect their feelings of loss and grief. However, Nirit's anger also seems to have stemmed from her concern with her image as a social worker. Her highly charged concern with the image of the social worker substituted for the expression of emotion in response to her friend's brother's death and was one of other manifestations, discussed below, of her assumption of the social worker's identity.

Doubts about their professional competence are quite common and entirely normative among undergraduates. These doubts are a natural outcome of the students' position as trainees whose skills are not yet honed, whose working experience is limited, and whose professional identity is still being formed. However, as can be seen from the students' assertions, these doubts were intensified by the terrorist attacks, which overburdened their emotions, drew their attention and energy, and raised the specter of their having to perform tasks, that is, dealing with newly bereaved and often traumatized individuals, which even professionals find extremely difficult.

CARVING OUT PERSONAL SPACE

Two of the students who sustained a significant personal loss coped with questions involving how they could carve out the personal space that they needed and the legitimacy of doing so, given their responsibilities as social workers. Yael showed intuitive awareness of the need to make space for herself before she tackled her personal and professional obligations. When her parents phoned at 5:00 a.m. with the news of her nephew's death, she said to herself, "You're not getting out of bed now. You will stay right here in bed, next to your boyfriend, and cry" and proceeded to do so for three hours. She related to the class that she had explained to herself that she had to take care of herself before she would be able to be with others. "I knew that, when I reached my sister's home, I'd have to be supportive of her and her kids, and of our parents." Yael took the space she needed, by crying and cuddling with her boyfriend, with full awareness of what she was doing and without any apparent guilt or other emotional hindrance.

Anat, when her best friend and her fiancé were killed in a terrorist attack shortly before their wedding, did not so much carve out personal space as allow her feelings to carve it out for her; she allowed herself to give into her anxiety attacks and to engage in regressive behaviors. As Anat recounted in my office, she was afraid of staying alone at home and did not do so. She was afraid of the dark and would not get out of bed at night without waking her husband to put on the light. This way of carving out the space that she needed constituted a partial loss of control, which seems to have stemmed largely from her emotional flooding and heightened vulnerability (e.g., the loss of her sense of safety) in the wake of the deaths. There also seems to have been, however, a certain relinquishment of control, that is, not a loss, but a giving up of control. Her regressive behavior was confined to her home, where it would not jeopardize her, as she could rely on her husband to accept her behavior and to take care of her. It did not extend to the classroom or other places. It may be conjectured that she used the controlled regression to make space for her feelings because she was not sure that making space for them was entirely legitimate. Instead of giving herself permission, she allowed her feelings to take over, without taking responsibility for them. Without self-legitimization, she sought legitimization from me. She repeatedly told me that this wasn't the self that she knew and that she was afraid that something was the matter with her. When I assured her that her responses were in no way abnormal, given what had happened, she was somewhat relieved. About a week later, she told me that my telling her that her responses were normal very much helped her.

Nirit did not take space for herself but rather threw herself into the social worker role while avoiding any contact with her own feelings of loss or anxiety. She told the class that, from the time that she learned of her friend's brother's death all through the next morning, she devoted herself to helping the family, especially the father, who was concerned that his wife's unemotional response (no tears and cool, collected functioning) was abnormal. Nirit reported that she calmed him down and assured him that it was a completely normal reaction and that everyone responded to such things in their own way. This statement, while valid and sympathetic enough, is the statement of a professional and not of a friend who herself grieves the loss. When I asked her in class how she felt, she simply repeated how angry and disappointed she was at the unprofessional way that the hospital had notified the family of the boy's death. She continued to play the social worker for some weeks, at one point intervening in a dispute between her friend and her father, to advise him, "You're not listening to her. You should listen to what she's saying." While this may be good professional advice, it is inappropriate for a young student to give to a grieving man over twice her age.

DOING FIELDWORK UNDER TERROR

Each of the four students who had suffered a meaningful loss related somewhat differently to the issue of going on with her fieldwork. Yael, who feared that she would not be able to cope with her fieldwork clients after her nephew's death, asked her supervisor for help. Her supervisor suggested three alternatives: to continue as if nothing had happened, to stop working with clients until she felt that she was able to, or to continue working with them while checking out how she was managing, with the option of stopping at any point. She selected the third option: self-monitoring while leaving an exit open should she feel that she could not cope. This flexible solution dissipated her anxiety about her capacity to cope and enabled her to continue working.

Netta, who was profoundly upset by the death of the son of her child's babysitter, said that she had changed nothing in her outward behavior as a student professional, even though it was extremely difficult for her to continue to work as though nothing had happened. Whether she actually comported herself as though no internal upheaval had occurred and whether and how well she was able to contain her clients' feelings are beyond our knowledge. What is relevant here is that, even though she was aware of her own needs, she felt strongly that it was her duty to continue to function as a professional. Her choice may indicate that she gave greater weight to her fieldwork obligations than to her personal needs and/or that her continued working served as an important source of inner sustenance and organization that helped her to cope with her pain.

Anat took a day off from her fieldwork after first asking me whether I thought that it would be all right and whether it would bring down her fieldwork grade. These questions may be understood on two levels: as a request for legitimization for her carving out space for herself at the expense of her fieldwork obligations and as a reality-oriented request for assurance that she would not be penalized for doing this. In addition, it should be noted that she took the day off, not in the midst of her upset, but afterwards and after she had already had a fair amount of time off during the semester break. She seems to have wanted the day, which is a very short time for self-healing, not only as a respite but also as a marker of her loss and grief.

Nirit notified the class that she had decided that she would continue to meet with her clients after her friend's brother's death, but that she would not write up the required reports on them. She presented this as a decision to continue with the social worker's key task of working with clients, while easing up on a rather peripheral and meaningless matter. Nirit's choice to stop precisely this aspect of her fieldwork, and no other, highlights her concern with how others see her as a professional. Although she projected the sense that she was dedicating herself to others, she was actually focused on her professional identity.

All four students who sustained a meaningful loss continued with their fieldwork, despite their distress and despite their concern that they would not be able to contain their clients' feelings. Although two of the students took a slight respite, this did not really disrupt their fieldwork. Their statements also reflect the value that they placed on continuing their work. This was clearest in Netta's insistence that her behavior did not and would not change, but the feeling was also conveyed by Yael, who told the class that she was pleased that the arrangement she had reached with her supervisor enabled her to continue working with her rehabilitation clients.

Summary and Conclusions

This study, based on statements made by students in the course of the semester, is inevitably impressionistic and inductive. One certainly cannot conclude that the students' responses convey the variety or proportion of social work students' possible responses to bereavement through terrorism or in other collective traumatic events. Nonetheless, the study sheds some light on the issues of social work students who lose meaningful others in a terrorist attack that has not received the recognition that it merits.

The experiences of these students present one aspect of work in a shared reality, a condition in which the clinician is exposed to the traumatic situation both as a private citizen and as a professional. They are exposed to it as private persons by the very fact that they are part of the community that was hit and, moreover, by the fact that somebody significant to them was killed. The students whose experiences were presented experienced a particularly sensitive situation as they were burdened with what Doka (1989) designated as disenfranchised grief, a grief that does not entitle one to publicly mourn one's loss.

At the same time, they were also burdened as professionals because they were already working as a social worker intern/student and were already in the process of developing a professional self. Thus, they suffered from a heightened level of personal conflicts.

While these examples shed some light on the special difficulties of students doing their field training, it also directs our attention to an aspect of work in a shared reality. It seems that a shared reality may involve conflicts, not only between the roles the clinician holds in different groups and social settings, but also an internal conflict between the professional self and the private self.

To conclude, there are a good number of professionals who may lose meaningful others outside their immediate families in situations of shared traumatic reality such as the course of terrorist attacks or in other catastrophes. The indications are that these individuals may suffer considerable distress as a result. Their special plight, however, gets short shrift in the research.

On both sides of the Atlantic, researchers generally ask whether their study participants were caught in an attack, whether they knew someone who was injured or killed in an attack, and whether they worked with casualties or their families or treated patients or clients who had been exposed to an attack (Adams et al., 2006; Adams et al., 2008; Boscarino et al., 2004; Cohen et al., 2006; Dekel et al., 2007; Eidelson et al., 2003; Lev-Wiesel et al., 2008; Shamai & Ron, 2009). Many of these studies ask separate questions tapping the loss of a first-degree relative and a more distant relative or friend. Most, if not all, however, combine the two categories for the purpose of analysis. The combining may stem from the difficulty of getting large enough samples to divide into the number of subcategories that would be needed to make the distinction. The result is that the special plight of those who lose meaningful persons outside their immediate family is not given adequate attention.

As for the practical level, while there is ample legitimization of the grief of mental health professionals who lose a first-degree relative in a terrorist attack, the grief that follows upon the loss of someone with psychological proximity tends to be disenfranchised (Doka, 1989). The issue of legitimization is very important. The literature on bereavement emphasizes the importance of legitimization, manifested in social recognition of the loss and due sympathy for it, to the mourning process (Murray, 2001; Worden, 2002). Without legitimization, it is very difficult to mourn the loss and come to terms with it. Loss that was not mourned may have deleterious consequences not only for the individual as a private individual but also in terms of the individual's professional performance (Gerson, 1996; Gold, 1993; Mendelsohn, 1996). Organizational awareness both by managers and supervisors to situations in which mental health professionals suffer a loss with psychological proximity might alleviate their stress.

The clear distinction between victim and professional helper no longer exists when dealing with situations of shared traumatic reality caused by terrorist attacks, wars, and natural disasters. The boundaries between these two are blurred twice over when the mental health professionals suffer a loss as do their clients.

In summary, "shared traumatic reality" is a concept that describes a situation whose central axis involves a blurring of boundaries. The clear distinction between victim and professional helper no longer exists. Rather, we find situations in which both are exposed to the same threat or injury, and the boundaries between them are blurred. At the same time, the inner boundaries within the professionals are also blurred. We have only begun to understand the implications of the blurring of these interpersonal boundaries between helper and client as well as intrapersonal ones within the mental health worker.

REFERENCES

Adams, R. E., Boscarino, J. A., & Figley, C. R. (2006). Compassion fatigue and psychological distress among social workers: A validation study. *American Journal of Orthopsychiatry, 76*(1), 103-108.

Adams, R. E., Figley, C. R., & Boscarino, J. A. (2008). The compassion fatigue scale: Its use with social workers following urban disaster. *Research on Social Work Practice, 18*(3), 238-250.

Altman, N., & Davies, J. M. (2002). Out of the blue: Reflections on a shared trauma. *Psychoanalysis Dialogues, 12*(3), 359-360.

Ayalon, O., & Lahad, M. (1995). *On life and death: Encounters with death through stories and metaphors.* Tivon, Israel: Nord (in Hebrew).

Baum, N. (2010). Shared traumatic reality in communal disasters: Toward a conceptualization. *Psychotherapy: Theory, Research, Practice and Training,* doi:10.1037/a0019784

Bleich, A., Gelkopf, M., & Solomon, Z. (2003). Exposure to terrorism, stress-related mental health symptoms, and coping behaviors among a nationally representative sample in Israel. *Journal of the American Medical Association, 290.* 612-620.

Boscarino, J. A., Figley, C. R., & Adams, R. E. (2004). Compassion fatigue following the September 11 terrorist attacks: A study of secondary trauma among New York City social workers. *International Journal of Emergency Mental Health, 6*(2), 57-66.

Cohen, M., Gagin, R., & Peled-Avram, M. (2006). Multiple terrorist attacks: compassion fatigue in Israeli social workers. *Traumatology, 12*(4), 293-301.

Dekel, R., Hantman, S., Ginzburg, K., & Solomon, Z. (2007). The cost of caring? Social workers in hospitals confront ongoing terrorism. *British Journal of Social Work, 37*(7), 1247-2261.

Doka, J. (Ed.). (1989). *Disenfranchised grief: Recognizing hidden sorrow.* Lexington MA: Lexington Books.

Eidelson, R. J., D'Alessio, G. R., & Eidelson, J. I. (2003). The impact of September 11 on psychologists. *Professional Psychology: Research and Practice, 34*(2), 144-150.

Figley, C. R. (1995). Compassion fatigue as secondary traumatic stress disorder: An overview. In C. Figley (Ed.), *Compassion fatigue: Coping with secondary traumatic stress disorder in those who treat the traumatized* (pp. 1-20). New York, NY: Brunner/Mazel.

Galea, S., Ahern, J., Resnick, H., Kilpatrick, D., Bucuvalas, M., Gold, J., & Vlahov, D. (2002). Psychological sequelae of the September 11 terrorist attacks in New York City. *The New England Journal of Medicine, 346,* 982-987.

Gerson, B. (1996). *The therapist as a person.* London, UK: The Analytic Press.

Gold, J. H. (1993). Introduction. In J. H. Gold & L. C. Nemiah (Eds.), *Beyond transference when the therapist's life intrudes* (pp. 125-140). Washington DC: American Psychiatry Press.

Keinan-Kon, N. (1998). Internal reality, external reality, and denial in the Gulf War. *The Journal of American Academy of Psychoanalysis and Dynamic Psychiatry, 26,* 417-442.

Kretsch, R., Benyakar, M., Baruch, E., & Roth, M. (1997). A shared reality of therapists and survivors in a national crisis as illustrated by the gulf war. *Psychotherapy, 34,* 28-33.

Lev-Wiesel, R., Goldblatt, H., Eisikovits, Z., & Admi, H. (2008). Growth in the shadow of war: The case of social workers and nurses working in a shared war reality. *British Journal of Social Work*. Advance online publication. doi:10.1093/bjsw/bcn021

Mendelsohn, E. M. (1996). More human than otherwise: Working through a time of preoccupation and mourning. In B. Gerson (Ed.), *The therapist as a person* (pp. 21-40). Hillsdale, NJ: The Analytic Press.

Murray, J. (2001). Loss as a universal concept: A review of the literature to identify common aspects of loss in diverse situations. *Journal of Loss and Trauma, 6*, 219-241.

Myers, D., & Wee, D. (2002). Stress responses of mental health workers following disaster: The Oklahoma City bombings. In C. Figley (Ed.), *Treating compassion fatigue* (pp. 57-84). New York, NY: Brunner Routledge.

Ostodic, E. (1999). Some pitfalls for effective caregiving in a war region. *Women & Therapy, 22*(1), 161-165.

Pulido, M. L. (2007). In their words: Secondary traumatic stress in social workers responding to the 9/11 terrorist attacks in New York City. *Social Work, 52*(3), 279-281.

Saakvitne, K. (2002). Shared trauma: The therapist's increased vulnerability. *Psychoanalytic Dialogues, 12*(3), 443-450.

Schlenger, W. E., Calddell, J. M., Ebert, L. B., Jordan, K., Rourke, K. M., Wilson, D., et al. (2002). Psychological reactions to terrorists attack: Findings from the National Study of Americans' Reactions to September 11. *Journal of the American Medical Association, 288*, 581-588.

Schuster, M. A., Stein, B. D., Jaycox, L. H., Collins, R. L., Marshall, G. N., Elliot, M. N., et al. (2001). A national survey of stress reactions after the September 11, 2001 terrorist attacks. *The New England Journal of Medicine, 345*, 1507-1512.

Seeley, K. (2003). *The psychotherapy of trauma and the trauma of psychotherapy: Talking to therapist about 9-11.* Retrieved from http://www.coi.columbia.edu/pdf/seeley_pot.pdf

Shamai, M. (2005). Personal experience in professional narratives: The role of helpers' families in their work with terror victims. *Family Process, 44*(2), 203-215.

Shamai, M., & Ron, P. (2009). Helping direct and indirect victims of national terror: Experiences of Israeli social workers. *Qualitative Health Research, 19*(1), 42-54.

Somer, E., Maguen, S., Or-Chen, K., & Litz, B. T. (2007). Managing terror: Differences between Jews and Arabs in Israel. *International Journal of Psychology*, 1-9. doi:10/1080/00207590701609076

Tosone, C. (2006). Therapeutic intimacy: A post-9/11 perspective. *Smith College Studies in Social Work, 76*(4), 89-98.

Tosone, C., & Bialkin, L. (2003). The impact of mass violence and secondary trauma in clinical practice. In L. A. Straussner & N. Phillips (Eds.), *Social work with victims of mass violence.* New York, NY: Allyn & Bacon.

Tosone, C., Lee, M., Bialkin, L., Martinez, A., Campbell, M., Martinez, M. M., et al. (2003). Shared trauma: Group reflections on the September 11th disaster. *Psychoanalytic Social Work, 10*(1), 57-77.

Warren, T., Lee, S., & Saunders, S. (2003). Factors influencing experienced distress and attitude towards trauma by emergency medicine practitioners. *Journal of Clinical Psychology in Medical Settings, 10*, 293-296.

Worden, W. (2002). *Grief counseling and grief therapy: Handbook for the mental health practitioner.* New York, NY: Springer.

Part Five:
Conclusion

Chapter Sixteen
From Helping to Changing

Roni Kaufman, Richard L. Edwards, Julia Mirsky, and Amos Avgar

In this conclusion, we present two strategic approaches for post-disaster inter-vention: the "helping and saving" approach and the "changing and developing" approach (Bates & Peacock, 1987; Cuny, 1982). Both approaches are relevant for post-disaster intervention policies and programs of various change agents: local and external, governmental and voluntary. However, in the spirit and the "opportunity oriented" approach of this book, we advocate that change agents adopt a "changing" approach to post-disaster intervention. We will demonstrate the relevance of the "changing" approach in each of the three phases of interven-tions in post-disaster situations: the emergency or rescue phase, the recovery or restoration phase, and the reconstruction or renewal phase.

CHANGING OR HELPING

The "helping" approach views disaster as an unfortunate event that requires rec-tification. The aim of the intervention is to restore community life to the status quo ante and to ensure the reversal of the devastating effects of the disaster. The "helping" approach is common in post-disaster situations and is often shared by both local and external change agents. By adopting this approach, change agents avoid the social tensions and conflict that are associated with the introduction of changes and developments that steer away from the pre-disaster situation. Be-cause this approach does not involve extensive planning and does not have to overcome significant opposition, it facilitates the achievement of quick results.

A major limitation of the "helping" approach is that it prevents the influx of new external and internal resources that are drawn to the community following the disaster and that create a rare opportunity for development and change. An-other limitation is that the "helping" approach is not sufficiently aware of the danger that weak communities are exposed to following major disasters, i.e., a hostile "takeover" by major external economical forces (corporations) that are interested in gaining control over valuable community resources such as open land and empty beaches (Klein, 2007).

The "changing" approach also views disaster as an unfortunate event. However, it takes into account the potential for growth and acts as a catalyst for social change and community development (Kreps, 1995; Rubin & Barbee, 1985). Similar to the "helping" approach, the "changing" approach responds to the immediate needs of the victims but carefully selects and directs the recovery processes with a premeditated attempt to achieve desired goals and an improved alternative state of affairs for the community. The aim is not merely to restore social order but also to seize opportunities for long-term development (Britton, 1999; Rossi, 1993). Contrary to the "helping" approach, the "changing" approach necessitates a crystallized vision of alternative community development or of improvement in community services, employment, infrastructure, and so forth. This approach not only enables the identification and materialization of vast opportunities but also encourages a positive attitude to offset the prevailing sense of pessimism and despair that characterizes post-disaster situations.

"CHANGING" IN THE DIFFERENT PHASES OF POST-DISASTER RESPONSE

In this section, we demonstrate the relevance of the "changing" approach to post-disaster intervention. Progression of post-disaster intervention has been analyzed in different ways (Boehm, 2002; Dodds & Neuhring, 1996; Drabek, 2005; Ferberow & Frederick, 1996; Kreps & Bosworth, 2006). We adopt the classic division that identifies three distinct yet interconnected phases (Mileti, Drabek, & Haas, 1975): the emergency or rescue phase, the recovery or restoration phase, and the reconstruction or renewal phase. Each phase presents opportunities for development and special challenges to social change agents.

"Changing" in the Emergency Phase

The response activities during the relatively short emergency or rescue phase concentrate predominantly on saving lives and providing for basic human services such as shelter and food. This phase is characterized by confusion, uncoordinated response, and fractured, often ineffective, leadership. At the same time, it is the phase that attracts significant funding and draws a large number of volunteers. It is during this phase that windows of opportunity for long-term development are opened. Yet, because the pressing life-saving challenges often take precedence, the response at this phase is highly specific and task-oriented, and long-term considerations and planning are overlooked. As a result, resources are wasted, leaving the development needs of the community without sufficient funding. A major criticism of a large-scale international evaluation venture of the post-tsunami response efforts (Tsunami Evaluation Coalition, 2007) focused on the issue of distribution of funds across the various phases. It was unequivocally stated that too much funding was allocated to the emergency and recovery phases, leaving insufficient funding for development.

During the emergency phase, the resources that are drawn to the region often, by far, exceed the capacity of the organizations operating at the scene to spend them in a productive and effective manner. At the same time, the implementing organizations are under considerable pressure to spend the funds and to show results. The challenge at this stage is to engage in a more in-depth resource allocation process, taking into account the needs across phases.

An example of such an approach is "cash for work" programs. These programs, particularly those based on the establishment and utilization of local "cooperatives" in the relief efforts, serve both the emergency as well as later phases of the response. Employing local youth groups to build temporary shelters integrates the phases of recovery. It increases the income level of the affected population, trains people in new skills, empowers the local community, and reduces the level of delinquency while responding to an urgent need of the victims. Another example of such integration is organizing and/or mobilizing local community organizations and volunteers for immediate relief activities, such as delivery of food, clothing, and building materials. Utilization of external change agents for the distribution of assistance misses the opportunity to structure the energy of the volunteers and harness the capacity of local organizations; both are critical for the long-term recovery of the community.

"Changing" in the Recovery Phase

The recovery or restoration phase lasts for several months, and often well over a year, and focuses on resuming basic life activities. At this point, tensions develop between forces that push for restoring the pre-disaster status quo and resuming pre-disaster conditions and the forces that push for introducing social, organizational, and environmental changes. The long-term consequences of adopting a helping rather than a changing orientation during this phase become evident. The recovery phase presents opportunities for development and sets the stage for renewal; however, adopting a "helping" approach that aims to restore the status quo prevents social transformation from taking place. Alternatively, change agents involved in recovery can adopt a "changing" approach with long-term development potential that seizes the newly presented opportunities while responding to the urgent recovery needs.

The successful adoption of such a strategy is contingent upon the existence of strong local leadership with a crystallized development vision, the ability to mobilize support for the new direction, and the capacity to withstand pressures to resume the status quo. When the "changing" approach is adopted at this stage, the major dilemma facing the leadership is whether it is justified to delay the response to some of the immediate needs until solutions better suited for the long run are developed. A common example is whether to resettle as quickly as possible the displaced population who is living in temporary housing, with a return to the same pre-disaster housing conditions, or to wait for the resettlement until better building codes and zoning ordinances are developed and adequate materials become available. A "changing" approach would involve conducting training for the local population in the building trades and mobilizing them as labor in the construction process while taking the risk of delaying the availability of permanent housing. Another dilemma is whether to allocate all the available resources for activities aimed at easing the immediate conditions of the population or to allocate funds only for the more basic social-economic and infrastructural needs and save some funds for development activities that would have significant social impact and benefits in the long run.

"Changing" in the Reconstruction Phase

The reconstruction or renewal phase following disasters often lasts for years. During this phase, opportunities for development can be fully materialized and can help reshape communities and organizations (Coghlan, 1998; Drabek, 1986). The seeds of these opportunities, as we suggested, should be detected during the emergency and recovery phases. If the structural, organizational, and physical constraints for development that existed before the disaster are detected early in the recovery process, they may be removed or weakened, and alternative future scenarios introduced. It is during this period that the new linkages that were established following the disaster and those that were strengthened can be further mobilized and committed to the implementation of development programs.

The scope of social change and development that occurs during this phase depends on the ability to identify opportunities during earlier phases and to adopt a "changing" strategy throughout the recovery process. A major dilemma facing intervening agencies at this phase is who should be responsible for the planning and act as the decision maker on the cardinal issues of the direction, final outcomes, and the means to be selected for the renewal and development programs. Similarly, a major consideration is who should lead in the implementation process. The "changing" approach calls for dialogue and cooperation between local and external change agents and between local and national leadership. The authentic local leadership, which represents the interests of the community, should be the major decision makers in regard future development to ensure that local community interests are met, cooperation with local organizations is achieved, and local capacities and assets are harnessed.

Because the active role of an authentic local leadership is critical, external change agents who are committed to achieving the goal of local development should invest the necessary resources to work with and strengthen such leadership. It is important to note that disasters can play a significant role in overcoming local controversies and conflicts, draw groups together due to the realization that "we are all in the same boat that needs to be rescued," and thus promote the level of community integration.

CONCLUSION

In conclusion, we recommend that the three phases of post-disaster response are regarded as continuous, interrelated processes (Boehm, 2002, 2004). Although some activities in each phase are distinct and may be implemented in an unrelated fashion, it is important to understand that the actions in earlier phases are often irreversible and have a significant long-term impact on later phases. Viewing the three phases as a continuum facilitates the adoption of an approach that enables the integration of emergency-relief with community development efforts. The road to development and change is harnessing the emergency-relief efforts and mobilizing them as a platform for development. Similarly, leveraging and harnessing local capacities and assets from the early stages of the recovery provides opportunities for long-range development. The "changing" approach requires long-term planning of the allocation and distribution of funds among the various post-disaster phases. Such long-term planning must take place very early in the recovery process, when the resources are in abundance and before they are potentially wasted. During the emergency phase, the level of funding from local as well as outside sources often exceeds the organizational capacity to implement, while the pressure to quickly disburse funding is high. During the recovery and development phases, the availability of funding declines, yet the funding needs are substantial. The challenge is to ensure a more balanced distribution of resources over time.

There are two major types of relationships between external and local change agents in post-disaster interventions. External change and intervention agents can seize and maintain direct control over the allocation and utilization of the resources that they have mobilized while bypassing local community leadership and organizations that remain less active. Alternatively, external change agents may adopt an institution-building approach that relies heavily on local capacities agencies and organizations for the implementation of recovery programs. Operating through local instrumentalities reinforces the growth potential of local communities.

In the wake of a major disaster, especially in the emergency phase when life is at risk and local capacities are severely damaged, a direct intervention strategy often cannot be avoided. However, from the long-term perspective of organizational and community development, an institution-building strategy is preferable. The direct intervention of external change agents often creates dependency and apathy and can even breed animosity between outside assisting organization and local ones. An important finding of the Post-Tsunami Recovery Coalition Evaluation Study (Tsunami Evaluation Coalition, 2007) was that a critical factor that inhibited post-tsunami development of the affected areas, despite the vast resources that were made available for the recovery, was the tendency of external change agents to assume direct control over the planning, intervention, and implementation activities. Little attention, the study concluded, was paid to harnessing and building local capacities, relying on local capabilities, or involving local organizations.

Direct intervention and institution-building strategies of outside organizations following disasters are correlated with the two intervention approaches discussed in this chapter. The "helping" approach often leads to direct intervention of outside bodies, while the "changing" approach is often associated with institution building.

The windows of opportunity following disasters are time-limited, may be short-lived, and are not always self-evident due to the confusion and disorganization that characterizes the situation. However, if they are identified early enough and acted upon in a timely fashion, they can bring about long-term post-disaster development and renewal, thus improving pre-existing conditions and promoting social growth.

We hope that this book will assist various post-disaster change agents to better understand the processes and dynamics at play following disasters. We believe that such understanding can lead to better decision making and interventions and facilitate not only post-disaster recovery but also long-term development and renewal.

REFERENCES

Bates, F. L., & Peacock, W. G. (1987). Disaster and social change. In R. D. Russell, B. DeMarchi & C. Pelanda C. (Eds.). *Sociology of disasters: Contributions of sociology to disaster research* (pp. 291-330). Milano, Italy: Franco Angeli.

Boehm, A. (2002). Participation strategies of activist-volunteers in the life cycle of community crisis. *British Journal of Social Work, 32,* 51-70.

Boehm, A. (2004). *Community intervention in the life cycle of a community crisis,* Journal of Social Research and Evaluation, 5(1), 5-19.

Britton, N. R. (1999). Whither the emergency manager? *International Journal of Mass Emergencies and Disasters, 17*(2), 223-35.

Coghlan, A. (1998). *Post-disaster redevelopment* [Conference paper]. Victoria, Australia: Australian Emergency Management Institute.

Cuny, F. C. (1982). *Disasters and development.* New York, NY: Oxford University Press.

Dodds, S., & Nuehring, E. (1996). A primer for social work research on disaster, *Journal of Social Service Review, 22*(1/2), 27-56.

Drabek, T. E. (1986). *Human system responses to disaster: An inventory of sociological findings.* New York, NY: Springer-Verlag.

Drabek, T. E. (2005). Predicting disaster response effectiveness. *International Journal of Mass Emergencies and Disasters, 23*(1), 49-72.

Ferberow, N. L., & Frederick, C. J. (1996). *Training manual for human service workers in major disasters.* Washington, DC: Government Printing Office.

Klein, N. (2007). *The shock doctrine: The rise of disaster capitalism.* New York, NY: Knopf.

Kreps, G. A. (1995). Disaster as systemic event and social catalyst: A clarification of subject matter. *International Journal of Mass Emergencies and Disasters, 13*(3), 255-84.

Kreps, G. A., & Bosworth, S. L. (2006). Organizational adaptation to disaster. In H. Rodríguez, E. L. Quarantelli & R. R. Dynes, R.R. (Eds.), *Handbook of disaster research* (pp. 297-315). New York, NY: Springer.

Mileti, D., Drabek, T. E., & Haas, E. J. (1975). *Human systems in extreme environments: A sociological perspective* (Monograph #021). Boulder, CO: University of Colorado Institute of Behavioral Science.

Rossi, I. (1993). *Community reconstruction after an earthquake: Dialectical sociology in action.* Westport, CT: Praeger.

Rubin, C. B., & Barbee, D. G. (1985). Disaster recovery and hazard mitigation: Bridging the inter-governmental gap. *Public Administration Review, 45,* 93-100.

Tsunami Evaluation Coalition. (2007). Retrieved from www.alnap.org

200

EDITORS

Amos Avgar, Ph.D., currently serves as Chief Operations Officer for TAG International Development. He served for the past four years as Executive Director of the International Development Program at the American Jewish Joint Distribution Committee (JDC), where he was responsible for strategic planning and implementation of all JDC nonsectarian programs worldwide, including those in countries such as Sri Lanka, Indonesia, Thailand, Myanmar, Pakistan, South Africa, Ghana, Rwanda, Kenya, and the Former Soviet Union Republics. He is a co-editor, with Julia Mirsky and Roni Kaufman, of *Social Disaster as an Opportunity: The Hesed Model.*

Richard L. Edwards, Ph.D., is Dean and Professor of the School of Social Work at Rutgers, The State University of New Jersey. He previously served as Dean at Case Western Reserve University and at the University of North Carolina at Chapel Hill. From 1989 to 2001, he served as president of the National Association of Social Workers and was a member of the Executive Committee of the International Federation of Social Workers. He was editor-in-chief of the 19th edition of the Encyclopedia of Social Work and has numerous other publications, including books and journal articles. He has been a visiting faculty member at universities in Canada and Romania, and served as a Fulbright Senior Specialist in Israel.

Roni Kaufman, Ph.D., is a Senior Lecturer at the Department of Social Work, Ben Gurion University, Israel. He co-edited, with Julia Mirsky and Amos Avgar, the book *Social Disaster as an Opportunity: The Hesed Model.* He also has authored numerous papers on social work education for social action, community work and organizing, social change organizations, university-community collaboration, and intervention in social problems, such as food insecurity.

Julia Mirsky, Ph.D., is Associate Professor at the Department of Social Work, Ben Gurion University, Israel, and has been a visiting scholar at universities in the United States and France. She is a clinical psychologist and specializes in the psychological aftermaths of migration, which is conceptualized as a major life crisis. She has published extensively on this subject in international professional periodicals and authored the book *Narratives and Meanings of Migration.* Along with Roni Kaufman and Amos Avgar, she co-edited the book *Social Disaster as an Opportunity: The Hesed Model.*

CONTRIBUTORS

Ahangamage Tudor Ariyaratne, M.D., Ph.D., started the Sarvodaya Shramadana Movement 50 years ago, and it is now of the world's largest people's participatory development movements. For Dr. Ariyaratne's work, the President of Sri Lanka has awarded him the highest national award (SriLankabhimani). He is also the recipient of many other international awards, including the Ramon Magsaysay Award from the Philippines (1969), King boud uwin Award for International Development (1982) Belgium, Niwano Peace Prize (1982) Japan, and the Mahatma Gandhi Peace Prize (1992) India.

Johny Augustine, Ph.D., is an Assistant Professor at the School of Social Work at St. Ambrose University in Davenport, Iowa, in the U.S. His recent research includes a study that investigated the increasing role of personal resources, family strengths, and social capital in promoting the growth of survivors of a major disaster. He has worked in a variety of clinical settings with the mentally ill, including inpatient facilities, outpatient clinics, and community mental health centers.

Yehuda Baruch, M.D., is the Medical Director of Abarbanel Mental Health Center and a lecturer on psychiatry at the School of Health Management, Ben Gurion University of the Negev, Israel. Previously, he served as a Deputy CEO of the Israeli Ministry of Health and as Chief Psychiatrist of the Israeli Defense Forces. He is the author of a number of professional articles and books.

Nehami Baum, Ph.D., is a senior lecturer of the School of Social Work at Bar Ilan University, Israel. She is a social worker as well as a family therapist and a psychotherapist, with experience in both public and private practice. Her main areas of interest are men's way of mourning and non-death related losses as well as situations that mental health professionals confront in their practice. More specifically, in the last few years, she has been studying the influence of professionals' private experiences (e.g., pregnancy) and environmental conditions (e.g., terror, war, and political conflict) on their professional functioning.

Mihir R. Bhatt, B.Arch, MCP, started the All India Disaster Mitigation Institute with a team of three after repeated droughts in the late 1980s. He is a recipient of the Russell E. Train Institutional Fellowship from the World Wildlife Fund, USA (1997), the Eisenhower Fellowship, USA (2000), and the Ashoka Fellowship, USA (2004). He is now a Senior Fellow of Humanitarian Initiatives at Harvard University. He has worked with disaster-stricken communities throughout India and other parts of Asia and is often invited to evaluate strategic initiatives in disaster preparedness and relief.

Miriam Ben-Oz, Ph.D., is a senior lecturer in the Department of Social Work, Tel Hai Academic College, Israel, and senior supervisor at the School of Social Work, Field Work Unit, University of Haifa, Israel. Her fields of expertise are supervision and the development of Social Work curriculum, and she serves as the academic advisor to the school of supervision in the Tel Hai Academic College.

Joanne S. Caye, MSW, is a Clinical Associate Professor in the School of Social Work at the University of North Carolina at Chapel Hill, where she teaches in the master's program. She is a co-author of *When Their World Falls Apart: Helping Families and Children Manage the Effects of Disaster* and is a frequent presenter at national and international conferences. Her areas of interest are disaster response, helper self-care, child welfare, and community organizing.

Howard S. Feinberg, M.S.Ed., currently serves as President/CEO of the Jewish Federation of San Antonio, Texas. He has over 30 years of leadership experience in organizational development, fundraising, strategic planning, emergency preparedness, and disaster response. Previously, he served in key executive capacities for United Jewish Communities, including Managing Director, UJC Consulting and Lead Staff, UJC Emergency Committee, and as a President/CEO of HSF Associates, LLC, a private consulting firm specializing in Emergency Preparedness and Disaster Response.

Patricia A. Findley, DrPH, is an Assistant Professor in the School of Social Work at Rutgers, The State University of New Jersey. She conducts quantitative analyses on disability and chronic illnesses, examining disparities in access and co-occurring physical and mental illnesses. She holds a research scholar position with the Veterans Administration, where she explores both physical and mental health as well as gender among the veteran population. She has a long clinical history in working with those with disabilities in medical rehabilitation settings and more recently co-authored a book, *The Cancer Survivor Handbook: The Essential Guide to Cancer Survivorship.*

Brian W. Flynn, Ed.D., currently serves as an Associate Director of the Center for the Study of Traumatic Stress and Adjunct Professor, Department of Psychiatry, Uniformed Services University of the Health Sciences in Bethesda, Maryland. He is a retired Rear Admiral/Assistant Surgeon General in the United States Public Health Service. He is an internationally recognized expert on the individual, family, and community psychosocial factors in large-scale trauma, disasters, and emergencies. He has served as an advisor to numerous national and international organizations, states, academic institutions, practitioners, and government officials in many nations.

James Halpern, Ph.D., is the Professor of Psychology and Counseling and Director of the Institute for Disaster Mental Health at the State University of New York at New Paltz. He co-authored the book *Disaster Mental Health: Theory and Practice* and is a frequent presenter on trauma and disaster mental health throughout the US and abroad. He has consulted for the United Nations on assisting victims of terror and serves on the Advisory Committee to New York's Veterans Mental Health Project. He is a member of the psychosocial planning group of the World Association of Disaster Emergency Medicine and has developed curricula for the United Nations Emergency Preparedness and Support Team. Dr. Halpern has provided direct service at many local and large-scale national disasters.

Shira Hantman, Ph.D., is an expert in gerontology, with over 40 years of experience in the field. She is currently the Dean of the Faculty of Social Sciences and Humanities at Tel Hai College in the Upper Galilee, Israel. She also chairs several committees in the field, among them the Gerontology Accreditation Committee at Israel's National Association of Social Workers, and is a member of the Advisory Committee to the Minister of Aging Affairs. Dr. Hantman is the author of the book *The Sandwich Generation* and has published extensively in the field of gerontology.

Jessica C. Jagger, MSW, has been engaged in research and practice on disaster management and disability policy since 2005. She has conducted this work in the US and in Jamaica as a Fulbright Fellow. She is a Ph.D. Candidate at Virginia Commonwealth University, with an expected graduation date of May 2011.

Vivek Chemmancheri Kokkammadathil, MSW, is a professional social work consultant from India with more than 10 years' experience working in the development sector. He has worked intensively in the disaster management sector in over 20 countries in Asia, Africa, and the Americas. He has supported several international non-governmental organizations, including Action Aid International and Plan International, both based in the United Kingdom, in developing Disasters and Emergencies Preparedness Plans.

Mooli Lahad, Ph.D., is a Professor of Psychology, founder and president of the Community Stress Prevention Center in Kiryat Shmona, Israel, and the Vice President of the Israel Trauma Coalition. He is the author or co-author of 28 books and numerous articles on trauma, resiliency, the healing effects of the arts, and the power of imagination. He also is a consultant to governments and professional bodies worldwide, and he has developed novel models and methods for coping with and treating psychotrauma.

Dmitry Leykin, BA, is a research fellow at the Community Stress Prevention Center in Kiryat Shmona, Israel, and is a co-author of several articles on psychotrauma measurement and treatments. He is currently studying for an MA in Psychology at Tel Aviv University, Israel.

Ronald E. Marks, Ph.D., is Dean of Social Work School at Tulane University, New Orleans, Louisiana. After the devastation of New Orleans caused by Hurricane Katrina in September 2005, he has been actively partnering with many international aid organizations to assist in the recovery of the city and surrounding areas, and he has worked to provide field sites for Tulane's students and research collaborations for Tulane faculty. Over the last ten years, Dr. Marks has been working to establish an international social work program as part of the MSW program at Tulane. He has led programs in Central America, Cuba, and, most recently, in north India, where he has worked for several years to aid in the development of a project with Tibetan refugees.

Benon Musinguzi, MA, has been the Dean of Social Sciences at Uganda Christian University for the last six years and has taught at the university for the last 13 years. He has submitted his PhD thesis on "The Implications of HIV/AIDS on Households in Uganda."

Nitsa Nacasch M.D., is a psychiatrist and the Director of Prolonged Exposure (PE) Treatment Center at Sheba Medical Center in Tel Hashomer, Israel. She is a senior supervisor, trainer, and researcher on PE with war veterans and victims of terror and has authored a number of papers on these topics.

Shulamit Niv, Ph.D., is a psychologist, therapist, and trainer in marital and family therapy and a senior member of the Community Stress Prevention Center, Kiryat Shmona, Israel. An expert in stress management and psychotrauma treatment and an international trainer for professionals working in post-disaster areas, she has authored several articles on crisis intervention in schools.

Lilach Rachamim, Ph.D., is a clinical psychologist and supervisor for cognitive-behavioral therapy and prolonged-exposure therapy, including special experience with the pediatric population. She manages the Cognitive Behavioral Therapy (CBT) training at Schneider Children's Medical Center of Israel and specializes in community-wide disaster interventions.

Ruvie Rogel, Ph.D., is the Deputy CEO of the Community Stress Prevention Center, Kiryat Shmona, Israel, and is a senior trainer on community psychotrauma and the recovery of communities. He led several international missions in disaster areas. In the past, he served as an advisor to the Israeli

Prime Minister's committee on the relocation of evacuees from Katif-Gaza Strip.

Yehuda Shacham, Ph.D., is a psychologist and a school counselor specializing in marital and family therapy. In the past, he served as the Deputy Director of the Community Stress Prevention Center, Kiryat Shmona, Israel. He participated in and led special projects for training and empowering psychologists and other professionals following disasters worldwide and authored a number of articles and book chapters on crisis intervention and crisis management.